Stop Training Your Dog

A Guide to Connecting Beyond Commands, Understanding Behavior, and Becoming the Change You Both Need

Jaime Caponetta

STOP TRAINING YOUR DOG: A GUIDE TO CONNECTING BEYOND COMMANDS, UNDERSTANDING BEHAVIOR, AND BECOMING THE CHANGE YOU BOTH NEED

JAIME CAPONETTA

For more information: Jaime@PawsomeUniversity.com

ISBN (Paperback): 978-1-962280-37-2
ISBN (eBook): 978-1-962280-38-9

Reflek Publishing.

Introduction

Are you immediately confused by the title of this book—*Stop Training Your Dog?* After all, it sounds counterproductive. Most people looking to train their dogs are looking for an actual dog training book. You know, with basic obedience and step-by-step training methods to correct their dogs' bad behavior.

Well, this is not one of those books.

You've been warned! This behavioral dog training book is about teaching, not training. This is because after almost ten years in this field, the number-one problem I have identified with the dog training world is that most people and trainers in it focus on training the dog and not the parents. Which is bullshit! Honestly, the one-size-fits-all dog training ideologies are detrimental to both dogs and humans. Which then, of course, trickles down to our children and so on and so forth. We just pass down garbage training methods to our kids, who then pass them to their kids.

Yes, crappy dog training *can* be a generational curse!

Getting a dog is one of the most exciting times in a person's life. I remember the first puppy my parents gave us. I was ten years old when a floppy seven-week-old chocolate Lab came fumbling toward me with a big bow around his neck on Christmas morning. To date, that's one of my favorite childhood memories!

Dogs are magic. They bring an effortless comfort and connection that we sometimes have a hard time finding human to human. In our loneliest moments, our dogs are there for us. They always forgive us. Dogs elicit a joy like no other, like a newborn baby—just pure magic!

So if dogs are so pure and bring us such happiness and fun, shouldn't the way we teach and work with them feel the same way? Shouldn't it feel good? Shouldn't it elicit joy and bring happy tears to your eyes?

If that's what you're looking for, you're in the right place! This dog training book is going to meet you where you are, help you put aside societal pressures about what makes a "good" dog parent, renew your hope (regardless of how big the hole is that you think you're sinking in), and recreate a bond with your dog in the easiest, most pain-free, most fun ways possible.

Soup to nuts, I will cover everything in this book!

Now, let's get some things straight before we drive in!

- This book will read like you're talking to your bestie. But I will also be dropping science-based knowledge—just without all the fancy words you don't understand or care about. Yes, deep breath. This is going to be real fun!
- This book is also going to cover all positive reinforcement methods. I do not use any aversive tools or techniques. I will get into the *why* throughout the book. Just know that you will not be using any techniques that make you feel icky and gross. Again, it's about fun!
- At times, this book may test your ego, the way you were raised, and your attachment styles. It may also make you feel slightly defensive at first. *Good!* Sometimes, hearing the truth hurts a little, and that's okay! If you sit with those feelings and figure out why you feel that way, you'll be able to put your best foot forward for you and your dog. And please know that I know how hard it is to come to some of the conclusions you might come to. I congratulate you for wanting to keep going for your dog! Keep going!

- I compare dogs and kids quite a bit. This is because they are extremely similar in how they learn and think. It's also because I treat my dogs like I treat my kids. To me, there is no difference. I will be humanizing dogs as much as possible. So, if that bothers you and you don't want to better yourself, put this book down.
- There will be some cursing. I am a fluent curser when I am passionate about something. We are all just trying to figure this shit out in life, and I think cursing makes many points sound more like real life. Plus, I want you to feel like you are talking to me one-on-one. Well, how I wrote this is how I talk. I also was told intelligent people curse a lot, so I'll just leave it at that!

I'd also love to tell you a little about myself so you can get a good idea of who is talking to you, what got me where I am today, and where the passion and visceral need to write this book came from. I have been working with dogs for almost ten years now.

I was one of those people who went to college because everyone else was. I pretty much hated school, but I didn't want to break my mother's heart. I didn't know what I wanted to do, but I knew I did not want to be a corporate worker. So, I majored in art. Painting was my major, and I loved it. But the starving artist thing wasn't something I was terribly comfortable with. After I graduated, I took a job at my sorority's headquarters in Philly. Didn't mind the job as much as I minded catty girls wearing dresses and heels. I knew I needed out. I knew I needed to figure out what I wanted.

When I was growing up, my mom and I were obsessed with the TV series *Pit Bulls and Parolees*. I thought if I could be anywhere and doing anything, it would be rolling up my sleeves, getting dirty, taking care of animals, going on rescue missions, and saving lives.

So that's what I did! I quit my job, found an online training program, and decided to start working at a doggy day care in the meantime. I quickly moved on from that job and started working at the local SPCA shelter as a handler in canine care. It was the most fun, most rewarding job I'd ever had. I had never before felt more at home in my twenty-three years. It's also where I met my husband, John.

It was one of those fairy tales in which someone falls in love at first sight. (Yeah, I have me one of those far-fetched love stories, and it lives up to the hype.) John was my boss (scandalous, I know!) and was a humane police officer while running animal care. Within two years, we were married!

I couldn't be more blessed with how my life turned out. We now live in central New Jersey on a nine-acre farm—the dream! We have two sons (JJ and Joey), a third baby boy on the way due August 2024, three rescue dogs (Pudgalina, Oaklee, and Tishi), and a cat (Salem Rae). We also have ten goats and a pig—all rescues! On our farm, we took the horse barn and converted it into large dog kennels. We use these to board rescue dogs that are on the chopping block and at risk of euthanasia due to behavioral issues. They join our rehab rescue program, get a chance to decompress away from all the stress and noise of the shelter, and learn how to trust. This usually gives them a better chance at adoption. It can also give the rescue a better idea of what the dog's limitations are and where they would fit in best, family-wise.

So, what made me want to write this book?

Ever since I was a kid, I thought how cool it would be to write a book. I'm dyslexic, so this was a dream I thought would never be attainable due to that disability. But here I am. I know this book will change lives. So I am writing it for all the dog parents who truly want help, want to better their relationship with their dog, want to change up their training style, and need to know that there is someone out there (me) who believes in them and knows that any situation with a dog is fixable.

I will say it again—any situation with your dog is fixable if you are committed! This book is made to shift your thinking, throw all the dog training myths that have been used since the 1960s out the window, and start a dog training transformation for generations to come. This book should leave you feeling knowledgeable, empowered, hopeful, and confident in your choices moving forward. You should also feel like you not only understand your dog's specific behaviors but can make them the happiest and healthiest versions of themselves. Plus, this means you'll be able to identify dog behaviors to help friends and family make better choices for their pups in the future!

This stuff matters.

I hope you enjoy this book!

Part One:

Everything You Know about Dogs Is Probably Wrong

Chapter 1:
How Dogs Think

I think this is the perfect way to start! Understanding how a dog thinks and learns is imperative to creating a respectful and authentic relationship with your dog. Skipping this step is like throwing the car manual out and yelling at the car for not fixing itself. Can you frickin' imagine doing that? I know all you dads and car fanatics with teenagers are shaking your heads!

Did you know that every dog learns at a three-year-old level for their entire life? Level of intelligence, breed, or age does not change this fact. Your dog—all dogs—are forever toddlers. I know that seems super weird to think about, but when I dive in deeper, you'll understand better. And it will blow your mind.

Dogs and toddlers learn by association, not cause-and-effect thinking. What do I mean by this? You're relying on cause-and-effect learning when you think, *If I yell at you enough or you are uncomfortable enough, you will eventually stop doing the thing I want you to stop doing.*

But this is how adults learn, not how young kids or dogs learn. Not effectively, anyway. If you are a parent to children, I'm sure you can think of the times you have yelled at your toddler not to do something, and absolutely nothing changes. You can threaten them, take things away, and scream your head off, but your kid still does the thing.

Why? Because this approach is just not how they learn. This is fear-based learning. You didn't fix the problem, which is the thing that drives the action in the first place!

For example, let's say my eldest son is feeling insecure, jealous, and angry every time his baby brother gets attention. So, in his three-year-old brain, hitting his little brother is the best way to deal with these negative feelings. Obviously, as a parent, I want to yell and punish this "bad" behavior, which is unacceptable. (Some parents still spank their kids. So they're hitting their kid for hitting. Yep, that'll show them not to hit.But my yelling just causes a fight and many tears. The next day, it happens again. And again. No matter how much I yell, take things away, or send him to his room, it gets worse.

Crap! Neither of us is having fun anymore. I feel like all I do is yell, and it is a constant battle. He may even start to hate his little brother more for being the thing that came along and disrupted his perfect one-kid household of constant love and attention he didn't have to share.

When I switch up my brain from thinking, *Why is he doing this? This is unacceptable!* over to *I wonder what he is feeling right before he does that, and I wonder what I can do to help him work out those feelings better*, it gets a lot easier as a parent.

Let's back it up to pinpoint the problem. The actual problem is that my eldest feels negativity about his brother receiving attention because he isn't receiving any at that time. This is not something I can shield him from. Jealousy is a normal emotion!

It will pop up his whole life. My job as a parent is to help him *deal* with the negative feelings and control his emotions. I don't want him to bottle them up so that he erupts one day like a volcano. If I can help him change his negative emotions to positive ones, the problem goes away, right?

Easier said than done, I know. My lord, toddlers can be hard. But when we start to break it down, we can build confident, self-regulated, empathetic little humans. (And dogs—stick with me.) I can work through the problems with him, make him feel seen, let him know that those are all normal emotions, and show him by words and actions that he is still loved regardless of his brother's existence.

But I also put firm boundaries in place. I'll say, "You can be mad, but you can't be mean." This lets him know that his emotions are valid but his hitting is not. I can also say, "I see you are feeling jealous and angry. What do you think you can do differently to calm down and tell Mommy what's going on?" This way, I can give him some action he can take to change the way he is feeling physically.

Now, for some of you, it may be simple to relate this to dogs. If so, a light bulb may have immediately turned on. Others may be scratching your heads. Totally fine! I'll give you some dog-related examples. And no, I won't be expecting you to ask your dog what they can do differently next time.

Let's say you have an eight-month-old puppy, and she is meeting your loud, talks-with-his-hands, tall, sunglass-wearing, bearded uncle for the first time. Your puppy sees your uncle and immediately growls, retreats, and gets low to the ground with ears back.

You immediately yell at her. How dare she act this way! She's embarrassing you. She may stop growling right after you yell, but she does not warm up to your uncle and doesn't take her eyes off him. She won't come within fifteen feet of him either. You start apologizing to your uncle because she's never acted like this before, and you are so disappointed in her behavior. You start calling trainers because you want to "train out this behavior."

Now, let's break it down. Your uncle *scared* her. He is big and loud, and he came in hot! No one prepared her for this visitor or what he would look like. She has survival instincts that pop up when she feels threatened. We *do not* get to dictate what should or shouldn't frighten dogs. Even if you do not find it scary, you don't get to say she can't be scared. Your emotions do not matter here. Only hers matter. She wasn't being aggressive, and she did not approach him. She gave a warning. She communicated her fear, and then she got reprimanded for showing emotion.

It's like when we tell kids to stop crying because we're unable to deal with their sadness because somewhere along the line, someone told us to stop crying. (These were the attachment styles I told you I was going to bring up. Yes, it hits hard, and we're gonna keep it real AF through the whole book, so buckle up!)

We don't get to shut a dog's emotions off because we never dealt with our own! When we do this, we are suppressing their emotions. We are saying, "It is not safe for you to communicate honestly. Your emotions are not welcome here." This is the start of a snowball effect I see more often than I'd like. Four months later, you have a dog that's reactive to people (which means they are fearfully vocal—barking, lunging and growling), and you "have no idea where it came from." But humans have a direct hand in this problem. When you are an emotionally unavailable parent, this is the result.

Now, let's bring it back full circle so you can understand what happened. Where is the negative association? Your dog will start to associate certain people with negative emotions and being yelled at. Over time, she may associate these feelings with other dogs or anything else that frightens her. She does not understand that your corrections are because her behavior is affecting others negatively or that it is inappropriate and rude to growl at someone. All she knows is that she was living a lovely life with you (her person) until your uncle came over. Then you (the one she trusts most in this world) just turned on her in five seconds flat for seemingly no reason. So, what you are actually doing is saying, "Every time someone you don't like is around, you're going to get yelled at, and you are unsafe." This makes her hate those people more.

In reality, as dog parents, that's not what we intend to say. But that is what they interpret. What we really want to say is that our dogs are safe with people we allow inside and that we will prove that fact to them by not yelling at them for showing emotion. We want them to *like* the person! When you were a kid, were you ever *forced* to hang out with a kid you disliked? Did you ever change your mind and ever truly like them? Probably not. Same thing with activities. Have you ever been forced to play a sport you didn't fancy? You probably didn't come out of it with a newfound love.

I will give you another example: the dreaded mail carrier!

I think everyone would agree that most dogs dislike the mail carrier. There is a real reason for this. I think there is a part of every one of us who likes the idea of having a dog for protection. If it isn't full-out protection, it's at least the idea that a dog will alert us if something is going down that shouldn't be, like someone breaking into our home. Now, dogs bark constantly at the mailman. Day in and day out, it's the same song and dance. They bark, we yell, they may stop, or they may not. But they know you're not happy, the mailman goes away, they stop, and the next day, it repeats.

Why? It's so damn simple you're going to laugh at yourself.

When. The. Mail. Carrier. Shows. Up. You. Start. Yelling.

They hear the mail carrier pull up, and they see them approaching the house. This makes them feel uncomfortable, protective, or scared. The front door can be a barrier to a lot of dogs, eliciting barrier frustration and making them more reactive than they are when the door isn't closed. And if your dog is slightly friendly, there could also be some excitement mixed up in there, which gives them a tornado of emotions, such as fear and excitement. So they bark, lunge, and growl. You start yelling and correcting them the second they start reacting, so they think, "My parent was fine before the mail carrier got here, and now they're angry and yelling at me. The mail carrier sucks."

Then the mail carrier leaves! Their reactivity saved the whole family! It worked! They did their job.

Dogs do not understand that mail people come on our property just to deliver the mail. They don't understand that it is an occupation or what mail is. All they know is this: "That person was on my property. I didn't like it. I reacted, and they left. I will continue to keep me and my family safe."

This is why it never changes or gets any better. And we have a direct hand in making it an awful situation for everyone involved.

(Spoiler alert: we can make this situation so much better. We will dive way deeper into this rabbit hole of associative learning in Chapter 11, and I will tell you exactly what you should be doing instead!)

The moral of the stories above is that you are molding a living, breathing, feeling creature. Yours is not a military or police dog. Yours is a *family* dog, so you need to treat them like you treat a beloved family member. Moving forward, we will throw corrections and perfection out the window and focus on helping your dog with their emotions and setting them up for success with all the empathy you can muster up!

Why though? Why do we *need* to throw the old ways out the window if they have made dogs behave and be obedient for so long?

That is also a simple question to answer.

Because your dog didn't ask to be here.

Yep, I said it. Your dog did not ask to be a part of your family. They didn't get to choose. I believe that if you are going to get a pet or have a child, you better have the highest intentions to give them the best fucking life possible. *No exceptions.* Otherwise, why get one? No one forced you to get a dog. You're not required by law to have one. So, if you are choosing to bring a pup home, you should be making the vow "In sickness and in health, for better or for worse, till death do us part."

For the most part, we are all pretty intelligent humans. We know that dogs cost money, time, and energy. We know they need food, water, shelter, treats, and vet care. But their health is usually the first to be put to the side if the money needs to go somewhere else. We know they need to be trained. We know dogs can be difficult for us, and we know that we need to be consistent and present. But instead, many people either look to ship their dogs off to a board-and-train program or want proper, high-caliber training for less than $200 (which does not exist).

We want our dogs to be exactly how we want them to be. But can you imagine doing that with a child? I have two boys, and I fully accept that they are different. I *chose* to have a second child. (And a third.) And in doing so, I agreed to the possibility that he could be a different ball game in personality, learning, sleeping, eating, crying, and growing than his older brother. And I was right: they are different kids, but I never put expectations on him just because his brother did or didn't do something.

This is something we do constantly with dogs. I've so often heard someone say, "I have had dogs my entire life, and I've never had a dog do this!" Why do we expect all dogs to be angels 100 percent of the time and grow up the same as each other, no matter what season or life stage their parents are in?

I will use my own parents as an example for this one!

Let's get one thing straight first: I love them dearly, and they are my best friends. I would not be where I am right now without them, and I am severely proud to be their daughter. That being said, they're not that great at being consistent with dog training. And, like a lot of couples, they aren't always on the same page about things with the dogs.

When I was sixteen, I got a beautiful pittie puppy named Dottie for my birthday. She was a dream—a unicorn dog. No real training necessary, potty trained in two weeks, never super bitey, respected our older dog, slept in bed, and didn't wake in the night. Just an angel!

Well, now I am thirty-one, and last year for Christmas, we gifted my parents another beautiful pittie puppy named Sage Marie after fostering her and making sure she was the right fit for their family. She is also a very good girl! But she was bitey; could be a little rough on their older dog, Gatsby; had some random accidents on a few beds; and was a pretty consistent jumper on people. The number of times I had to retrain my parents' brains to not compare her to Dottie—yikes. But here is the thing: their life is so different now than it was back in 2008. They're in their sixties, they have two grandsons, they're tired, and I no longer live there. Dottie was my dog, and I took care of her full-time! Things are just different, and it was hard for them to come to terms with that.

It's easy to compare, but we are the ones creating these unrealistic expectations—not the new puppy who just got here. When we bring in a new dog, we need to have the idea that we will do whatever it takes to help them or get them the help they need while also being open to changing or admitting we are wrong. If you don't want to do these things, please do not get a dog.

I know it sounds a little harsh, but I will probably say that multiple more times throughout this book, so buckle up. But for real—if someone you knew was having a baby and admitted they didn't care what happened to the kid or didn't want any involvement in helping them learn or become a functioning person in society, I bet you'd think that was fucking strange and would be disgusted. You'd probably say, "So why did you choose to have a baby then? That kid deserves to be loved and cared for 100 percent." And I would wholeheartedly agree!

Another example of unrealistic expectations that hurt the dog and the human is the emotional support or therapy dog. This one slightly boils my blood, so I will try to keep my frustration to a dull roar!

Many people have the idea that you can turn any dog into an emotional support or therapy dog, but this is false and dangerous. There's a new trend of people getting emotional support dogs for their own mental health needs but not getting their dogs formally trained or assessed to see if they are even capable of giving the support their parents are asking for. The same goes for therapy dogs. I was a certifying therapy dog trainer for our local SPCA, so I know from firsthand experience the horrible, unrealistic expectations humans can put on their pets.

I will never forget this story. I had one dog mom who trained her dog on a prong collar for over a year to teach her how to behave in public so she could be a therapy dog. In the therapy dog program, aversive hardware and tools were not allowed, so this dog mom had to walk her dog on a martingale collar. When dogs are tested, they are put through socialization situations of all kinds—tons of school-aged kids running toward them, lots of aggressive petting, loud noises, kids screaming and skipping, another dog being in the same room, old people with wheelchairs and walkers coming near them, and someone pretending to push them and their parent from behind to see if the dog will become defensive or aggressive. For lack of a better phrase, to be a therapy dog, they need to be bombproof. Well, the second this poor dog came into the room, she took one look at the kids and was petrified. The dog mom yanked this dog all over the place, trying to get her to obey her commands and let the kids pet her, but this dog looked like she wanted to be anywhere else. It was honestly so hard to watch. At one point, Mom leash-popped the dog and said, "We've trained for over a year for this. You will *not* fail."

True story. My heart broke for this dog. You want a therapy dog to volunteer and make other people's day better, but you couldn't give a rat's ass about how you are treating your dog or how they feel? Red flag. Swiping left. This dog's entire one and a half years of life had been dedicated to this one thing that Mom was forcing her to do, and she looked like she wanted to crawl out of her skin. This dog did not ask for this. She deserved better. She also did not have the personality, temperament, or type of brain for this type of work.

This, to me, is abuse.

What do I mean by this? Well, to be a good emotional support or therapy dog, it's kind of like that old Maybelline ad—"Maybe she's born with it!" You cannot *teach* a dog to be empathetic and resilient. You cannot teach a dog to not leach emotions off another living, breathing thing.

Now I will use my own life as an example. My dog Oaklee is a therapy dog. We adopted him in 2018, and he was a stray from South Carolina. We call him a "happy dummy." Honestly, I mean this with the utmost love and respect. Oaklee is one of the *happiest* dogs I know, and it's because he is a happy dummy. We say, big head, no thoughts! But that is exactly what makes him one of the best therapy dogs I have ever seen. He was born an extroverted and empathetic dog. He can identify someone under stress and give them exactly what they need in the moment. This is also not something we have practiced or trained for. The only thing I had to help him with was not jumping on people or giving his paw without being asked for it. (So he doesn't accidentally cut an elderly person or a child.) I identified Oaklee as a therapy dog almost instantly because of his ability to give a person the type of therapy *they* need, not something rehearsed that is given over and over again.

If my husband, John, is upset, Oaklee will sit in front of him with his big, beautiful eyes, waiting for eye contact. Then he will nudge John with his nose to get him to pet his head. If he thinks John can make a quick turnaround, he will try to engage in play, which always makes John super happy. They like to roughhouse together. It gets John every time!

If I'm upset, Oaklee will sit next to me and just wait without any direct eye contact. He lets me come to him when I am ready. If I am really upset, he will nudge my underarm with his nose, wedge his face between my rib and arm, and just rest his head lightly on my heart or knee.

My best friend, Kirstin, is a middle school counselor and understandably has a lot of emotions to get out. Oaklee will rest his head right in her lap, make eye contact, and not move until she's calm. The number of times he has done this to her makes us all laugh because she immediately realizes how much she needs him at that moment.

Oaklee can walk away from any high-stress, sad, depressed, anxiety-ridden situation, and mentally, there is not a scratch on him. There is still elevator music playing twenty-four/seven, and I wouldn't have it any other way. He was born to do what he does, and I am so proud to be his mama!

Now, I explain all this because the new trend is to get just any dog in the world and make it do these things Oaklee does, whatever the cost. But it can be detrimental for both dog and dog parent. If you are looking for this for yourself or have dreams of volunteering with your dog, then you need to find the right fit. Therapy dogs that volunteer should *love* it! They should see their vest and want to do nothing else but help people by getting poked and prodded.

Emotional support dogs also need to have the right bones for the job. With anxiety and PTSD at an all-time high in humans, an emotional support dog needs to be like Oaklee—have a marshmallow brain, be intelligent enough to learn any cue, but not be so intelligent that they are reactive, anxious, or fearful themselves. They need to be unconditionally friendly and emotionally neutral in high-stress or high-excitement situations.

They also need to *love* you. If your emotional support dog is not being treated with TLC and receives aversive training instead, they will disengage from you and most likely give you more anxiety and frustration, and thus come to hate you more. So many dog parents come to me with this situation. They got a dog to be their therapy or emotional support dog, but they use aversive, punishment-based techniques and then want devotion and unconditional love in return. This is absurd to me. Would you ever expect an emotionally or physically abused child to love or trust their parents?

No way.

Another thing an emotional support dog cannot be is an emotional leech. You could have the best dog in the world, but if they leach your emotions, anxiety, and stress, they cannot help you. And now you both have anxiety. Unfortunately, I have more clients than I would like to admit who now have a reactive, fearful, overprotective dog because the client struggles. Now the dog won't let anyone come near their parent because they constantly think they are in a dangerous situation due to the parent's mental health state.

I'm sure you know at least a handful of dogs that meet the emotional state of the household or people around them. Unfortunately, these dogs are not fit for this type of work or lifestyle. I think putting them through it is cruel and selfish unless you have the death-do-us-part theory in your head, meaning you will still love and support them whether they can meet that need you intended them for or not.

Which brings me back to the big picture—the whole enchilada! Are you prepared to give this dog the best life possible? As humans, now more than ever, we want the very best. This goes for pretty much everything—food, products, education, technology, cars. The list goes on and on. It's also true of dogs. I probably see at least five commercials a day for the good, natural, refrigerated dog food that costs as much as my mortgage each month.

Clothing for our pups? Some of the pajamas out there are top-notch, with great material. They even offer matching outfits for humans. I mean, genius.

How about bedding? There's memory foam for the pampered princes and princesses. Or the ballistic material beds to ensure that those dogs with separation anxiety aren't sleeping on a cold crate tray.

Now, more than ever, we are going above and beyond for our dogs when it comes to nutrition and products. But why do we not do this with training and education? Why are we so quick to do what our parents did back in the 1970s or listen to any dog trainer without checking credentials? Why do we think that putting a metal prong collar around a dog's neck is proper and ethical? Why are we checking ingredients and wanting the best in every other aspect but are so willy-nilly and comfortable when it comes to handing the leash over to harsh, restrictive, and abusive outdated methods?

I believe the answer to this stems from old-school training methods and myths that, for many reasons, we just can't get rid of for good. Our society loves instant gratification and quick, easy, sexy, DIY. Thirty-second videos are currently up on the pedestal for providing dog training content. This works so well for the aversive or balanced dog training community, as their techniques are quick, physical, and easy to videotape. We have many "trainers" who got themselves famous by going on national TV and teaching people how to be unkind to their dogs. And everyone glorified them.

One clear and well-known example of this is Cesar Millan, the so-called dog whisperer. He's admittedly self-taught and has no certification or educational background in behavior or dogs. The pause button is his best friend, yet people think he fixes dogs in thirty minutes. In reality, it's days and days of emotional suppression and being jabbed in the ribs by someone's fingers that lead these dogs into quiet anguish—not proper or science-based training. Millan's own dog, Junior, mauled Queen Latifah's dog to death while it was in Millan's care for training. Afterward, Junior attacked the teenage daughter of one of Millan's employees when the girl came to see her mother at work.

The world is idolizing someone whose training methods are, first and foremost, inhumane and abusive. They're also extremely dangerous, resulting in numerous lawsuits and payoffs. Many trainers follow his lead and try to make excuses and defenses for why this type of training should still be the go-to way. These people and methods should not be the picture of dog training or something to follow if you want to learn how to parent your dog. *Parent. Not Owner.* Please, for the love of God, simply wipe these methods and people from your mind when you think of good dog training.

Don't worry—I am going to explain all the reasons why!

This type of training is called aversive or balanced training, and it can be extremely damaging to your dog. Balanced training simply means using rewards and punishment together, which is just trying to make it sound better than it is. This punishment-based approach tries to train out bad behavior. Using these methods and wanting a behaviorally sound, happy, well-rounded dog do not go together. To quote my husband, "Suppressing emotions with correction-based training is like taking the tick away from a ticking time bomb. It *will* explode eventually, with no warning."

You see it in the news all the time. A reporter will say, "A dog attacked a child out of nowhere," but what they never reveal is what kind of training methods were used on the dog prior to the incident. They only like to mention the breed, as if that has anything to do with it.

Imagine a dog growling at a kid and being reprimanded over and over again. Maybe a prong collar or shock collar is being used to correct the dog's communication and warnings as well. Every time this dog sees a kid, they are in pain and scared. One day, someone leaves the front door open, there is a kid across the street playing basketball, and the dog gets out. I am pretty sure you can connect the dots of what happens.

If we do not allow dogs to show emotion, those emotions get stuffed into a little box and will be unleashed one day. It's like little boys who are told their whole lives to "toughen up." They hear:

- "Stop crying!"
- "Don't play with that. It's too girly."
- "Don't yell and scream. Only I am allowed to do that."

These little boys turn into angry, angsty, misunderstood men with horrible tempers. That's when it becomes unacceptable, and they get called aggressive, abusive, and dangerous. They can't find a spouse or don't know how to properly raise their children, and they get looks in public.

They deserve better. From an early age, all these young boys deserve nurturing, loving, and empathic homes where they are allowed to *feel.* Instead, they grow up feeling misunderstood and like they can blow at any moment. Add the stress of daily life, work, and kids, and you have yourself a mess. Our little boys who turn into men deserve better.

So do our dogs. Not being allowed to show emotion and feelings leads to aggression, depression, anxiety, and disconnect. I think we can all agree that this is not what we are looking for.

The most commonly used tool for aversive training is the prong collar. It has a series of fang-shaped metal links, or prongs, with blunted points that pinch the loose skin on a dog's neck when pulled.

The first myth I'd like to debunk is the excuse that every pro-prong-collar dog parent or trainer makes when confronted about this: "It doesn't hurt."

If you simply do your research, you will find it tremendously easy to locate evidence to the contrary. "Prong collars work by inflicting pain as punishment in an attempt to correct unwanted behaviors." This is the first definition that comes up when you google "What is a prong collar?" The prong collar was created decades ago and was never intended for everyday use. It was intended to deliver discomfort while training but was not designed for long-term use. It should never be used as your dog's primary collar and should not be used on casual walks or outings. It was intended to be used for no more than one hour and only during designated training sessions. Using the collar any longer could irritate your dog's neck. If placed incorrectly, it can injure the trachea. Personally and professionally, I do not think that anything that can break a bone in your dog's neck, affecting their windpipe for life if simply positioned wrong, is an appropriate training tool.

My next counterpoint to the pro-prong people is that if it doesn't hurt, how does it work? If there is no pain involved when it is tugged as intended, why does the dog stop the behavior? No one has been able to give me an understandable or decent answer yet! And don't give me the fucking bullshit response that it is like when the mother scruffs them when they are babies. Rubbish! Their mother's teeth didn't go all the way around their neck and weren't straight-up metal. Your dog is no longer a baby or as tiny as they were back then, and the mom damn well didn't leash-pop the crap out of her kids.

Another prong collar myth is that it is the only way to successfully walk a large dog that pulls or has aggressive or reactive tendencies on a leash. Yes, you will most likely be able to control them better during their reactivity outburst, but if the prong collar wasn't being used, would there be an outburst at all? Did the collar, in fact, create the problem you now feel cornered with? Either way, there are other, safer options, like front-clip harnesses that are pain-free and extremely durable.

I am also going to say something a few people may not like. If you are not strong enough to walk your dog on an appropriate, humane harness or your dog is so reactive that you are nervous to walk with anything else, I urge you to stop walking your dog until you can safely get their reactivity under control. Your dog most likely isn't enjoying that walk either. I can put money on it.

I'm sure you've noticed by now that I talk a lot about emotions and feelings, but I haven't talked much yet about cue-based dog training. Isn't dog training about telling a dog to do something and they just do it?

No.

Everyone's main goal is to have a happy, healthy, well-rounded, and safe dog, right? So, if we can agree on that point, let me ask another question. Has learning how to do math ever helped you not get into a blowout fight with a friend or significant other? If it has, send that info my way!

If you catch where I am going with this, you'll start to understand that feelings and emotions are the most important parts. But the goal is not for dogs to blindly follow our cues regardless of what they are feeling or doing. The goal is to use those cues to gauge where we are in our emotional regulation. Is it great to have dogs successfully learn and then execute cues in stressful times?

Sure, but again, it may not fix the problem and may only mask the issue with obedience. Do you want to *have* to use obedience cues on your dog their whole life? Or do you eventually not want to have to do or say something to live a peaceful, meaningful life with your dog?

Did you know that allowing your dogs to sleep in your bed or be on your furniture makes them think they are the alpha?

No? Good. Me neither, because it's a dumb fucking myth. The next chapter will clear this up for you immensely, but I wanted to touch on it a bit here first. I have had dogs my entire life. All types of dogs—reactive ones, perfect ones, big, small, sweet, and sassy. Never once has letting a dog sleep in bed been an issue. When I get a new client, the first session is always a complete overview of their dog's life, history, training, and issues. I need to get the whole picture, not just a snippet of the issue that's a problem now. Most of the time, when someone is explaining what they're struggling with, they'll say, "Well, they sleep in bed with us. I know that's probably the problem." Or, after saying the dog sleeps in bed, they will wince, thinking I am going to start yelling at them. This is because so many aversive trainers live by this rule, and so does anyone who is stuck in the old-school training way.

Currently, I am looking at my three rescue dogs, who have different backgrounds and who are snuggled in my bed. That is where you can find them 80 percent of the time. The little Chihuahua is there 95 percent of the time. And she's the one I am going to use as an example here.

John and I fostered Pudgalina, or Pudge for short, in 2016. She is from a hoarding case of over three hundred dogs in one house. Yes, I said three hundred. That is not a typo. And the house was a three-bedroom, so don't go thinking it was a mansion! I physically plucked her out of garbage and debris inside this dilapidated house as little dogs ran around, panicked and biting any chance they could. I was wearing a full hazmat suit and garbed up in the dead of June. She was covered in thousands of fleas, was about only two weeks old, and her eyes were barely opened. I quickly realized she wasn't breathing. So I rushed her outside to the medical tent, and she was immediately whisked off to the local ER. It was one of the longest days of my life. From eight a.m. to ten p.m., the SPCA cleared this house of dogs and tried to get them to triage and safety.

That night, after dropping the last lot of dogs off at the shelter, I couldn't get Pudge out of my head. When I'd found her, she'd given a little scream, then was nothing but a limp body barely holding on. I decided I had found her for a reason and made the decision to foster her if she was still alive.

A week later, she came home with me—bottle-and-milk feedings, warming disk, and all. I had my first foster. Cute, right?

But what in the hell does this have to do with dogs not being allowed on the bed?

Well, Pudge, as cute as she was in the beginning, became more and more difficult. In her defense, her genetics were crap. She was inbred to start with. Her parents were cousins! All three hundred dogs stemmed from eight purebred small dogs. And to follow it up, none of her family members were socialized properly. They were basically feral dogs just living indoors. They'd never been outside, and the majority of them were untouched by humans. So let's just say Pudge does not fall into the "easy" dog category I was talking about earlier. She was feisty, reactive, and sassy. She held her ground when she wanted something badly enough. She absolutely gave John's patience a run for his money in the first year or two, but all in all, she was our baby, and we worked with her.

If there was ever a dog to become dominant or guard resources, it would be Pudgalina. She came from a home and had a genetic background in which resources were extremely scarce. Guarding comes second nature to dogs like this. But she does not guard the bed or furniture.

Why?

There are many reasons, but the short answer is that we make sure none of her basic resources (food, water, high-value toys, enrichment, love, etc.) are scarce. And we never once forced her to move off the bed or furniture out of pure dominance or to prove that we could. I will talk about this more in Chapter 12.

This was a long-winded way of saying that just because you allow your dogs on the furniture or in bed with you does not mean it will affect your relationship and training poorly. This is an extremely outdated myth that old-school trainers use to bully dog parents. They also use it as an excuse when their other methods aren't working. This also goes for the myth that you need to assert dominance over your dog to train them and get them to obey you the right way. This type of training includes flipping a dog on its back for misbehaving, pinning them on their back, and holding them down until they submit to you.

Disregard this ridiculousness! This is abuse and is *never* necessary.

Next myth to break: some dogs need a heavy hand. I scoff at this one! This is an old and poor excuse to use a prong or shock collar or use a physically heavy hand on a dog because the trainer simply is not educated enough to fix the problem without it. This goes back to my comparison with kids. No child needs to be physically hurt to learn properly. That just shows the child that it is okay to hurt others when they aren't listening. No child needs a heavy hand. What children and dogs both need is firm, clear, and unwavering boundaries. I have trained dogs from four pounds to two hundred and fifty pounds, and I have never once had to use a heavy hand, aversive tools, or techniques. If someone tells you that a certain breed needs this type of method, run for the hills, and take your dog with you! As you continue to read, you will understand all the other ways we can go about correcting unwanted and even aggressive behaviors without meeting them with aggression in turn!

One of my other favorite myths is that a dog is too old to learn or change (as in you can't teach an old dog new tricks). False! My favorite rebuttal is to ask if a sixty-year-old person can still go to therapy and make huge, positive changes in their life and other lives around them. Absolutely they can. So can older dogs because this isn't about trick training. This is behavioral, and you can always change behavior, emotions, feelings, and associations no matter how old you are!

Many of these unhelpful and abusive myths originate from the ideology that since dogs are descendants of wolves and this is how wolves act in the wild and in their packs, we should act that way too.

That's another myth! Actually, both parts are. First, that's not how wolves act in the wild. And second, we have so thoroughly domesticated dogs that we cannot fall back on wolf pack behavior modification, thinking this is the correct way to go about training our family dogs. This is known as the alpha theory, and Chapter 2 will tell you all the reasons it sucks!

Chapter 2:
The Alpha Theory Is Wrong

Have you ever heard a dog trainer, family member, friend, or random person on the street give you the unsolicited advice of "You *need* to be the alpha?"

If you answered no to this, consider yourself lucky! This is probably the worst advice anyone can receive when it comes to their relationship with their dog. Before I go into why, I want to explain a little about the alpha theory's background and where it came from. I think it will help a lot of you who might be holding on to this as truth because it may be all you know and grew up with. Also, it may help you if someone says this to you in the future!

In the context of dog training, the term *alpha theory* is often associated with dominance-based or pack leadership theories. This idea suggests that dogs form social hierarchies similar to wolf packs, with the assumption that a dog parent must establish themselves as the alpha, or dominant leader, in the relationship to control their dog's behavior. If not, they will never have a well-behaved dog, and problems will continue.

In the 1990s, L. David Mech, one of the original researchers on wolf behavior, revised his views and disavowed the concept of a strict dominance hierarchy in wolf packs that he'd come out with a decade prior. He stated that the idea of an alpha wolf was misleading and did not accurately represent the cooperative and family-oriented structure of wolf packs in the wild and dogs in the home. Why did he change his mind? Well, it turns out that the dynamics of wolf packs in captivity do not necessarily reflect natural wolf behavior.

To dumb it down a little, homeboy David Mech created the alpha theory and then realized, years later, that he was *wrong*. Then he *owned up to it*. He debunked his own theory!

To explain this a little further, Mech had taken one wolf from each wolf pack and put them in captivity together. So the wolves that were in captivity together were not blood relations or from the same family pack. So, of course, there were fights and killings. Certain stronger, more confident, and intelligent wolves were the ones to not cross or mess with, giving the illusion they were in charge. Have you ever seen the reality TV show *Big Brother* or any reality TV show where people who don't know each other are inside one house together? These are good examples of what Mech's experiment showed him. *Total fucking chaos!* We all know that these people are not acting like they normally would at home with their mothers, where they are safe and loved. These people are fighting to marry the most good-looking contestant or win $50,000. So yeah, they're gonna get a little rowdy and cutthroat!

Now, think about the contestants who "win" by being the most popular among the group. Are they truly the most loved and admired? Or are they feared?

It is the latter.

After a while, Mech realized the problem with this theory. It's just not realistic, and these circumstances do not happen in real life. So we can't use this theory to construct our everyday, normal behavioral training.

Wolf packs in the wild function much like human families. The parents teach their young how to function in society, but there is not one set of parents in charge. They function as a group, and certain tasks and jobs are delegated to individuals as they teach their young to one day take over their role in the pack. They do not thrive as a pack by focusing on punishment-based parenting. They correct pups with proper communication to allow them to understand and do better the next time. This builds trust. The mild correction fits the situation. The parents give alternative opinions and reassure the pups that they are still loved but that what they did is a hard boundary. This is necessary in all societies. The wolves prove that firm boundaries and proper communication are necessary—not pain and dominance. But humans make it sound so vicious and aggressive.

Additionally, if we want to compare wolves to dogs, we need to consider all that we have done by domesticating them and bringing them inside because it's not fair to compare two kinds of animals that are living different lives. John and I got to see Sindhoor Pangal present at the 2023 Aggression in Dogs Conference, and it was eye-opening.

Sindhoor lives in India and was telling us about India's large population of street dogs, better known as "streeties." These are not stray or feral dogs. They live peacefully and harmoniously in the neighborhoods and are loved by the human population. She told us about her dog, which lived indoors, and how she interacted with the streeties that lived just beyond Sindhoor's property. It was so fascinating. In the beginning, although her dog didn't get the subtle, nonverbal cues from the resident mama dog in that pack, her dog tried to play and be social with them. Sindhoor observed from afar and did not physically or verbally get involved. She got to see all the ways the streeties communicated as a family and how drastically different it was from how our inside dogs communicate. These streeties, by comparison, were so in tune with each other.

The streetie mama could move ever so slightly, and a pup that wasn't even hers would know to stop playing too roughly with a sibling too close to the mama. She did not need to bark or get physically aggressive. It was such a subtle movement that it took Sindhoor herself a while to pick up on it. But she took videos so she could study them. The biggest takeaway was how little her own dog picked up on these subtleties. This was because her dog did not grow up that way, similar to a lot of dogs, except for maybe rescued strays or city dogs that are constantly around other dogs in large groups.

By domesticating dogs the way we have—bringing them into our homes, pampering them, and feeding them at the same time every day with seemingly no struggle for them at all—we've removed their need to harness or utilize these communication skills for survival. Have you ever had a dog that never socialized with other dogs before? Such as in the first three or four months of their lives or even a few years. Then they get into a situation where they need to interact with one or more other dogs. Maybe you get lucky and they do well. But the majority of the time, one of two things will happen:

- Your dog is super awkward and submissive because they're terrified and realize they can get hurt.
- Your dog is super reactive or immediately aggressive upon approaching and getting sniffed.

This is not their fault! This is like keeping a kid inside their entire life—never letting them leave the house or interact with any other humans. All of a sudden, you send them to first grade, and they have a mental breakdown and don't know how to socialize. This happens because they did not learn the social skills they need to be with other humans, especially kids their own age.

Another example is kids who are only children. They are stereotyped as bratty, spoiled, type A control freaks who can't share or delegate. This stereotype isn't based on nothing, and it's not their fault! (This isn't always the case, but it does happen often. So, if you are an only child, please don't be offended!) They did not have siblings to share toys with, they didn't have to let a sibling pick what to watch on TV, and they didn't have to deal with someone else getting all the attention. That's because their parents had only them to worry about. They never learned how to calm down when they're upset, when they don't get their way, or when they aren't getting their needs immediately met. We are all products of our environment, as are our dogs!

So the moral of the story is that basing training for our inside dogs on what wild animals do or don't do does not check out. Unfortunately, regardless of all this science-based information and debunking from well-known and credited scientists, most aversive or balanced dog trainers lean extremely hard into the alpha theory. They do this even though subsequent research, and Mech himself, debunked the strict dominance hierarchy concept in wild wolf packs and its correlation with dogs. Mech has been documented on many social media platforms trying to tell the world he was wrong. But the aversive trainers of the world try to act like this is not true.

Why?

Because if they were to listen and agree, their entire training and business model and what they do would crumble! So they ignore it and keep abusing dogs. And honestly, we are all just letting them do it. We don't do research. We think that because someone owns a business and talks confidently, they must be right. We are so naive. It will never stop until dog parents wake up and demand better.

Many of these trainers use the alpha theory at the forefront of every move they make—physically with the dogs and mentally with their human clients. They come off as confident, assertive, and aggressive, creating the illusion that they know what they are doing. They bully not only the dogs but the parents as well. During their training, they do not ask anything about the dog's history, past, or emotional struggles. They do not take into account if a dog has anxiety, suffers from stranger danger, or was previously abused or in a traumatic situation. They use the same punitive techniques on any dog that exhibits "bad" behavior.

This is abusive and unethical. Relying on dominance-based methods is considered outdated and harmful, and many modern animal behaviorists and trainers have criticized dominance-based training methods. Using punishment-based techniques to establish dominance may lead to negative consequences, such as fear, anxiety, and aggression in dogs. Isn't this the exact opposite of what we want for our dogs?

Current approaches to dog training emphasize using positive reinforcement and building a strong bond based on trust and cooperation rather than attempting to dominate the dog. If any of the methods you have been told to use consist of anything you could see your childhood bully doing, run for the fucking hills!

Here are some old-school training red flags and things to avoid:

- "When they do something wrong, stare your dog down." This is where you make direct eye contact with a dog, usually standing over them, and wait for them to submit to you.
- "Dogs are not allowed on furniture or in bed with you. They'll think they're your equal." Again, utter bullshit.
- "Dehumanize your dog. They are not human and should not be treated the same." This is asinine! Your dog's needs and emotions are just as important as yours. I had a client tell me that their previous trainer said this to them, and I almost puked in my mouth. Disgusting!
- "Prong collars don't hurt. It mimics when their mothers correct them by scruffing them." So many things to say. 1) They *do* hurt. Otherwise, they wouldn't work. 2) No mother dog scruffs her puppy past a few weeks old. 3) You are not a dog or that dog's real mother. Stop! 4) There are so many more humane ways to show a dog you do not like a certain behavior without pain. Grow up.
- "This breed always needs a heavy hand." More bullshit. No breed needs a heavy hand, ever. I have trained more "aggressive" breeds than I can count, and I have never had to resort to aversive techniques. In reality, this phrase equates to "I have no idea how to help your dog, so I'm just going to be a bully. When it doesn't work, I'll just blame it on the parents." *Run*, please! For the love of God, run.
- "The prong collar doesn't seem to be too effective for your dog. Let's switch to the shock collar. It's just a vibration." This is a straight-up lie. Shock collars absolutely hurt. Fit one properly on your neck,

shock yourself, and let me know how it goes. And the trainer never just keeps the vibration. They will always kick it up to a shock and keep going till your dog submits to the pain.

Not all the time, but the majority of the time, aversive trainers or any dog parents who refuse to change from aversive techniques get a serious personal high off this type of training. I have concluded that most of the ones I have met were either bullies in high school or got bullied in high school and think now it's their turn. If you still agree with aversive training after learning about these facts and studies and do not think you are a bully, please tell me why you would choose these options over a more humane technique for your dog. I want to know!

Ultimately, this goes back to childhood. I'm sure you can remember that one schoolteacher you hated. What kind of personality did they have? How did they teach you? I'm sure they humiliated you, embarrassed you, punished you unfairly, and shamed you. If you did listen to them, it wasn't out of respect. It was out of fear.

My most hated teacher was my freshman math teacher, and the first thing that comes to mind is, *What a horrible human being she was!* But once I stop thinking back as my fourteen-year-old self and think now as a thirty-one-year-old wise and enlightened me, my second thought is, *She must have been an unhappy, unfulfilled, damaged person who needed to do a whole lot of emotional work.*

I remember saying to my mom, "Why would someone like that want to teach kids if they're just going to be so mean all the time?" My mother didn't have an answer for me. Partly, I think she was thinking the same thing. My mom always taught me to have good manners and not be disrespectful. She did not jump to her kids' defense just because. She always wanted to know the facts and make sure I wasn't the one creating the problems. Basically, she didn't want me to be a menace to society, and in her defense, I was an outspoken, somewhat difficult kid growing up. She knew I could get a little rowdy. I just really liked to talk! I also didn't take shit from anyone, especially just because they were in an authoritative position. I am still like this. Just because you are "important" does not mean you get to be an asshole to everyone. That's a hard *no* for me.

After many conferences with that teacher, even my mom disliked her. She was still in her position due to tenure. She just made everything more difficult, tense, and less fun. Before freshman year, I loved math. I was good at it despite my learning disability, but she ruined it for me. I didn't retain anything that year, and I believe it hurt me for the rest of my high school career. I didn't fully understand what I learned that first year, and everything after was built on top of prior knowledge. So I just kind of skated by the next three years.

After that, I behaved in her class, but not because I respected or liked her. It was honestly out of avoidance. I didn't want to have to talk to her or interact with her at all. After going back and forth with the conferences and standing up for myself in the beginning, I was shut down for the rest of the year. I just didn't want to deal with her horribleness anymore. So yeah, she looked like she got what she wanted—a seen-and-not-heard student. But I didn't learn a thing. She should have wanted to teach children the way they learn and thrive—not with her my-way-or-the-highway type of teaching.

This goes for dogs as well. Why would someone become a dog trainer if they didn't want to help dogs the right way? The science-based, vet-approved, humane way? It still baffles me, but I know why. People love instant gratification and quick fixes. Unfortunately, this is how our society has become. And it's even more so after COVID because everything during the pandemic was online and done super quickly. Look at dog training TikTok! It's all thirty-second snapshots of how to eliminate bad behaviors. It's just not real. It's not normal, authentic, empathetic training. And frankly, it's dangerous! When you give people blanket advice on how to fix issues when you don't know where the issues stem from, it is unethical. That's thirty seconds of fixing an issue. But I want to see how the next year pans out for that dog and their family due to laziness and lack of education.

Did you know dogs can experience PTSD like humans do? It is extremely common and not some far-fetched myth. Have you ever seen a dog wince when you go to pet them?

We adopted Oaklee in 2018. Since then, he has never known a bad day in his life. Pup has the dream life, for real! But, still to this day, he jumps a little when he feels my hand on him. I could be petting him consistently—pets that he asked for—and when I release him and come back down to his fur, he still jumps. My poor boy. He was abused before we got him. Someone was mean and rough with this sweet soul. When we first got him, he looked like he wanted to give kisses, but then he'd shy away. So we let him come to it in his own time. When he finally got up enough courage to kiss, he would wince and cower like he was going to get hit across the face. It was one of the more heartbreaking things to watch. I think he'd lived with a family that had young kids. He's just so amazing with them, but I think he got hit if he kissed them. It took us years to show him he was allowed to kiss whoever he wanted without someone taking out aggression on him. I could see how hard it was for him to fully trust that he wasn't going to get hurt.

It takes time, empathy, and consistency to help a dog with PTSD overcome something done to them in a matter of seconds. It's like gaining weight. You could gain twenty pounds in a few weeks, but it may take you a full year to lose it.

I try to get this point across so often, but a lot of people want help only once the damage is done and they are in a hole. If more people understood what to watch out for from the very beginning with dogs—such as who not to turn to and what kinds of techniques to avoid like the plague—we could avoid so many struggles!

PTSD in dogs can show up in many different ways. Remember how we discussed in Chapter 1 that dogs learn by association, not by cause and effect? This means they remember events and scenarios through emotions instead of logic. This seems to be a tough concept for humans to wrap their heads around. But just keep telling yourself over and over again, "My dog thinks like a toddler." But dogs cannot scream, cry, or ask for help like a toddler can, so they react. They bark, lunge, and growl. This is their only form of communication! This is extremely important to remember as I give more examples of PTSD and what it looks like.

I have a lot of clients who tell me, "I've had my dog since they were eight weeks old. I don't know why they are so scared of _____." Well, my response is usually that eight weeks is a decent amount of time to be treated poorly and develop aversions to certain things, don't you think? Have you ever dated a narcissist for two months? Zero out of ten recommend. Maybe your dog is a purebred and was with a breeder before you picked them up. There are many different scenarios that can happen in a short period. (These can also happen in rescue situations!)

- The breeder had a heavy hand and was rough with the puppies, so now your dog is scared of men who look a certain way.
- The breeder had young kids who handled and played rough with the puppies, so now they're terrified of young kids.
- The breeder used a vacuum to clean up their area every day. It was loud and scary, so now your dog hates the vacuum and tries to attack it.
- Your puppy was the runt, and none of their siblings let them nurse on Mom or get to food. Now they're a food guarder and will go after anyone who goes near them when they have food.
- Your dog had a long flight or car trip to get to you. Now they're anxious or stressed, and they hate to travel or leave the house. Super fun!
- Your puppy was picked on by all its siblings and didn't know how to defend themselves. Now they are terrified of other dogs and come off aggressive, but they're just scared.
- Mom was a stray and had her puppies on the side of the road. Mom passed away, and the puppies were left to fend for themselves. This can leave you with a dog that has abandonment issues, resource guarding, and fear of pretty much everything.

When dogs experience PTSD or act on feelings and emotions, we don't get to disagree. If a dog is food guarding because they were the runt of the litter and never got to eat, we don't get to say, "Well, you have food now, so get over it." We have to *prove* to them with consistency, compassion, empathy, and love that they will always have food and no one is going to take it from them. We have to heal the wounds, even if we weren't the ones who wounded them. It's kind of like when you get into a new relationship, and your new partner has some trust issues from their past. You weren't the one who caused that trauma, but if you love that person, you want to prove to them that you aren't like their ex. Is it frustrating to have to bear a cross you didn't create? Hell yes! But this is what we do for the ones we love, and it only builds a deeper bond. Dogs are the same way. They just can't understand our English or why they shouldn't feel so bad about something, so it needs to come more from our actions than our words.

PTSD and aversive training go hand in hand. Some people get so mad when I say this, but it is ridiculously true. If you have an aversive trainer, your dog is accustomed to thinking, *I better do _____ right away so I don't get a leash pop or a shock.* That's already fear-based thinking, but then there is another component.

What is the trainer asking them to do? Maybe they want your dog to go in the crate. Your dog already doesn't love the crate because when they go in, you leave for work, and they just sit there, stressed, until you come back hours later. So you hire a trainer so you can stop chasing your dog into the crate every morning before work. After the training, your dog goes into the crate only when you pick up the remote to threaten a shock on their collar, so they run in.

You got what you wanted, right? You guess so, but then you see how sad your dog looks and how much they howl when you leave. Or maybe they shake or drool or have diarrhea daily now. You're having second thoughts. Was this really what you wanted? Did you want to have to threaten your dog to get in the crate? Or did you want your dog to like their crate better and have less anxiety about you leaving for work?

I believe you were looking for the latter, but because you wanted it done so quickly and are so busy, you wanted someone else to do it for you. Now you're worse off. You're not only more stressed when you're leaving for work, but you also feel awful for threatening your dog so you can leave the house.

How did this happen? Unfortunately, you were bamboozled by an aversive trainer who promised you results their methods can't attain. You also got greedy, and the quick fix looked good.

Imagine if your boss or significant other threatened to hurt you every time you didn't do something the way they wanted, even though you said you didn't like doing it. I'm pretty sure you'd run.

So, what's the right way to train a dog?

It's called positive reinforcement behavioral training, and in my professional opinion, it is the only way dogs should be trained, no matter what you are dealing with. Cradle to grave, start to finish, it's always the best approach. I absolutely love my job, and I'm going to show you all the reasons why.

Positive reinforcement is based on the principles of operant conditioning, which emphasizes the positive consequences of behavior to increase the likelihood of its recurrence. It is considered a humane and effective training method that promotes a strong bond between the dog and the trainer or parent while minimizing stress and fear. But let's be honest. Positive reinforcement training can also get a bad rap because the connotation is that dogs are being bribed, spoiled, or made dependent on treats to do what we want them to do.

I have so many things to say about this!

- If I had to choose something for my dog to be dependent on, I would want it to be treats and not a metal or shock collar.
- Dogs don't live very long, so you bet your ass I'm gonna spoil them as much as I can, while I can. But that's not the reason they listen to me.

- Using reward-based training is not bribing them. Rewards mark good behavior, but they also can change associations from bad to good—which is really the moneymaker!
- If you train the right way—with rewards, love, and empathy—your dog won't rely on treats at all. That's because they have a great life and they love you. End of story. You think I walk around my three dogs all day with a treat bag on? Absolutely not. My dogs listen because I work on building a bond with each of them, and I uphold my part of the bargain daily.

Positive reinforcement training is also said to be mostly cue-based training, which is not what I do. For example, a trainer who is certified in positive reinforcement might just work on the place and stay cues for a dog that struggles with greeting people and jumps when guests come in. There is a huge difference between regular positive reinforcement dog training and positive reinforcement behavioral training. The behavioral component changes things drastically, for many reasons.

Behavioral training is more like therapy and comprehensive care, all rolled into one. I don't just look at the fact that my clients' dogs have low impulse control and can't calm down when guests come over. But I am going to look at the whole dog and the whole big picture. I'm going to ask a lot of questions about the dog's daily life and what enrichment activities they receive. I am going to ask what the family does proactively to get their dog ready for guests coming over so they're in a good mental space. I am going to look at their background and what their socialization looked like early on. For example, were they a COVID puppy and had zero interactions with guests for their first two years? Are they now unable to settle down when friends come over?

All of these things matter when we are trying to do effective behavioral modification. By just forcing place and stay cues, I can actually create more anxiety and frustration when guests are over. I also do not find place and stay cues to be super natural for families. They're not authentic, and it seems to become more and more stressful for families over time as they try to greet their guests and manage a dog that's a millisecond away from ditching their stay and pummeling the guests. It's just not realistic, especially if you add a dog or two to the mix, along with little kids running around.

Believe me, I am not trying to knock cue-based training! It absolutely has its place, and cue training is definitely necessary if we want dogs to know what the hell we are asking so they aren't confused. It's the foundation of most training!

I think the biggest difference here is that I would not ask for a sit-and-stay if I knew a dog was fearful, overstimulated, anxious, or stressed in any way. Many people ask me, "Why would you not continue to ask for those cues when the dog is too ___ to listen? Isn't the whole point to get them to listen to you, no matter what?"

The answer is no. That's not the whole point, and this is where we go wrong. The actual goal is not what we say out loud. Clients will say, "I want my dog to listen when guests are coming in the door." And I say, "No, what you want is a calm dog that greets people without jumping and doing crazy zoomies, not a dog that pushes its own emotions aside to obey you. You want a dog with impulse control." This cracks me up because the latter is so much more attainable than a dog that listens to you when guests come over. Would you ever expect your kid to be able to listen to everything you say the second their favorite grandparent or best friend from school comes in the door?

Hell no! You wouldn't even attempt it until your kid calms down a bit and comes down from the high of seeing their favorite person. You'd smile at the love they have for each other and feel grateful for the excitement.

I know this because it happens at my house at least four times a week when my parents come through the door. It's one of my biggest blessings. And the same goes for my dogs. They *love* my parents. Now, in our society, it is acceptable for our kids to run into the arms of our parents. But for our dogs, it's a big no-no. They get deemed untrained and wild, but it's simply untrue!

Pudge spent the first year of her life living at my parents' house. She thinks the sun rises and ends with the two of them. She'd pack her bags and move there tomorrow if we let her! When my parents come in, she loses it. Her blond twelve-pound body is a blur as she tears all around the living room. Then she runs up to them and waits to be picked up. I'd never ask her for any cue during this time because it would never happen. And I honestly don't have to. She gets her zoomies out, which we allow, and she doesn't jump or nip. We've worked on helping her control her excitement to the point where it's perfectly appropriate, and everyone wins! We all get such a kick out of how excited she is.

Some may say, "Well, she's twelve pounds. Good luck getting away with that with a bigger dog!" Okay, so Oaklee is around ninety-five pounds, and he gets just as excited when my parents come in. He does not jump or knock them over. He will excitedly come over for pets and love. He may squish them on the couch a little bit, but never in a dangerous way. We've taught him how to naturally control his impulses and enjoy all the love from his grandparents without pushing them down the stairs!

So, how did we get to that point with dogs? We worked with them in a natural, helpful, empathetic way, using behavioral modification. Let me explain!

In reality, we yell cues at dogs when they are jumping on the grandparents, day after day after day, and nothing ever changes. Dog parents don't get it because their dog understands "Down" every other time, and the dog doesn't jump on them when they come home. But when the grandparents come in, all hell breaks loose. And they're right! A dog's impulse control goes out the window for any type of excitement that's over a seven on a scale of one to ten, with ten being the most excited. But they understand the down cue, right? So why can't they calm down?

I asked this question earlier, but I need to ask it again. Does knowing how to do math ever help you not get into a fight with your significant other?

No, not at all. Because math has nothing to do with your emotions. Has it clicked yet?

Math and *cue training* have nothing to do with *emotions* and *impulse control.* It is so simple. Meanwhile, what we learned growing up and what we see on TikTok and TV is glorified. It's like sticky candy stuck on the inside of our brains. But it's time to clean it out if you want true, long-lasting results that end in you and your dog having this blissful, read-each-other's-thoughts type of relationship.

Don't worry. We will discuss guests and impulse control more in Chapter 9.

As I stated earlier, behavioral training is more about the big picture and less about fixing a situation the moment you are in it. There are no band-aids here. We stitch up big wounds. It is a lot about setting dogs up for success and preparing them for the things they struggle with. It is a lot of Systematic Desensitizarion and working our way up to what I call the "big kahuna moments," which are the moments that currently cause them the most stress or trigger low impulse control. And it involves a lot of making sure we are meeting a dog's needs before we ask them to meet ours! Systematic desensitization therapy is a type of cognitive-behavioral therapy (CBT) that is used to treat anxiety disorders, phobias, and other conditions that involve excessive fear. It works by gradually exposing the person to their feared object or situation in a positive, controlled and safe environment.

In behavioral training, there isn't anything we can't fix or improve. It is important to give each dog and situation all we have before throwing in the towel or thinking this is just the way things are. It is about diving deep and doing anything we can to help improve the most intense behaviors. Behavioral training is all about figuring out the best plan and protocol for your family, not the family down the street.

We will discuss in depth how to meet your dog's specific needs in Chapter 5!

Chapter 3:

What Kind of Dog Parent Do You Want to Be?

Now that we've gone over how dogs learn and think—as well as all the ways you can unnecessarily fuck up your dog—let's figure out what kind of parent you want to be moving forward. Let's figure out what you are made of!

Embarking on the journey of dog parenthood is a commitment that mirrors, in many ways, the complexities, rewards, and consequences of human relationships. It is a *commitment.* It requires a blend of empathy, understanding, extreme self-awareness, and a willingness to grow alongside your dog. And yes, that means taking responsibility for situations you may have accidentally created. We all make mistakes, but how you make up for them and change your behavior for the future is what matters. If you suck at apologizing when you hurt someone's feelings, pay attention. In my experience, dog parents generally fall into one of four categories. Recognizing where you fit—or where you aspire to be—can profoundly affect the relationship you build with your dog. Time to get real and buckle up!

First are the dog parents who approach their role with open hearts and minds. My *favorite* kind of dog parents. They're ready to listen, learn, and apply new knowledge for the betterment of their dogs. They take responsibility and own up to the things they may or may not have done that have contributed to the issues they are now dealing with. I respect this so much! This group thrives on empathy and compassion, understanding that successful dog parenting is about guidance rather than control. They are not interested in control whatsoever because they have unconditional love for their dog and only want the best for them to be happy. When faced with challenges, they seek solutions that prioritize their dog's emotional and physical well-being. If you're naturally empathetic, this path offers a fulfilling way to deepen your bond with your dog. These are my badass parents who are a joy to work with, and I can tell you, their behavior modification process always goes way faster than all the rest. If this is you, pat yourself on the back. I love you. Stay golden!

The second set of parents adore their dogs but find it challenging to adapt their behaviors and responses to meet their dogs' needs effectively. These parents spare no expense on premium food and veterinary care, yet they struggle with their dog's lack of emotional regulation, often resorting to yelling or blaming their dogs for misunderstandings or misbehaviors. This disconnect usually stems from unresolved personal issues or learned behaviors that obstruct empathetic communication, usually learned in childhood. Recognizing this pattern is the first step toward making change, but this group of parents has a hard time having empathy for their dog. It is kind of like a brick wall for them. They can be on board and understand that their own behavior is why the dog's behavior is not changing for the better. They will actively tell me they understand and agree, but then they have an extremely hard time remembering what we discussed. They can change how they react in the moment and need to be reminded multiple times. These parents want to help, but they struggle to mentally help themselves because they may have deep-rooted attachment styles to reprimanding and assuming ill intent. Their brains do not know how to play detective and get curious when they are overwhelmed or frustrated. If this is you, you have to remember that your dog isn't the problem and that the solution has to start with you. This will take time, so give yourself grace. All you can do is put 100 percent effort in. You got this!

Third, we have the authoritarians. These are the parents from Chapter 2—the alpha theory lovers. They believe in a hierarchy in which dogs are seen and not heard and are expected to obey without question. This approach often relies on intimidation and punishment, ignoring the dog's emotional state and well-being. It's a perspective rooted in control, not companionship. These parents think that because it is "just a dog," they can do whatever they want and the dog should tolerate and allow it. They believe they are alpha and that the dog needs to listen all the time, no matter the circumstances and whether they have taught the expectation or even earned the dog's respect. As with my second set of parents, this is usually rooted in how they were raised or how their parents treated animals. This group suffers from narcissistic tendencies. If you find yourself or a family member leaning toward this style, it's crucial to immediately reevaluate it. Although, if this is you, I highly doubt you are reading this book. (But your spouse probably is.) It is always extremely hard when someone in the family has these views and just blatantly refuses to get with the program. This group *hates* taking advice or orders from anyone else. And, just like a misunderstood child, they will do the thing you are asking them not to do just out of pure spite. So we need to tread with caution with this group—but not because we are scared of them. Screw that! We are treading lightly for the dog's sake. We will eventually win them over throughout this book. We will teach our own boundaries with parenting and training in a healthy, caring, empathetic way (and a little bit of reverse psychology). And after that, if they don't get on board, I highly suggest leaving! I'm kidding, but I'm also slightly serious. It has been said that the way someone treats animals when they are young is a good way to gauge how they would treat their own children when the going gets tough. I'll just leave that there. At the end of the day, dogs are sentient beings deserving of respect and kindness. Period. Transforming this mindset can not only improve your dog's quality of life but also unlock a level of companionship you might not have imagined possible. By not cutting off the bad fruit, you may infect the whole tree, if you catch my drift. Our children watch everything we do.

Fourth, we have the poor novices. But everyone has to start somewhere, right? If you are a first-time dog parent and are reading this before even getting your dog, *bravo*, my friend. You are going to shine! First-time dog parents are a group beaming with enthusiasm and high expectations but often lacking in practical experience and the ability to be realistic. Their hearts are in the right place, yet they might harbor unrealistic expectations about dog parenting, which, I am sure you can guess, sets everyone up to fail miserably. This experience needs to be more like having a human baby. I think almost every new parent, right before giving birth, is just hoping and praying the kid comes out with all their fingers and toes while knowing there will most likely be a struggle, or twenty. They are not expecting to sleep or be able to take a shower. I think most first-time human parents have proper expectations before bringing their first baby home.

First-time puppy parents? Hell no. I have no idea why, but every new puppy parent is confused when the dog nips them, pees in the house, tears up their stuff, and doesn't listen when they don't nap. The utter befuddlement on parents' faces when they come to me with their four-month-old-puppy problems is comical. Most of the time, I have to keep in my laughter and refrain from saying, "But seriously, what were you expecting they were going to be doing at this age?" Did we think we'd be brewery hopping? I mean, seriously! Truly, though, the key for first-timers is education and openness to learning, but being realistic is most important. Understanding that puppies and dogs require time, patience, and consistent training is vital. You have to be committed to that and to the fact that there are no guarantees. No one can guarantee you a well-rounded dog with a chill personality—even if you do tons of research on a specific breed.

You will see stories in this book about purebred dogs that are the exact opposite of what the big book of dog breeds says they should be. Do not be surprised when your doodle mix is an anxious mess that doesn't want to be touched! You have to adjust your expectations or simply have none at all. It's just like having kids. You may think you are getting one type of kid but get the opposite. Does that baby deserve less love? Absolutely not. And they should not have to stand up to expectations they never agreed to. Have an open mind and be willing to adjust without holding on to resentment. Every puppy deserves a fresh start and an open future. If you are a first-time parent, welcome. I can't wait to teach you *everything*!

As you move deeper into this book, you'll need to make some decisions and ask yourself some pretty big questions. Reflecting and answering out loud or on paper can be ridiculously helpful and enlightening. So, it's time to ask yourself some critical questions:

What are you seeking in a dog?

Why do you want a dog?

What are your expectations?

These reflections are crucial in ensuring that you're ready for the responsibilities and joys of dog parenthood. If your answers sound more selfish and egotistical than selfless, please reconsider getting a dog. I know that sounds fucking harsh, but it is just the truth. And we all know the truth hurts sometimes. No one should have a life and a family just to meet other people's needs and fit into a little box without room to grow. And here is why.

At the heart of all these reflections is a fundamental truth: dogs are not possessions but beings with needs, desires, and rights. You do not own them. You notice I call you a "parent" and not an "owner." Embracing this mindset is the first step toward becoming a dog parent who not only meets their dog's needs but also respects their autonomy and individuality. Whether you're seeking a companion, a protector, or an emotional support animal, remember that the relationship must be built on mutual respect and understanding. You cannot *make* them into what you want just because you are a human and they are a dog.

I could never make Oaklee into a guard dog in a million years. And it would be even more difficult to make Pudge into a therapy dog. Honestly,

I'm laughing at the thought. Pudge would bite someone immediately! They are just simply not built for those jobs.

Similarly, I could never be a humane police officer. I would have murdered someone on my first day. But John was, and he did it for years with poise and grace. It wasn't that he didn't care or didn't also want to give those horrible people what they deserved for abusing animals. It was because he knew if he didn't do the job right, there would be many other dogs he couldn't save. *Selfless and proper perspective.*

Me? No proper perspective over here. Just beating everyone up for hurting animals, and that's why I am not a cop! And John does not do the one-on-one training with clients because he hates talking to people. It's just not his thing! That doesn't mean he's not an excellent trainer or good at talking to people. He just does better in group settings with me leading or just one-on-one with our rehab program dogs up for adoption. We all shine in different ways, and so do our dogs! But I can assure you, no dog can shine under the force and pressure of trying to be something they are not. Remember the poor pup who was being forced to be a therapy dog? Is that what you want to do to your dog? I hope not.

More questions you need to answer are:

Are you ready to be an advocate?

Are you ready to stand up for your dog?

Are you ready to put them first, no matter what the situation?

Are you prepared to respect their communication, boundaries, and wishes?

Are you ready to put your own bullshit aside when your dog appropriately tells you they don't like something?

Are you ready to get your dog the help they need, medical or behavioral?

Are you ready to question and second-guess outdated advice, then do your research on medication and technique?

Are you ready to love this dog unconditionally and not give up on it when you have a baby, decide to move, get married, the dog gets old, or it's Monday?

The answer should be yes to every single one of these!

Deciding what kind of dog parent you want to be is a personal journey that can profoundly impact both your life and your dog's. It's about more than just training and putting the time in. You can put in all the time in the world, but if the type of training you're using is trash, you are going to get garbage results.

Being the best dog parent you can be is all about building a relationship based on *mutual* respect, understanding, and love. For anyone who doesn't know, mutual respect is when you respect your dog as much as you'd like to be respected! Respect isn't demanded. It is earned. As you navigate this path, remember that growth, learning, and adaptation are part of the process. This may not be the way you thought this would go, but isn't that just the way the world works? Be kind to yourself and your dog, and embrace the journey with an open heart and mind. Always give yourself some grace. But most of all, go on and be a badass, love-them-and-never-leave-them type of dog parent!

Chapter 4:
Digging up Your Dog's Life

Now that you understand more about how dogs think and how not to be an asshole dog parent, let's look at your dog in particular and dig up their specific underlying issues. This part is so ridiculously necessary. You can't skip this part!

Understanding your dog goes beyond simply recognizing their current behaviors and reactions. To connect and address underlying issues, we must engage in comprehensive care. Comprehensive care in dog training means looking at the whole picture of a dog's life—including their physical health, emotional well-being, environment, and history—to provide a holistic approach to training and care. It's about addressing specific behaviors but also understanding the underlying reasons behind them in order to ensure that the dog's needs are fully met for a happier, healthier life.

The plan moving forward should be tailored to your dog's life and your family's lifestyle. Don't base it on the dog down the block that seems to be struggling with the same behaviors. Their lifestyle could be different from yours, and their reasoning for the struggles may be different from your dog's reasons!

This chapter is dedicated to unearthing the layers of your dog's history, personality, and experiences so you can tailor a behavioral training approach that meets their specific needs and helps them live a happy and healthy life.

Doesn't that sound fucking awesome?

Even though we domesticated dogs long ago, humans are so dense about dog behavior and what it means. Many seemingly innocent behaviors—such as constantly following their parents around, excessively licking themselves or their parents, or appearing overly clingy—are often misinterpreted as signs of affection. However, these can be attempts at self-soothing or indicators of stress or anxiety. They are all a cry for help and go unnoticed because they are "cute." Authentic affection is different; it's relaxed and not driven by anxiety. To address the root causes of such behaviors, a thorough understanding of your dog's background, genetics, and life experiences is essential.

Before diving into solutions or training protocols, I always conduct a discovery call with each client. This virtual session allows me to gather critical information about a dog's life.

Some new clients are adamant about coming here with their dog so I can assess them "at their worst, so you know what you are dealing with." This is one of my biggest pet peeves, but I can't be mad because people just don't know any better.

Let's break it down.

Why can't you just tell me exactly what your dog does? Why do I need to physically see it and put your dog through more stress in a situation I already know they can't handle?

From the moment people sign on with me, there is no more setting up a dog for failure. We have to back it up and mentally give them only what they can handle, then slowly work our way up to the bigger moments. To give blanket advice or put a dog through a situation "just to see how far they will take it or how bad they will be" is disgusting to me. It is not that hard to describe what a dog is doing, especially when I am asking all the right questions to get the information I need. That's my job! It's reckless to prescribe changes without understanding the whys behind a dog's actions.

If your dog *hates* people and you bring them to meet me without doing any of the groundwork and prior necessary steps to bring down their anxiety, they may really fucking hate me moving forward. Or we can simply take the way more fun route and set your dog up for success so that the first time they meet me, they *love* me. (And, as the parent, you are baffled.) I get to say, "See, they *can* do it! We just needed to tweak some things."

Boom! No extra trauma, no extra stress for either of you, and no extra frustration. Just a set, easy-to-follow protocol that has a great future. Sometimes, the best action stems from inaction, especially when someone is uninformed. A trainer should learn about your dog from afar before trying to change their life.

Now, how do you even begin to examine your dog's background? For starters, we need to dive into your dog's past and present environment.

Genetics vs. life experiences: The debate of nature vs. nurture applies to dogs. Genetics can predispose dogs to certain traits and behaviors. For instance, herding breeds, like border collies, may have a natural tendency to chase moving objects due to their genetic background in herding livestock. This is a behavior rooted in their DNA. As a real-life example, our Pudge was a hoarding dog found in a house of three hundred dogs, but she was only two weeks old. She didn't suffer like the others did, but she still has the tendency to hoard and hide food even though she doesn't need to.

On the other hand, life experiences shape behavior through learning and adaptation to the environment. A dog that has been rescued from a neglectful situation may exhibit fear or anxiety around humans, which isn't inherited but developed through negative experiences. Understanding the balance between what behaviors are inherited and which are learned or conditioned helps us tailor an appropriate training and socialization plan. Some dogs have both inherited and conditioned traits. It doesn't need to be one or the other.

Previous living conditions: A dog's behavior can be significantly impacted by their living conditions prior to their current home. For example, a dog that has moved from an apartment, where they had limited space and fewer opportunities to exercise or potty efficiently outside, to a single-family home with a yard may exhibit changes in energy levels, exploratory behavior, or even anxiety due to the new, more open environment, which is loaded with more space and responsibility. Conversely, a dog that's used to a large fenced yard may find the transition to an apartment challenging. They may show signs of restlessness or destructive behavior due to the reduction in physical space and the stimulation that comes from excess noise from neighbors.

Household dynamics: The makeup of your household and any changes to it can influence your dog's behavior. Your dog's age is significant. Puppies and younger dogs might display more energetic and exploratory behaviors, while senior dogs may prefer a calm and routine life. The composition of your household—such as the presence of children and other dogs or pets—can affect social dynamics. For instance, a naturally jealous, needy dog that's used to being the only pet might struggle with sharing attention after a new pet is introduced. Or a new baby! By that same token, an older dog may not be too keen on the sights and sounds that come with babies and toddlers running around, which can make them more stressed and snippy. Recent changes, like a family member moving out, can lead to separation anxiety or depression in dogs that have formed strong bonds with that person.

Life changes: Significant life changes can have a profound impact on a dog's emotional well-being and behavior. Moving to a new home disrupts their sense of security and routine, potentially leading to anxiety. Again, the introduction of a new baby might lead to jealousy or stress due to sudden shifts in attention and sleeping patterns, as well as the home's sounds, smells, and overall routine. Similarly, the loss of a family member can result in mourning behaviors in dogs, such as searching, listlessness, depression, or decreased appetite, as dogs can form deep emotional attachments and experience loss.

Triggers and fears: Understanding your dog's triggers and fears is crucial for managing their behavior effectively. Fear-based triggers might include loud noises like thunderstorms or fireworks, leading to panic or hiding behaviors. Overarousal can occur in overly exciting situations, such as visiting dog parks, leading to uncontrollable behavior or reactivity, which can result in PTSD. Overexcitement triggers, like greeting family members, can result in jumping, excessive barking, knocking people over, or even dogs injuring themselves. I'm working with a dog that has an anxious and insecure response to his family playing video games and "ignoring" him. Recognizing these triggers allows us to develop strategies to help the dog cope, such as desensitization and counterconditioning training

By examining these areas more closely and understanding their impact, dog parents can create a more supportive, understanding environment that addresses their dog's individual needs, leading to a happier and more balanced relationship. The more you know and understand, the better you can do!

Another big help is diving deeper into your dog's early life, temperament, and key experiences to shed light on current behaviors:

Early socialization: The opportunities your dog had for early socialization; any illnesses, like parvo; or experiences with littermates and parents can leave lasting impressions. I work with many dogs that almost died from parvo, which is a deadly virus that affects only puppies. When a puppy is positive for parvo or in a litter of positive puppies, they get quarantined and have minimal socialization, even with humans. This is because caregivers have to garb up to make sure no healthy dogs are exposed to the virus, so cuddling and natural interaction are limited. These puppies grow up struggling with socialization and impulse control.

Experiences with shelters or breeders: Not all of these experiences are positive, and they can contribute to your dog's current state of mind. Over the last few years, I have had to learn that not everyone is a good person. Not everyone loves dogs and is incapable of being horribly insensitive to them. This was an enormous pill for me to swallow. Many people in the animal world are not gentle, sweet, or affectionate. Some are there just to make a buck or because they need to pay the bills. Some people do not know how to compartmentalize their emotions, which can result in an undeserving dog being at the end of a bad day. In my opinion, there is no excuse for that. But unfortunately, the animal world is flawed. These dogs can be scarred from the beginning of their lives, petrified of being handled, leashed up, walked, or approached. Getting a dog at eight weeks does not make them immune to this. Eight weeks is a long time to be in someone else's hands.

Personality traits: Understanding what kind of dog you are dealing with is extremely helpful. Whether your dog is shy, assertive, independent, standoffish, or needy helps tailor our approach to their care. Because so many dogs have anxiety and stress from the beginning, many parents think these are personality traits. But they aren't. Once we figure out what is a personality trait and what is a trigger response, we can begin to watch dogs transform and shine. For example, being clingy is not a personality trait. Being clingy is a response to trauma or general anxiety. Once we use behavior modification to help a dog, we generally start to see that codependency trickle away.

I know I sound like a broken record, but by understanding the why behind your dog's behavior, we can approach their care with way more intentional effectiveness. We can do the damn thing because we *get* it. Otherwise, you may wonder, *Why am I doing this again?* and half-ass it. Only whole-assing it is allowed over here!

Just as human therapy often explores one's childhood to understand present behaviors, it is also a crucial step in helping dogs. You can't work on why someone gravitates toward people who treat them like crap until you figure out why. Did they have an abusive parent or first partner, so that's what they think love is? The way people treat them makes them believe that is all they are worth. You NEED to know that part first before diagnosing their challenge and trying to help them produce long-lasting change. They need to say something like, "Oh, my dad was an asshole. That's why I want to date assholes. Makes sense!" Now they can finally *stop* dating assholes. Sometimes, a little perspective is the exact thing we need to get over the hump of avoidance or ignorance.

Digging into a dog's past gives us that same clarity and direction for the future. With this comprehensive understanding, we're better equipped to meet their needs and adjust expectations and strategies accordingly. *Crucial!*

Armed with the insights we gain from delving into dogs' lives, the next chapter will focus on meeting their everyday needs and setting the stage for positive behavior changes. Fulfilling these needs is foundational; without this, any expectation for change is unacceptable.

Let's move forward with this knowledge and be ready to make informed decisions that help dogs be the best versions of themselves!

Chapter 5:
Filling Your Dog's Cup

This might be my favorite chapter and my favorite thing to talk about, so buckle up and get ready!

Filling your dog's cup the way they want it filled is the least discussed topic in dog training, but it is the *most* important thing for every single dog, behavioral issues or not. This is the answer to most of the issues dogs give us at home and the way to avoid those typical attention-seeking, destructive, annoying behaviors.

Now you're excited, right? Yeah, we're gonna fix all of that!

Picture a cup. We all have one of these cups, every single one of us. This cup is filled with all the things our lives consist of—family, friends, significant other, kids, career, house, hobbies, pets, etc. The cup must *always* be full, no matter the circumstances.

For instance, let's say I don't like my job. So, after a long, horrible day, I come home depressed and binge eat my entire pantry or have way more adult beverages, all alone, than anyone should on a weeknight before work the next day.

What happened here? My cup is depleted because I hate my job. But remember, my cup must always be full. So I filled it with quick and easy things, but in the grand scheme, they didn't fix the fact that I hate my job. And the choices I made were unhealthy. Instead of getting drunk by myself, I should have been on LinkedIn searching for a job that would bring me joy. Like Marie Kondo asks, "Does it bring you joy?" If not, toss it!

But as we all know, staying consistently negative is easier than changing. Anger, bitterness, and avoidance are the easiest go-to coping mechanisms. Routine feels safe, even if it's a negative one.

Now, what does this have to do with dogs?

Come on, don't you trust me by now? I always make my points. Just stick with me!

There is a basic list of dog needs that must be met. Others can be added to the list, depending on the dog itself, but these are consistent across the board. First is food. (The only thing that trumps this one is staying alive.) Water. Shelter. Mental stimulation and enrichment (work-to-eat toys, sniffing, puzzle toys, etc.). Love and positive attention the pet parents give willingly from the start. (The dog did not have to beg or do something naughty to get it.) Exercise and play. Proper sleep and a nap schedule.

These are all the things that make a dog happy, content, and well-rounded. Again, there may be others, but these are the basics that every dog needs.

Now, let me give you an example of a dog's needs not being met.

Mom comes home from a long day of work, says hello to her one-year-old pup, and lets him out of the crate to go outside to go potty. He comes back inside, and Mom immediately starts prepping for dinner. This pup misses his mom and hates it when she cooks because she doesn't pay attention to him. So he starts to go through the song and dance they go through every night. First, he grabs Mom's shoes and makes her chase him around the house. Then he goes into the bathroom and steals the toilet paper because someone left the door open again. Mom has to clean that up. Finally, as the grand finale, he stands in the kitchen and barks at Mom, making her turn around every other minute to tell him to stop until she loses her mind.

This causes Mom to lose a whole twenty minutes while she's trying to get dinner together.

What could Mom have done differently?

For starters, this pup didn't get proper love and positive attention when Mom came home. Even a quick ten to fifteen minutes can make a world of difference to a dog that has been alone all day. This doesn't have to involve crazy exercise or extra effort. It could just be some love and pets on the couch—super simple and something the mom could physically and emotionally do at that moment. Additionally, this pup didn't have anything productive or appropriate to keep him busy while Mom cooked. He is only a baby! Mental enrichment is an absolute must for *all* dogs. Age and issues do not matter.

Let's get one thing straight though: this dog is in no way naughty! So many people will say, "My dog is an asshole every time I try to do ________!"

Stop it! Stop saying things like this because you are only lying to yourself to make your shortcomings more tolerable. Everything this dog does is a cry for help and attention. His needs are not being met on a consistent, daily basis, so he will do anything he can to get his mom to turn around and pay attention to him. He learned that the only way to get his needs and wants consistently met is to be as annoying as fucking possible.

But he doesn't realize he's being annoying. Dogs do not understand that their actions can negatively affect us. He just thinks that this is how it works and Mom is having just as much fun as he is. Dogs, just like children, are products of their environments! They cannot change unless we model or offer a different behavior. As parents, we hold the key to the secret, and it is so frickin' simple: be proactive, not reactive!

What does this mean? Let's go through it!

Mom should have come home and given her pup ten to fifteen minutes of undivided attention and love, then immediately gone to the freezer to get a frozen marrow bone. He could have enjoyed it near the kitchen and still been by Mom while she cooked. But the important part is that he could be busy doing something that filled his cup while she did what she needed to do without having to exile him to the crate.

Many times, we expect our dogs to just sit there. Can you imagine asking a toddler to just *sit* there while you make dinner? Hell no, and you'd never even ask because that's absurd! Young dogs need something to do. If Mom had done this initially, she would have saved a lot of aggravation as well as the twenty minutes she spent chasing him around with shoes and cleaning up toilet paper. Plus, her dog would have been happy as a clam and wouldn't have learned any new negative attention behaviors!

The goal is to show them what awesome behaviors we want them to lean into when we are doing things that prevent us from giving them attention. We hope they'll realize that doing things on their own feels good too! If we forget to give enrichment after several weeks of daily consistency, they'll look at us like, *Uh, you forgot my marrow bone*, instead of falling back on those old attention-seeking behaviors. That's because we broke the cycle.

Okay, so maybe most of that makes sense to you, but the enrichment part doesn't. What is mental stimulation and enrichment? It's an absolute lifesaver and game-changer all rolled up into one! Most of the time, when I say, "mental stimulation," everyone thinks I'm talking about playing, throwing a ball, or going for walks and letting a dog sniff. Yes, all of those things are technically mental stimulation, but a lot of the time, these activities might inadvertently hype a dog up. You were trying to tire them out, but instead, they're overstimulated, and you are left befuddled. When I talk about enrichment, I am looking for your dog to sit down calmly for twenty minutes to an hour instead of biting, chewing, and licking something!

You might ask, "But why can't my dog just run around and get tired? Isn't that how you tire a dog out?"

Good question! There are many working dog breeds that everyone feels need to run for one to two hours a day or more. I look at it this way: people who are training to run a marathon may not be good at running a 5K in the beginning. But the more they run, the better they get at running. After a while, a 5K is not as difficult, and they're not as tired after. They may need to run more than a 5K to feel tired.

This is why I don't believe in running dogs long distances to exhaust them. I feel like it backfires after a while. In many cases, it might overtire a dog mentally or overstimulate them so that when they come home, they can't calm down or settle.

Day care is a slightly different story. I have lots of clients who say day care is a godsend and their dog is exhausted for *days* after. This is most likely caused by the mental component of it. There's mental effort in constantly making good decisions to keep friends, not make enemies, watch for social cues, and stay safe by not pissing another dog off. *This* is what exhausts them. It's not all about the physical component. It's similar to how people work: if we have a good balance of physical and mental activity, we can usually fall asleep quickly.

Now, why is the mental part so important? Biting, chewing, and licking all naturally release serotonin for dogs! Not to get too scientific, but if you are into that kind of thing, serotonin is a monoamine neurotransmitter. I call this the happy hormone! It carries messages between nerve cells in dogs' brains and throughout their bodies, which helps them regulate their emotions and calm themselves on their own. When we give high-value mental stimulation in stressful situations, we are giving our dogs something more appropriate to do than jumping all over guests, chewing the furniture while we're gone, nipping hands and feet as kids run, etc. We *cannot* just expect our dogs to just sit there and not have emotions about stressful situations. This goes for *all* stress, not just the typical fear type of stress. This is for excited stress too. (Which I call positive stress!)

So, how do we do mental stimulation the right way? What are the best forms, and how do we make sure they are high value?

Great questions! The best enrichment for your dog will depend on *your* dog and what they like. My first go-tos are marrow bones and the Pupsicle. You can find both of these on our recommendations list! Not just any marrow bones will do. The ones on our list are my favorite—the Pawstruck brand. For a good reason! They are thick and sturdy, and they do not crack easily. In fact, I've been using this brand for over four years, and I think maybe fewer than a handful have cracked. And those cracked straight down the middle. Thankfully, they did not shatter into pointy, dangerous pieces. This brand is top-notch.

Marrow bones are my top choice for a few reasons. I find they last the longest and are financially the best option because you can restuff them, refreeze them, and reuse them over and over again. The key is to get a good-quality bone that you can hollow out. Many bones from big-box pet stores tend to be stuffed with nasty filling. Also, the center third of the bone is rock solid, and the bone is pretty much useless once your dog gets an inch or two in. This is the opposite of what we are looking for! The pre-stuffed inside of a Pawstruck bone is not a gross mixture known to irritate dog stomachs. (But if you are wary about what you feed your pup, scoop out the inside and stick the bone in the dishwasher!)

Once they get an inch or two down, I scoop out the residual because dogs get frustrated or lose interest when they can't reach any more. Many clients get confused about why their dog won't take the bone at this point, but you gotta scoop that ish out! Once I do away with that center third and restuff with my own concoction, I freeze them over and over again! Every Sunday night, I gather all my bones, make a big bowl of dog-friendly filling, and stock the freezer. This way, I am set for the week and don't have to think about it. I just walk to my freezer and pull out something fun for them. And they are *all* tail wags. It is *so* easy because I *make* it easy for myself.

You also want things that will work for you financially so you're not breaking the bank. You need to find something that you are comfortable with price-wise so you do not think, *I am spoiling my dog right now.* That thought is not true, and it's not helpful to your dog or you. It gets in the way of the goal, which is to help mentally stimulate your dog, which makes both of your lives so much easier. Plus, you're filling their cup! Enrichment is as important as food and water. It is a key component of happiness.

Just today, I had a conversation with my own mother about this. My parents' puppy, Sage, is over a year old now. She gets *really* nutty after she takes a poop. Yes, it is as funny as it sounds! She gets the zoomies and will knock you down without looking back. She even gets a little nippy and bitey, especially if their other dog, Gatsby, is around. She does this for negative attention. She knows that if she goes for him, my parents will get involved. So I told my mom that she needs to watch her outside. If she goes to the bathroom, my mom should be waiting by the door with a marrow bone or some other high-value goody that Sage likes.

She replied, "But she just ate dinner!"

"Yeah, *and*?" I said.

How can Sage change her behavior if we don't give her an alternate option? And what is easier than waiting at the door with a marrow bone?

This is not spoiling. This is not overfeeding. Especially for Sage. Her weight is perfect for her frame, and she is in tremendous shape. One extra marrow bone filled with nonfat yogurt right after dinner will not hinder her at all. It will only benefit her.

And, honestly, Gatsby. Poor guy can't even get out of his own way half the time! How else is Sage going to break this OCD habit she has? We have to step in and *help*, not set them up to fail. We have to retrain our brains to pick the correct battles. Think of the goal you want, then think of what thoughts are standing in the way of meeting your dog's needs.

Now, throw them away!

This is why I always say to choose an enrichment that you emotionally, mentally, and financially can keep up with without making it harmful for your dog. Also, keep the ingredients as healthy as you can! The marrow bones work perfectly for our two big dogs. They are hard chewers, but they were both abused and neglected before coming to us, so their teeth are unfortunately down to the root and look like little nubs. Our dogs bite hard, but there isn't anything left to crack. I know some parents are worried about marrow bones cracking or filing down their dog's teeth, which is valid. If your dog is a savage or you're a helicopter parent, we have other options!

For my second favorite enrichment toy, we have the Pupsicle. John and I are so mad that we didn't come up with this invention first! It's a safe and ridiculously smart idea.

The Pupsicle is a round rubber ball that has open grooves on the top side for your pup to lick through. The lower part is a screw-off bottom that goes on perfectly, so your dog can't beat the system easily. If they want the enrichment, they gotta lick for it through the holes! When you unscrew the bottom, it has a little circular groove where you stuff whatever you like. The company offers many flavors of treat balls to place inside. These are great for dogs that do not like frozen stuff. (Such as Princess Diva Pudgalina the Chihuahua, who refuses to get a cold tongue. She's no peasant.) There's even a lavender coconut ball to help a dog relax and calm down! You can also wedge a bunch of treats in there. If I am in a pinch and don't have the treat balls or anything frozen, I will wedge a ton of the Stewart freeze-dried liver treats. Just make sure the Pupsicle is nice and full so they can't easily grab those treats.

And there's a black rubber Pupsicle for all you parents with savage chewers that don't take no for an answer and can tear up regular rubber products! Our pittie mix, Tishi, is thirteen and rips up a red Kong like it's cheesecake. It's impressive and slightly frightening—especially because she's the most gentle soul. She can't tear the black one though, so we were stoked!

For those dogs that like frozen enrichment, the company sells a four-cube silicone ice tray so you can make your own treat balls. This is so ridiculously money smart that it is mind-blowing. Again, I am so mad I didn't think of this product first. I just love it so much.

Every week, I use all my silicone trays (I have four currently) and fill them up with whatever I am filling my marrow bones with. I let them freeze, and *then*—here is the best part—I pop out all sixteen ice balls into a ziplock bag and leave them in the freezer. Now they are ready to go for the week! I just keep refilling the trays with leftovers. Maybe I have leftover toddler scrambled eggs—into the trays they go with some broth on top to freeze! I currently have two-gallon ziplock bags filled with doggy ice cubes right now, and the ease of it is so invigorating. But I can't even take credit for this beautiful idea. My best friend, Nichole, told me to do it, and I was again floored that I didn't think of it first. (Having two toddlers can make your brain a bit mushy!)

Now, some clients say their dog can get through the Pupsicle fast. And yes, some dogs are good at getting through it. But I always just tell those clients to use another one! The balls are much smaller and can be way fewer calories than other types of enrichment, like a bully stick. Those are high in protein and calories, and they're expensive to do every day. So, if your dog goes through a Pupsicle quickly, pick lower-calorie ingredients to stuff it with. This could simply be chicken or beef broth and a few kibbles or treats. Get creative!

There is no wrong way to do enrichment. If it can be stuffed and frozen safely, go for it.

Kongs are a great option, but they can be a hit or miss for some dogs. I think it's because a Kong has only one hole, and some dogs can't reach the bottom. The Topple is an up-and-coming enrichment tool. In my opinion, it is a wider, more open-faced Kong. It wobbles a bit if a dog doesn't have a tight grip, which increases the difficulty. Silicone mats are a cost-effective option, but I prefer the licky mat bowls! These are great for enrichment and meals. I like to prolong a dog's meal by making them work for it while having fun.

The night before, I take their kibble, put it in the licky mat bowl, and then fill it with broth or water. I use a decent amount of water; the kibbles should be floating, not just soaking in the liquid. Otherwise, it's just mushy, cold food in the morning. I want it to be a block of frozen food! When I take out the bowls, it takes my pups twenty minutes to lick and bite through that ice block of food. I call it frozen kibble soup! My dogs *love* it. Some of my clients do this, but their dogs look at them like, *You want me to eat this?* It's not for every dog, but it works for a lot of them—especially if they love food.

I will use slow-feeder bowls exactly the same way as the licky mat bowls, but the metal ones are better for this than the plastic ones. You don't want them to crack if you have an overzealous dog! Just pour a bunch of broth in there and freeze it; the dogs will work forever on it. Again, you can throw in a few low-calorie treats to make it more enticing. They're perfect when guests are over and I want to keep the pups occupied and with the group at the same time. Kong Wobbler and Snuffle Mats are also great for meals, as they can slow dogs quite a bit!

I feel like anything we give our pups should be made into a fun way to stimulate their brains and make them work for it. Why give a meal that is scarfed down in five seconds flat? Use it as enrichment! Work that brain!

Now, let's get into the slightly more costly options that are still great to have for special occasions!

The Bento Ball is similar to the Pupsicle, but to work properly, it needs the treat discs you push into it. And it can get costly. But a lot of dogs like them and can stay busy with them for some time. There's a vanilla-scented one that honestly smells so good that it's alarming that it's a dog treat! The Bento Ball also has a little cove on the back that can hold treats at the same time. I haven't used these in a while because I got tired of buying the inserts, but I do still use the empty ball to fill with frozen enrichment treats. So, overall, it's not a bad buy.

Next is the Himalayan yak chew. I really like this one. My dogs don't always go for these, especially if there is more exciting stuff. It is not the highest on the totem pole when it comes to enrichment, but these are great for lower-level days when I just want to keep my dogs cruisin'.

Thankfully, my dogs get along well, so enrichment can be left around without creating a problem. In fact, Oaklee and Tishi routinely switch bones and yak chews while they lie next to each other. It's always super casual and almost planned. So these are all over the house. If a dog finds one under the couch or the bed, they get excited and will work on it, but it is not as exciting as, say, a bully stick, which would *never, ever* be forgotten under the couch in this house. These are the holy grail for my dogs! This is the only thing Pudge will resource guard. She loves her bully sticks. We don't give bully sticks to Oaklee and Tishi for long-lasting enrichment. They're more of a nice reward when we want to say, "You guys were awesome today," or "I just love you so much!" That's because, for them, bully sticks don't last that long and are expensive.

We do use the Bully Buddy, which is a little dumbbell-looking contraption that clamps the bully stick to itself so the dog is unable to eat the end of it. This is helpful for dogs that tend to swallow big items, but it also drastically slows Oaklee down, so it is necessary. Oaklee will finish a bully in five minutes or less, but with the Bully Buddy, we get an extra ten minutes of him working on the nub that is stuck in the clamp! Another genius invention I forgot to come up with (sigh).

Next up, pigs' ears. They're high-value treats, but they may not last long, depending on the dog. Pudge can work on one for a while, but Oaklee and Tishi are done within minutes!

Now, what in the world do we put in the marrow bones, Pupsicle trays, Topples, Kongs, and anything else that's freezable and can hold a soft mixture? – **For a complete recipe guide, dont forget about your FREE gift listed in the beginning of the book!**But here are a few of my quick favorites:

Banana: Make sure you don't use one that's too ripe, as it can irritate some dogs. But these are my go-tos because they are cheap and healthy.

Sweet potato: There are two options for this one: fresh then boiled, or canned. The trick with canned, though, is finding them with no sugar or syrup added! If you find canned, drain them into a colander and squeeze all the extra liquid out!

Plain nonfat Greek yogurt: Get the huge tub—it's cheaper! Drain off that extra liquid at the top when you first open it. We want the mixture to be as firm as possible when stuffing. If the mixer is too soupy, it will run right out of the marrow bones. If you are using something like the Pupsicle tray, it will stand upright, so the liquid doesn't matter!

Pumpkin: It is important to use pure canned pumpkin and not pumpkin pie filling. Yes, I have made this mistake—ugh! The pie filling is delicious, but dogs don't need the extra sugar or calories. Ain't nobody got time for diabetes!

Applesauce and toddler pouches: These should be low in sugar. Many kids' pouches have natural and healthy ingredients, and these are a great way to get something stuffed quickly if you have extra lying around that your kids don't eat anymore.

Peanut butter: I don't use a ton of peanut butter, but if I am making a whole bowl of something, I will add a scoop or two to the mixture.

Leftovers: Yes, that is not a typo. Look in your fridge and see what's dog friendly and about to go bad (or won't get eaten before it goes bad!). Examples include strawberries, blueberries, apples, and other fruits that are on their way out. (*No* grapes, as these can kill your dog). But you can use avocado (*No* pit; this can also kill your dog), cheese in small quantities, turkey cold cuts about to go bad (this one's a crowd-pleaser!), and veggies if your dogs are not picky. If it's dog friendly and your dog likes it, stuff it and freeze it! I even go to the grocery store and buy the big bags of large carrots and freeze them. I also get cucumbers when they are on sale, then halve and freeze them! I just hand these off in the summer, and the pups have a little treat to cool down with.

Go with what is on sale and what is high value to your dog without breaking the bank. If it doesn't break the bank, you are more likely to do it willingly multiple times a day without flinching! Just make sure you don't use grapes, onions, garlic, chocolate, or avocado pits in anything. These are all toxic to your dog!

How often should you give enrichment each day?

Three to five times a day, every day.

Yeah, I am not kidding. Use two of those times for their meals, three if you feed lunch. Then you just need two other times each day when your dog can use some extra Zen time.

When are the best times to use mental stimulation with a dog?

All the time.

- When you want to relax, watch TV, or read a book, but your dog won't stop barking at you or nipping. Give the enrichment before you hit the couch. Don't wait for the barking or nipping to begin!
- When exciting guests come over and your dog has low impulse control. Hand high-value enrichment over as the really exciting guests walk in. This will help curb jumping, mouthing, and barking. This can also be used for dogs that don't like guests! Now we are pairing something previously scary with a positive resource.
- When crate training, especially with an anxious dog that's not a fan of their crate yet. This will turn going in the crate and you leaving into a positive thing.
- When you leave the house and your dog has separation anxiety. Give them something better to do than tear the place up!
- When you're doing homework with the kids and your dog feels left out and forgotten.
- When you're making dinner.
- When you're eating dinner.
- When the kids are playing rough and it overstimulates your dog or makes them anxious.

- When your dog needs a break from social stress.
- When your dog *is* the social stress.
- During the peak dog-walking hours in your neighborhood if you have a dog-reactive dog.
- When the baby is sleeping and you don't want your dog to bark and wake them up.
- When you want your dogs to chill out and stop playing for five frickin' seconds so you can think straight.
- When you want to shower and need to get the puppy used to being out of the crate for a little while without being destructive or having an accident.
- When it's five o'clock somewhere.
- *Every day.*
- *All the time.*
- *Anytime.*

Most of the scenarios above focus on helping our dogs avoid negative attention. Negative attention is basically a dog doing something "naughty" to get a response from you without understanding that they are being naughty. They just know that an activity—like demand barking, getting into the garbage, counter surfing, etc.—gets you to put your phone down, step away from the kids, stop watching TV, or get off the computer. It's for those times when they don't feel their needs have been met. Or their anxiety is tricking them into thinking they aren't getting their needs met. (We'll go over this in a little bit!)

So, the key to avoiding negative attention is to be proactive and not fuel the association. If you can start to anticipate when your dog will look for attention or tend to feel more anxious and needy, you can be proactive. It becomes pretty simple, seamless, and second nature! Let's walk through exactly how to do this effectively in normal situations.

I like behavior modification to be as realistic as possible. If you are having people over but know guests are an excitement trigger for your dog, this trick is so simple and easy. Let's say your dog usually demands attention from everyone and will just be all over them. Maybe there is demand barking or just crazy jumping on peoples' heads when they sit on the couch. Instead of using the normal "*No*, no jumping! *No!* Sit, sit, sit, *sit!* Why won't you listen? *Go lay down*" and constantly apologizing to your guests, why not try giving a marrow bone or any other high-value enrichment that gets their attention the second guests walk in the door? The guest can even be the one to hand it off! If your pup likes that enrichment enough, they will take it and most likely greet everyone more calmly. They'll still be excited and happy, but we usually see feet on the floor and hear no barking because the enrichment is in their mouths.

Genius!

I usually encourage guests to give calm pets and calm praise when they walk in. This encourages the pup not to jump. The dog is getting all their needs met—verbal and physical affection, along with something edible—so the jumping shouldn't happen after a period of consistency. Most dogs have to be vocal or nip when overstimulated, but that high-value enrichment toy helps them curb the oral trigger. Once everyone is settled in, your dog should be encouraged to enjoy the bone with the group or go off on their own to enjoy it. But you need to make sure it is high-value enough! Sweet potato most likely will not trump the excitement your dog feels when their favorite person in the world arrives. Be smart about this!

We do this with my parents' dog Gatsby when anyone comes over to the house. He used to be an excited jumper, and he is a big boy at a hundred pounds! My parents were never good at working with him at the door when guests arrived because they just had high expectations they didn't work for. They are human and would quickly get embarrassed and annoyed by this behavior, as most people do when guests come over. They were never on the same page and just were focusing on hosting versus one of them greeting and one of them helping Gatsby. So they would get frustrated in the moment, but it never changed anything over the long term. Which, honestly I can't fault them. No one really wants to be working with their dog when inviting guests into their home!

So, instead of battling with them and making them do something that did not feel natural and authentic, I figured out a way to help them that worked for *all* of them. I told them to use this trick a few years ago, and it worked like a charm! It was honestly so funny. They'd hand off a frozen treat to Gatsby when guests arrived. And homeboy *loves* food, so he was like, *Okay, love this very much.* People would come in, and he'd just greet them sweetly and excitedly—no jumping. Just a happy, wagging tail as he trotted around a bit. Then everyone would come in and migrate to the kitchen island, like most parties do. He'd lie down on his bed, eat his bone, and just wag his tail. He would look up occasionally and smile at all the guests, then go back to his bone. Once he was done with the bone, he would rejoin the party much calmer and get lots of pets from everyone.

Five years later, they don't even have to do this for him anymore if they don't need to, even though I tell them it doesn't hurt to keep up with it. His jumping has decreased tremendously. The only time he jumps now is when people hug for a long time. He likes to join in, which I think is sweet and only lasts two seconds.

Here is another example of something the majority of the dog parent world experiences regularly: the second you hit the couch at seven p.m. to decompress after a long workday, your dog is like, *Sike.* Maybe they demand bark at you, nip you, have an accident in front of you, bark at the back door, grab stolen contraband to get you to chase them, get into the garbage, pick a fight with their dog sibling, etc. So many families deal with this! It goes back to the dog not getting their needs met and having anxiety over you not paying attention to them. You were gone all day, and now they feel it is their turn. But here you are, relaxing. How dare you!

As annoying as this is for us, their feelings are valid, and yelling or ignoring them will not fix it. I promise you. If this is a daily trigger for your dog, being proactive is the way to go. Sometimes we go through seasons when we just don't have it in us to give our dogs 100 percent every day, all day. That's okay and normal. Maybe work has been difficult lately, maybe a parent or a kid is sick, you just had a baby and are in the newborn struggles, or you emotionally aren't doing so hot lately. Some days, we are just all hanging on by a thread, and the sound of a dog barking is like forks in our eyeballs. I've been here. I get it!

The only thing I ask you to do is hand off enrichment before your ass hits the couch! So simple. Most importantly though, it *has* to be before the negative attention. We don't want to teach dogs to do the things we hate to get the enrichment. So do everything in your power to grab that frozen bone or Pupsicle from the freezer before sitting down and decompressing. Set an alarm or make a written reminder near the couch, if you have to!

Also, just to reiterate and circle back, you are not bribing your dog to behave. So, if any of you were thinking that ridiculousness, you can relax. You are teaching your dog how to also relax while you are relaxing. It's more about teaching them that this is how we act between six and seven p.m. Over time, you break the negative OCD behavior urge. That one time you do forget to give it, your dog won't just immediately default to that old behavior. They may sit and stare at you instead or sit by the freezer or cabinet. But isn't that so much better?

Now, what if you are an imperfect person and forget to give enrichment? Welcome! You are indeed human!

First thing is, do not immediately respond to the negative attention. Ignore it for fifteen to thirty seconds—no eye contact or flinching. They can't know you can see them or hear them. Then, get up nonchalantly, and switch up the scenery. That means going to the bathroom, going into another room for something, or letting them outside to pee quickly—anything that will break their attention from what they are doing. After you do that, go to the freezer for enrichment.

The number-one goal here is that you do not want them to think the only way to get their needs met is to do something naughty. If they figure out that a few demand barks get them a treat, they'll do it all day long. And it won't be their fault—it will be yours! If your kid cries for a lollipop every day and you do it to shut them up, why would they not continue to tantrum for the lollipop?

The next question I always get during this talk is "What do I do if I've done everything for my dog? I've met all of their needs, but they're still demand barking at me or getting into stuff."

Great question! So, you've taken them to the bathroom, given them positive attention (play or cuddles), and given them a good amount of high-value mental stimulation (thirty to sixty minutes), and they're *still* barking at you?

Unfortunately, you must ignore them. I know no one wants to hear that, but it is necessary. Don't look at them, flinch, or respond in any way. They need to think you've gone deaf. They need to understand that their barking holds no value and will not get them the response or attention they are looking for. This is their anxiety playing tricks on them and making them believe they need your attention around the clock. If they don't have it, they think something is wrong, and they panic. This, in general, is not healthy for your dog or you. It can lead to codependency, which is when one can't function without the other. We want to avoid that for both of you. If your dog falls into this category, I highly recommend looking into help with anxiety. (See Chapter 13.) You don't want to use this method if your dog is struggling with anxiety and codependency. You don't want to feed into more abandonment and insecurity issues that your poor dog already has. So please, keep reading and finish the book before experimenting so you can properly understand your pup and what they need! Also, do *not* ignore them if you have not thoroughly met their needs!

One more example is jumping up on counters! Fun, right? Let's say you've done everything above and met all your dog's needs, but they keep jumping on the counter.

Let them!

Yes, I said *let them*!

And no, I am not insane. Make sure, first, that there isn't anything dangerous up there. Paper towels, tissues, papers that don't matter—all safe if your dog chooses to swallow them. Some people look at me like I'm crazy for this, but those paper products easily come out the other end! I'm definitely not saying your dog should be snackin' on a whole roll of paper towels and you should ignore it, but I am saying one or two sheets will not be life-threatening.

I am about to drop some real knowledge, so pay attention. There are only two reasons dogs jump on the counter: 1) to get something good or 2) to get your attention. If they get neither, they will eventually realize that there is no value in jumping up, and they will lose interest.

Reread that again, please! Once you play it out and watch it, it makes a lot more sense. If they don't get attention or a physical reward, like food, jumping on the counters is no longer valuable. So they just stop.

If your family consistently does not meet your dog's needs, you bet your ass they're going to find the most fun way to meet those needs—and that will absolutely be in ways you hate, like counter surfing. If I am a dog and I come down with something yummy every time I jump up on the counters, hell yes I'll continue every chance I get. It doesn't matter how many times I get yelled at because "Don't ask for permission, ask for forgiveness" seems to hold steady in this house.

On the flip side, maybe your dog knows that there isn't food on the counter every time. But they also know that you always put your phone down there. And they miss you. Next thing you know, they've grabbed a towel, and now you're chasing them. They think this is fun!

Do you see how that works out for a dog? We. Fuel. Their. Fire!

So, how do we do this the right way?

Start by puppy-proofing, to a point. I don't want you to remove everything, because that isn't realistic. Just push everything back so your dog can't reach food or items they shouldn't have. I want them to see it all because food and items on the counter are just life. So they still need to see those things. They just need to get to a point where they don't care or find value in them. So push everything back. And when your dog jumps up but can't reach, I want you to do nothing.

Yep, *nothing*!

Don't say anything. Don't look, don't flinch, don't watch, and don't stand up with hand motions. Nothing.

Why? Because they can't reach the thing, and you're not feeding into the negative attention bit. They. Will. Get. Down. On. Their. Own. I promise. Just wait them out. They may even look at you while they are up there and be like, *Hey, don't you see me up here?*

Continue to ignore them. They will get down! If you do this consistently for two to three weeks with no mishaps of food being in paws' reach, they won't be inclined to look much in the future.

Now, is this super realistic with kids in the house?

No. Honestly, kids don't listen! I can say this because I was one of those kids. I still struggle with not leaving food out on the counters, but I'm somewhat better since having Oaklee. When he is left out of our bedroom and we leave the house, he panics and looks for any food. It is his separation anxiety quirk. So, believe me, I know it's not the most doable with a chaotic lifestyle. But if you can attempt it for a few weeks and be super intentional, you can make a world of difference with this behavior!

The other big, important part of this is that if you see your dog going up there looking for stuff and you haven't met their needs yet, you still need to meet those needs even though they technically did something you don't like. The naughty thing only happened because you didn't meet their needs.

So put ya ego aside, nonchalantly switch up the scenery, and meet the needs after you ignore the jumping!

Here are some of the most frequently asked questions about enrichment and meeting your dog's needs:

- "How many times a day can I give enrichment?" I usually suggest three to five times a day, depending on the behaviors you are working on and your family's schedule. The important thing to remember is that you can't give too much. The key is being creative with how you give it and being ingredient smart. Giving five bully sticks or five full peanut butter bones a day will not end well!
- "Isn't this going to spoil my dog?" Nope, this is a necessity if you want a happy and healthy dog. Enrichment is just as important as food, water, sleep, love, and exercise.
- "Aren't I rewarding bad behavior?" No, just as long as you make sure to switch up the scenery and are super nonchalant about it. Make sure you are not going from A to B with negative attention to reward. There needs to be a C, D, or E involved in there to break up the connection.
- "My dog doesn't like enrichment. What do I do?" There can be a few reasons for this. Some dogs don't like anything frozen. Some are a bit pickier about what they like. Maybe the stuff inside just isn't high value enough for the situation they're dealing with. Or perhaps that enrichment tends to require them to shut the world off and sink their teeth in, which makes them feel vulnerable, so they just abandon it. This is because they're too anxious to let their guard down and relax, so they're disengaging altogether. If this is happening, continue reading the rest of this book to help you in other areas because there is probably more going on than just pickiness.
- "Can I give all the suggestions above when I leave them alone?" Yes, but I suggest never giving bully sticks or yak bones in the crate since

dogs can choke on them once they get down to the bottom. Use a Bully Buddy if bully sticks are your dog's go-to. The marrow bones and rubber options are the best options for safety!

- "What enrichment is unhealthy and harmful for our pets?" You want to watch where your enrichment is made. I do not purchase anything if it's made in China. The majority of bully sticks, rawhides, chews, and sticks are bleached animal skin and dyed to look more fun. This happens a lot during the holidays because people like to buy presents for dogs. The pet stores have stockings filled with white, red, and green rawhide bones that look festive, but they are extremely toxic. Any type of chew or dried meat should be given under supervision.

One last thing to keep in mind: Dogs don't have to-do lists, jobs, hobbies, or chores. If we don't give them things to fill their time appropriately, they will make our lives a living hell through no fault of their own. If there is one thing you do as a dog parent, this should be it!

Just meet their needs!

Part Two:
Specific Behaviors

Chapter 6:
Puppy Stuff

Welcome to Part 2! This is where we dive into specific behaviors. I will give you the lowdown on each and how it can affect different dogs and lifestyles.

The best place to start is the beginning, right? So first, let's begin to understand a puppy's developmental stages. A puppy needs proper, appropriate, and regular socialization to grow into a well-adjusted adult dog. These stages will explain the different things they need and at what time!

It is important to remember that many variables contribute to a dog's personality traits and to the way they function and act. We will get into this a little bit more in Chapter 10, but if a dog is genetically what I call a "smarty-pants," any mess-ups in the following developmental stages can be a huge blunder for that dog. The smarty-pants dogs tend to be more sensitive, intelligent, hyperfocused, and aware of scary, potentially harmful things, versus those happy-go-lucky puppies that have elevator music playing most of the time and are super go-with-the-flow. I call these pups the "happy-dummy dogs"—with the utmost love and admiration. It's not that happy dummies aren't smart. It's just that smarty-pants dogs have more advanced emotional intelligence. Also, let me point out that this is not an asset. It tends to be detrimental to a lot of dogs as they grow up, contributing to a lot of fear and reactiveness.

From zero to seven weeks, puppies learn social behavior from their mother and siblings. This is the most important time to learn how to manage bite inhibition, appropriately show they come in peace, ask for attention, and build confidence around other dogs by learning social cues. Orphan puppies may struggle with behavior issues in these areas without proper guidance. This was our Pudgalina. She was from that hoarding case, and we didn't know who her mother was because she was all alone under garbage. So, unfortunately, John and I had to show her the ropes, along with all the family dogs at the time: Gatsby, Burno, Zoey, and Chi Chi. We relied on them to show her what was okay and what wasn't in terms of socializing with other dogs. She struggled with bite inhibition at first, having never gotten to practice on other rambunctious puppies at such a young age, but she blossomed into a well-mannered dog.

Many breeders and rescues believe weeks seven through eight is the best time for puppies to go home. I thoroughly disagree. Yes, they can form strong bonds with people and are mentally ready for training and adjustments during this time. But professionally, I believe that if puppies get to socialize with their siblings and mothers longer, we'll have less reactive dogs down the line. Seven weeks is just not enough time to learn lifelong skills, especially if those skills aren't continued once they go home. Which, the majority of the time, they aren't.

Veterinarians usually say not to socialize puppies with other dogs until after they've had all their shots at four months, which is a *huge* gap of time. We are sending them home to not socialize for two months? What's the point of that? If you have a nice sibling for that dog, great. But that is not everyone's situation.

Weeks eight to ten are what is known as the "fear period." This is even more reason to let puppies be with mom and siblings during this time instead of flipping their world upside down. Puppies are extremely impressionable during these weeks. Positive experiences are crucial, as is avoiding scary situations until after eleven weeks. If a pin drops and they think it's scary, that's all that matters. So it is important to keep things calm, cool, and collected during this time—no vacuums or hair dryers. No little kids picking them up by the neck or big scary people coming in hot, manhandling them. We can't always control these things, and life is not perfect. But if they do happen, try to turn mildly unpleasant experiences into positive ones!

During weeks eleven through sixteen, puppies are most willing to learn and follow your lead! This is a great time to start working on cues and setting up boundaries that might be staples in your home so your pup doesn't get confused later on. Enrolling in puppy socialization classes can be helpful, but make sure sessions are fun and positive! I do not suggest classes that make dogs perform perfectly when they're all basically flipping out and can't calm down. This is hard for puppies and shouldn't be expected of dogs this young. They're infants! It should be more for fun than teaching cues. In my classes, I give cue training as homework, and in-person classes are for socialization and play! Avoid punishment at all costs! The more we separate them and make them focus on obedience, the more stressed they become.

Many will say to expose your puppy to various experiences as often as you can. Please tread lightly. We can actually create fear this way. If you push interactions that your dog is not enjoying, they may start to hate these situations and turn to reactivity. We'll touch on this more in a little bit and in Chapter 10.

In months four through six, puppies become more independent. Continue working with them on your household or personal boundaries, and continue with cue training. Eventually, you can incorporate distractions so they can learn better impulse control. And ensure that your puppy is spayed or neutered no later than six months (unless they are a giant breed). This is the time to strengthen your bond with positive rewards and trust-building with your pup before the tough months of adolescence come!

You can expect some challenges and changes in months six through twelve. Dogs this age start to realize that the things they do cause certain responses, good or bad. But mostly, they learn how to manipulate situations to get their needs met if they aren't already, like discussed in the previous chapter.) They start to feel BIG feelings and have the potential for traumatic, PTSD-type moments that can affect them over the long term, so it is important to keep socializing. But be cautious about throwing them into things abruptly. This is the time to have more empathy and patience for the random behaviors they throw at you. They are just trying to figure this whole thing out, and exploring and pushing limits is the only way to do that. Nothing they do is to purposely annoy or inconvenience you. During these months, provide tons of stimulation, companionship, and safe opportunities for play and socialization. *But no dog parks.* This is play-it-safe time, not a free-for-all! If your dog is unaltered, they may exhibit some not-so-great behaviors during this time. If your dog is struggling in certain situations, avoid those situations. For example, if your dog has poor recall, do not let them off leash at the park, then get upset when they don't come back to you. That's just asinine! You would think I wouldn't have to say that, but you would be surprised how many people complain about that scenario, not understanding how ridiculous they sound.

At months twelve through eighteen, dogs reach emotional maturity. Many want to say that this is when dominant tendencies emerge, but I disagree. What we are actually seeing is insecurity. Insecurity exists because of the developmental age, but it's also due to a lack of socialization, genetic and hormonal changes, or basic needs not being met. Remember what I said—there are many different variables to dogs and why they act the way they do. It is not black and white. To me, saying that behavioral challenges are just due to dominance is a disservice to our dogs and slightly offensive. They are so much more than dominance-oriented creatures looking to rule the roost all the time. They are real. They are scared, vulnerable, loving, and excited. And most of the time, they are all of these things all at once.

Additionally, their brains are bouncing around like pinballs, and they can't explain to us verbally what they are feeling. Stop looking for perfect behavior, and adjust your expectations to the actual situation. Recognize challenges immediately, avoid punishment, have empathy, and find a behavioral consultant immediately.

Do not DIY this! Do not ignore this! Behaviors you see during the six-to-eighteen-month time frame are usually not a phase. Which is why an entire chapter is dedicated to this time frame! Your dog most likely needs help and understanding that you can't give them because you are not trained in this, and that's okay! But you can find a trainer who can help you and your dog.

Your dog will thank you later for it!

Chapter 7:

Biting and Nipping

We are gonna get into nitty-gritty topics now and dive deep! Should we start with everyone's favorite puppy behavior?

I chuckled as I wrote that because all I can think about are the hundreds of consultation calls from potential clients who are almost sobbing on the phone as they say that their two-to-four-month-old puppy is aggressively biting them, and they are scared. I don't mean to laugh, but it is kind of funny! It was like no one told them anything about a puppy before they got one, and they are confused about why their Furby changed into a gremlin after midnight!

Just yesterday, I spoke to a man who told me his four-month-old puppy was biting him aggressively, and I was trying to get more information out of him. He said, "Well, he thinks we are playing, but we are definitely not." So I asked what was happening during this time. And he replied, "Well, I'm usually picking up a dog toy to throw it out."

No joke. I almost hung up the phone on this man! He picks up a toy, and he's confused as to why the puppy is engaging in play?

Then he told me ten minutes into the call that his puppy had been attacked by another dog, had a broken jaw, and had been in a muzzle and cone for the past few weeks. He didn't think that information was pertinent at all, I guess. But it absolutely can contribute to puppies biting more!

So let's get one thing straight: puppies bite. And sometimes, they bite fucking hard! If you have had a unicorn puppy or were lucky enough to have had previous dogs that didn't bite, you should thank your lucky stars because it is *very* uncommon to have a puppy that doesn't make you rethink why you thought getting a puppy was a good idea. I feel like this part is a rite of passage, but there are proper and easier ways to go about managing biting, so let's dive in!

There are multiple reasons why your dog is biting and nipping. The first one is that they have not learned bite inhibition. Bite inhibition refers to a dog's ability to control the force of their mouthing. A puppy or dog that hasn't learned bite inhibition with people doesn't recognize the sensitivity of human skin, so they may bite too hard, even in play or while receiving affection.

Bite inhibition needs to be taught. It is not learned just from passing time. Most first-time puppy parents do not realize this. That's why many of them panic when the biting doesn't improve after a few months. We tend to see bite inhibition issues in dogs that were separated from their mom and siblings too young, or before eight weeks, as discussed in the previous chapter. Some moms don't parent well enough and aren't interested in their puppies. Other puppies don't have a normal puppyhood. These are all young dogs that may not learn bite inhibition. So, how do we teach bite inhibition the *right* way?

Step 1: Make sure your puppy is not in Cujo mode. Cujo mode is when they are overtired, nipping like crazy, and won't calm down for anything. You have likely missed a nap, or they're overstimulated. This is not the time to teach proper bite inhibition! Pick a time when they are engaging in what seems like nice, genuine play.

Step 2: Make sure you are not playing too rough or without proper toys. Your puppy needs appropriate things to bite on other than you! If they do not have an appropriate toy or one that keeps their interest, they will absolutely bite you instead, and you can't get mad about it.

Step 3: When your puppy comes over and chomps down on your hand, stay relaxed, and don't move your hands. Then make a high-pitched *Yip!* noise. Not after or before the teeth bite down. It needs to be authentic for the puppy to understand what you're trying to communicate. Otherwise, they think you are just making weird noises at weird times.

Step 4: They should immediately stop and look at you like they're wondering, *What the heck was that? Are you okay?* This is when I want you to calmly say, "Thank you, good boy or girl." Then try to reengage in proper, calm play. We are not trying to provoke anything or get them to bite.

Step 5: If they attempt another nibble, make an *Eh-eh* noise before they make contact. If that doesn't stop them, attempt the *Yip!* again. If they bite one more time, do your *Yip!* Then disengage from play and walk away calmly. Do not hold a grudge! If they follow you, do not shun them or ignore them. They are still learning.

Many trainers will suggest that you ignore them and walk away, but there needs to be an in-between, where you hold your boundary of not getting bit while trying to proactively and appropriately teach them. Avoid sending them the message that you will abandon them the second they do something wrong. This is the exact behavior that provokes anxiety and insecurity in dogs like you see in people-pleasing kids! Have you ever seen a dog panic when you are mad or don't want love from them? All they do is try *harder*. It's unhealthy and leads to codependency. Instead, hold your boundary and get up, but don't leave them. Just disengage from the play, and don't put your hands in a place for more nibbles. They may need some calm pets or a walk outside if they are getting close to naptime. If that is the case, this is the time to transition into a nap or a calmer activity like enrichment.

Now, let's get into all the things you should *not* be doing. That's pretty much everything you'll read when you google this issue.

Do *not* bite your dog back. When I was young, my parents bought a chocolate Lab puppy from a breeder who told me to bite him back when he bit me. He said he'd never bite me again. At eight years old, I knew this was highly inappropriate and not true. Also, it's so fucking dangerous! I was eight, and this asshole set me up to get bit in the face! Now, truth be told, this may make some dogs scared of you, and the biting might decrease. But other dogs are gonna bite you back, and much harder than they did the first time. It's like a parent spanking a child for hitting. That's fighting fire with fire. You are saying hitting is okay. In a puppy's case, you're saying biting is okay. And not just play biting, but painful biting. Also, there are better, more humane ways to handle this. Don't bite your dog. End of story.

Do *not* hold their mouth shut, hit, spank, scruff, or physically punish them. Not only is this aversive and punitive, but it also does not teach your dog anything productive about bite inhibition. They do not correlate pain in this way with what we do not like, so it is a waste of your energy and ruins the relationship you have with your dog. If you go this route, they may fail to trust you moving forward, grow hand shy, or become defensive when touched.

Let's troubleshoot because it's not always that simple or black and white!

What if your puppy gets even more crazy after the *Yip!* noise? This happens to a small percentage of dogs, so don't be alarmed. If this happens to you, go through the other reasons for nipping and rule them out first. If it continues after you try these methods, give more enrichment and engage in play less often. I would also suggest contacting a behavior specialist to figure out the root of the problem.

Teething is another reason for nipping. This is when a puppy's teeth are actively trying to fall out, and it is painful. It's inevitable, but it's temporary, usually lasting only four weeks! Teething normally starts at four and a half months and ends around five and a half months, but the first two weeks of it are usually the toughest on both puppy and parent. The first week is when the tiny chicklet teeth are trying to come in, which gives a puppy a decent amount of consistent pain. In the second and third weeks, the canines are trying to make their way in. These are the four large, pointy motherfuckers that hurt the most. This is the most painful stage. Once these suckers are in, puppies tend to bite us way less because the pain is gone. The fourth week is all about the back molars, which don't seem to bother many dogs. If they do, it is hard for a dog to bite all the way back that deep on a human, thankfully.

The most asked question about teething is "Why is my dog chewing on me instead of the many toys I am giving?"

That's simple! First, we have human skin and blood underneath that. Duh! Stick with me. The way our skin feels on their teeth is like when we have a toothache and press on it to relieve the pressure. Have you ever had that? You have a toothache or pain in your mouth, so you press on it, and it feels so much better. Until you let go! So, long story short, your flesh feels a lot better on their teeth than that inedible, rubber-flavored chew toy you spent $20 on that they've picked up only twice.

Second, we tend to make funny noises and move quickly when being bitten, unlike that stagnant, non-yelping chew toy that does nothing. Point blank, you are just more fun to bite! The main thing to focus on right now is keeping your puppy as calm as possible, sticking to a solid nap schedule, and amping up the food-based enrichment as often as possible. Enrichment is a must, not only to keep them busy but to ease the painful gums with something frozen to help wiggle those teeth out quicker.

Top things to be aware of during this four-week period:

- Your puppy may have diarrhea from the pain. This is normal, so don't freak out. They most likely didn't eat anything bad.
- They will most likely swallow the loose teeth and poop them out. This is also normal, so don't freak out.
- You may see blood on chew toys. You guessed it—this is normal, so, seriously, don't freak out!
- They may be less tolerant of pretty much everything. This includes doing cues they already know, paying attention to you, and listening

in general. And they may have a shorter fuse than normal. Don't freak out and think they are regressing in training! This is the time to give them a little grace but still hold your boundaries with empathy!

The third culprit behind biting and nipping is usually an overstimulated and stressed-out puppy! As you probably know by now, puppies are easily overstimulated, so we must treat them like tiny infants in terms of their daily schedule. Which, shockingly, is hard for humans to wrap their heads around and stay consistent with.

If you have never had a baby, you need to know naps and wake windows are extremely important. This is not a suggestion. It is more of a lifeline! If you miss a wake window, which is the allotted time period during which a baby or puppy can be awake before needing another nap, you will, without a doubt, have a cranky individual on your hands! It is our job to keep an eye on these times to ensure a pup is set up for success.

The trick is disengaging from the play or activity before they become tired. It is also important to provide a transitional time frame. This is so they can go from energetic to cool down to ready for a nap. When you sprint on a treadmill, you don't just jump off and walk away, do you? No! You'd have jelly legs! How about when you watch an action-packed movie? Do you get right into bed immediately after and fall asleep easily? No! You'd probably still be a little wired and need some time to get tired mentally. Dogs absolutely need this too!

Here are all the ways puppies tend to get overstimulated:

Rough Play

If you are playing too rough with your pup, they may get a rush of emotions. The combo is usually a lot of excitement and enjoyment but also a tiny bit of fear. This is because they're still learning boundaries with you and don't yet know if they are safe during this type of play. They want to keep going because they're having a blast, but they also tend to get a little feisty due to that fear lingering in the background. So you may see a little bit of protectiveness come into play, or maybe the play intensity increases out of nowhere. If you see this after a few minutes of rough play, try to dial it back a little until your pup gets a little more comfortable with you and more confident in themselves and your relationship. Give them lots of love and reassurance during this time. To build trust both ways, you also need to listen to the boundaries they are setting as well. Throwing some encouraging words in there during play can also help so they know everything is okay. Talking to your dog sweetly during play is the biggest thing parents miss out on in terms of confidence building! Saying "Yes! Good girl" goes a long way in letting them know they are safe and it's all good.

Playing for Too Long

For some puppies, ten minutes is too long. I know this seems crazy because they have so much energy, but it's not a lack of energy that causes this reaction. It's the low impulse control and inability to manage emotions at this young age. They feel themselves getting worked up, and they tend to nip and bite to create serotonin naturally. That's that happy hormone we were talking about earlier, which helps them decompress and work themselves back down the ladder. Puppies have not yet gained control over impulses and emotions, so it's our job to see where they are emotionally, understand what they can handle, and start cutting off play around that time frame. As they get older, you can start to tack on minutes to play!

Too Many People and Too Much Excitement

Dogs. Are. Children. This one goes hand in hand with the other reasons above. When there are too many people and too much going on, puppies will start to feel overwhelmed, then they nip and bite to calm themselves naturally.

But they don't have the development to do it correctly. They don't know how to leave the room for a break or ask everyone to calm down and stop touching them. When you have people over, kids are running and screaming, you take your puppy out to a public place, or just abnormal craziness is going on, there are a few things you need to keep in mind. First and foremost, realize this situation is not normal for your puppy. They are processing and may be nervous because they don't know what to do with their emotion.

I can't believe how many times we've been to a brewery or winery and seen people bring in a puppy who is so fucking uncomfortable. I watch them cowering or barking, and the parents are just forcing it and getting so frustrated by these behaviors. It's like the dog is ruining their time, and the parents are inconvenienced. I just have to say that this is not okay. We cannot shame a dog or ignore their fears because we want to have a good time. Your puppy is not a trophy for everyone to goggle at. Yes, some puppies *love* that shit, but some of them don't. Like at all. You may need to work toward these goals before deciding to take your puppy to a brewery on the busiest day of the summer and plan on being there for three hours. Also, intoxicated people and a fearful dog make the worst cocktail combo ever!

When you do take your puppy out somewhere like a brewery or a winery, give them time to decompress after around fifteen to thirty minutes. This can mean creating space away from everyone or taking them for a calm walk around the block. If your dog has separation anxiety or you can't leave, even giving enrichment around everyone is better than nothing. Once they're done decompressing for thirty to sixty minutes, they can rejoin the party. Repeat decompression time as needed!

Too Much Physical Touch

This is pretty common but not often thought of. I know it sounds weird, but seriously, this one happens more often than you think! Some dogs are more sensitive than others. Some dogs are soothed by physical touch and crave it to relax or get to sleep. But other dogs seem energized by touch and will start to mouth you immediately. Then they go on their backs, and all hell breaks loose!

It is important to identify whether or not your dog gets overstimulated by physical touch. If they do, try to keep it to a minimum in the beginning. And know that this is not forever. Start by putting a large treat in one hand and holding it there. Don't give it up. Let them lick and bite at it to keep them focused on that treat, then calmly stroke them with your other hand maybe five times. Now give the treat. You can do this a few times and then disengage.

By bringing food into this, you are not bribing them so you can pet them. That would be ridiculous. What you are doing is splitting the brain into two parts—affection and food. When an overstimulated puppy's brain gets split and can put some of that energy into working for food, they can calmly allow and appreciate the petting without going apeshit! Their brains also then understand that when they are getting petted and don't bite you, it feels better. You are simply helping them get there instead of forcing your love until they "get over it." That never happens.

As they get older and you're consistently giving enough enrichment and positive attention, the mouthiness should lessen. Also, pay attention to dogs that go belly up on their own but quickly get nutty. Puppies tend to go on their backs a lot to be playful and submissive, then quickly think, *Uh-oh, this seemed like a good idea at the time.* Then they start to bite more because they're in a submissive position and get nervous. They are too insecure in general to feel submissive like that.

The happy dummies won't care though. These dogs will sleep belly up, not a care in the world. Most smarty-pants pups will roll up like a little cinnamon roll and keep all those organs tucked in tight. If your dog is a smarty-pants, they can get nippy while belly up. If their eyes are slightly bulging, either swiftly and calmly flip them back over as soon as you can or don't engage while they're in position. This was textbook Pudge when she was a puppy. I told everyone in the family to not play with her if she went belly up. She was too feisty to let us flip her back over. Homegirl was *fierce* as a baby. I crack up just thinking of it. Tiny Parana about sums it up, truly! So, any time we were playing and she gave her belly, we would all just have our hands off and wait for her to flip back over. She eventually got the point!

Puppies also bite because they are looking for attention. As discussed in Chapter 5, you *need* to meet their needs! If you are not willingly giving them enough positive attention, they will look for it in all the wrong ways. This is negative attention. And, like kids, puppies and dogs are products of their environments. If we are not giving them what they need, they will find a way to get it.

The best thing to do is document when your puppy tends to nip and mouth you the most. Is it when you sit down to decompress with TV or a book? Is it when you help the kids with their homework immediately after you get home from work? Try to pinpoint your pup's trigger times, then combat them proactively. Give positive, uninterrupted attention for five to ten minutes prior to the thing that you do that they hate, give them enrichment near you so they still feel involved, and then go do what you gotta do! This way, everyone is happy. If we are always reactionary, they will think that mouthing you is the only way to get their needs, which creates a negative habit that we tend to blame them for. Any attention is good attention!

Like I said, the final reason for biting isn't the most common, but it can be the case if you have family members who are too much. This could be kids or adults who are too touchy-feely, all up in your puppy's face, waking them from naps, wanting to hold them like a baby, and never leaving them alone. If this is your situation and your puppy is biting during these times, they are trying to tell you that they want to be left alone, but no one is listening to their warnings. This is something we severely struggle with as a society. We tend to not respect our dogs' space and emotions. Yes, they are here to love us and depend on us, but that does not mean they have to be okay with and accept everything we do to them. If we want to have relationships with our dogs that consist of mutual respect, we have to respect them back! They are definitely not an object to flaunt, and they're absolutely not a rag doll toy for your toddlers and kids. This can traumatize puppies for life and be one of the biggest reasons they get rehomed—"All of a sudden, not good with my kids." My first thought is always, *Well, what did your kids do to piss your dog off so much that they finally had enough?* Please teach your kids how to respect your dog and other dogs around them. The fact that your kids are kids is not an excuse to let them do whatever they please with no boundaries for other living creatures. Teaching kids boundaries for others and holding those boundaries with empathy is the kindest thing you can do for a child.

So, because this happens so often, I feel it wise for us to go over when to leave your dog alone. Most definitely, when they are sleeping. You would not be happy if your dog woke you up out of a dead sleep. This can become dangerous down the line because your dog may think it needs to bite to hurt when woken up. Also, leave your dog alone when they are chewing on something *they* deem as high value. This can be a marrow bone, Kong, bully stick, yak bone, or meal. Again, you would not be happy if your dog started putting their paws on your food or touching you while you were trying to eat or decompress. This creates unnecessary stress and can lead to guarding down the line, even if the dog seems unbothered by it now. We discuss this more in Chapter 12.

Another telltale sign that you should leave your dog alone is if they are nipping you, then release quickly back into themselves and come back for another nip when you continue to pet them, or something similar. This is not friendly, playful nipping. This is a warning bite. Dogs tend to get tense and low and have tight body posture when they're giving a warning bite. They can be looking at you with whale eyes (where the whites of their eyes are visible, making them look like a sad cartoon character) or actively trying to not make eye contact. When they look away, they're trying to indicate that they want to be left alone and are avoiding connection in hopes you leave.

Another indication that they want to be left alone is when they run away from you when you are playing too rough. If there are low growls and swift, sharp barks associated, back up and leave them be. Do not reprimand. They are trying to communicate their emotions honestly and effectively. This is a good thing, but if you don't wise up, you will have a more difficult situation on your hands because they'll get quiet and just go right to a real bite.

In conclusion, understanding and addressing biting and nipping in puppies is a fundamental aspect of their upbringing that requires patience, knowledge, proper expectations, and a bit of humor. Remember, biting is a natural phase for puppies as they explore their world and learn about bite inhibition. It's crucial to approach this behavior with empathy and effective training techniques rather than frustration or punitive measures. Don't punish your puppy for simply being a puppy!

By implementing the strategies outlined above—such as teaching bite inhibition, providing appropriate toys, and ensuring they are not overstimulated—you can guide your puppy through this phase successfully. It's also important to remember that each puppy is unique, and what works for one may not work for another. No training should be a blanket method for all dogs. Always keep that in mind when reading and listening to everyone's two cents. Therefore, observing and understanding your puppy's specific needs and triggers is key.

By creating a supportive environment that encourages good behavior while understanding the underlying reasons for biting, you are setting the foundation for a well-behaved adult dog. Above all, keep the lines of communication open with your pup, and remember that this phase, like all challenging stages of puppyhood, will pass. This is just a season! With consistency, love, and the right approach, you'll both emerge stronger, more connected, and with fewer accidental wounds!

Chapter 8:
Potty and Crate Training

Now that we've gotten biting out of the way, let's move to the second bane of every parent's existence:

Potty training. Lions, tigers, and bears, *oh my*!

For most of the following examples and instructions, I will mention crate training a lot because there are so many benefits of crate training when you're trying to potty train. I can't ignore how it positively affects the process. To many people's surprise, crate training can drastically reduce or eliminate separation anxiety if you use the crate properly. It can help negate issues with your pup for years to come if you just use it for a short period of time.

Some statements I hear constantly are:

"Crates are mean!"

"They're like jail for a dog."

"I feel bad when I use one."

Listen, I hear ya! And believe me, if you do it the old-school way, absolutely, a dog will feel like they're being punished and the crate is jail. I am not sure if you've realized it yet, but that's not the world you stepped into by reading this book! This is going to be way more enjoyable for everyone involved—most importantly, your dog.

Truthfully, if crate training is done properly, it can be amazing. In fact, it can be life-saving for a dog! I have a lot of clients out in California, which is extremely different from where I live on the East Coast. They have earthquakes and dangerous forest fires every other day. Unfortunately, this means they are moments away from an emergency evacuation at the drop of a hat. And if a dog isn't able to go into a crate or be separated from its parent, the dog may be left behind. Or the parents may not be able to leave. This can be scary! So, for my Californian clients, evacuation plans are always on our list of goals, as is working on crating, separation, and being less reactive to new people or chaotic situations. Like I said, it can be life-saving!

The crate is pretty essential in helping us potty train your pup! Thankfully, most dogs do not go to the bathroom where they sleep, so the majority of you will be able to use this to your advantage. Not wanting to be by their pee and poop gives them a reason to hold their bladder while in the crate, and this allows the body to learn how to hold it, which puppies have a hard time doing outside the crate and in the early months of their lives. Learning to hold their bladder for longer as they get older and go only outside are our two main goals. The crate will help with both and is imperative to the process!

Puppies tend to have accidents when they get distracted, which happens *often*. If they're in the crate when we can't watch them, we won't have unnecessary accidents that could have been avoided. By that same token, humans tend to get distracted easily—by our phones, TV, kids, laundry, cooking, mom brain, etc. If you don't know what mom brain is, it is when you are pregnant or have a kid or four, and your brain just goes to mush. You walk into rooms and forget why you went in there; you put plastic containers in the toaster oven; and mid-sentence, you forget the word of the thing you are talking about. So yeah, a mom with mom brain and a potty training puppy—hot mess express! These are all valid distractions, but if we don't do this the right way, our dogs are the ones that suffer the most. If you haven't noticed, this is a huge theme of the book! Silly humans.

Thankfully, the crate is a safe holding place for your puppy while you do all the many things you have to do in a day. I see this as a type of home base in the game tag! You cannot watch a puppy twenty-four/seven. It's impossible. Just like with a newborn baby, you have to put them down safely somewhere to get your own needs met so you can continue to be a good parent. It's the same with puppies! I tell all parents this: you cannot pour from an empty cup! And if you don't know how to do this, ooh, girl, you gonna learn today!

How can you fill your puppy's cup if you are burned out, frustrated, flustered, and sleep deprived? This is the same with kids, spouses, friends, and family. You *must* make sure you do not consume yourself with puppyhood. There needs to be a positive balance, not just for your sake but for the sake of not creating unhealthy codependencies you may later regret and become resentful of. I am specifically talking to the moms and dads who will lay their arms into the crate while sleeping on the floor all night to reduce their dog's anxiety! Sweet, yes. But also not healthy. My back hurts just thinking about it!

Proper crate training also helps avoid separation anxiety. I know, easier said than done with some puppies, as some puppies come with separation anxiety issues or are just anxious and clingy from birth. A big issue we see is puppies having separation anxiety or anxiety in general and not being able to hold their bladder due to stress and anxiety, inside or outside the crate. We will touch on anxious peeing a little later, but if you desensitize your pup to being in the crate and make it a positive, you can avoid many accidents. Keep in mind, not all puppies experience separation anxiety, but it is always good to get ahead of the game!

First things first, choosing the right crate can be crucial! If it is too big, the puppy can pee in one section and then go lie down far away from it. There is just too much room. The right-size crate promotes good potty training habits! Now, on the flip side, if it is too small, the puppy will not be comfortable or have a good association with the crate because they are cramped and won't be able to sleep well. They associate how they feel with people, places, and things. So, if they feel cramped and lonely in the crate, they'll think, *Screw this metal cage. I want out!*

So, what is the right-size crate? Your puppy should be able to walk into the crate and do a full 360, comfortably. They should be able to sit on their butt without their head touching the top and lie comfortably, slightly sprawled out. If you have a larger-breed dog that will grow, I suggest a larger crate that comes with a divider. These are a no-brainer in terms of not breaking the bank. The crate essentially grows with them instead of you having to update every few months. As you see it getting a little snug, you can move the barrier back a bit!

Now, if you are not a fan of the metal barred crates, as I know a lot of people aren't, you can purchase something a little more nontraditional. Airplane crates are an option. But my favorite alternative is a soft crate. They're not great for bitey puppies, but once your dog is out of that stage, these are super functional. They have PVC piping framing, and the shell is a tough but cute-looking canvas material that you can remove and wash! You can fold one nicely under a couch or bed when you are not using it. They also travel well! Unfortunately, again, these are not for intensely chewing dogs, so you would need to wait until your pup is slightly older or out of that phase.

The key to introducing your puppy to the crate and making it a comfortable, enjoyable space is making it super cozy—bed, blanket, toys (nothing they can choke on), blanket or cover over the top, sound machine, etc.

A sound machine can be a *huge* game changer, especially if people are home during the day or you live in a loud apartment building. The Hatch Rest sound machine is my favorite! It gets loud without hurting anyone's ears. A lot of people resort to music or TV, but it's not the same. Ambient noise makes all the difference because nothing gets in and nothing gets out!

The next key component to this process is, you guessed it—*enrichment*! You need to make the crate a positive and a resource versus the end of the world and stress city. Always give high-value, long-lasting mental stimulation and enrichment toys when you put your puppy in the crate. Every. Single. Time. This includes marrow bones, frozen Kongs, lick mats, etc. But I stay away from bully sticks and yak bones because they can be a choking hazard unless they're in a holder of some sort. And definitely, no rawhides!

The last piece of the puzzle is making sure the crate is not a stressful place and that you don't try to trick them to get into it. It's gotta be all good vibes! To start this off, just place some fun, enticing treats and the enrichment in the crate, then let your pup come and go as they please without shutting the door on them. Don't force them in physically. Let them go in and out naturally. A lot of dogs naturally gravitate to the crate and lie in there with the door open if this is done correctly. It is sweet to see. After a day or two, you can start to play around with shutting the door if they don't show much hesitation.

There are many ways to do this. Here are a few. Start by shutting the door and hand-feeding them treats through the bars for a minute or so. Then, casually open the door and let them come out. You can put enrichment and treats in there, then shut the door and walk around the room, tidying up. Or you can leave the room. After a minute or two, come back and let them out. You can close the door, sprinkle treats, watch TV, or leave the room and come back, sprinkle more treats, leave again, come back, and sprinkle. Just keep repeating while increasing the time you are away.

It is important to note that these techniques are for most dogs that severely struggle with the crate and show anxiety around it. Some dogs do come to us with no issues crate-wise. If that is your dog, still do treats and enrichment every time. But you do not need to do a whole charade if they are content with the door closed and go right to the enrichment!

Once you get your feet wet, the next step is gradually increasing crate time. You may need to go minute by minute or fifteen minutes by fifteen minutes. Or you may be able to jump big in terms of time if your dog is cool with it.

Now it's time to tell you all the things to avoid while crate training. Yay! These are so common, but I have to say them out loud.

- *Never* use the crate for punishment. Pups sometimes need a time-out. And we sometimes miss nap time by a little bit, and they need some chill time because they are in or close to Cujo mode. There's nothing wrong with using the crate for those situations. Take them for a quick walk, or let them outside to potty. Then grab your enrichment and put them in the crate with praise. Never with anger!
- *Never, ever* use it as a way to correct unwanted behavior. I promise you will not get the result you are looking for, and they may start to resent the crate. Then you are screwed. Just like we talked about with nipping and teething, try extra uber hard to put them down for naps before they get overtired. If the only time they go in the crate is when they're overstimulated and cranky, they won't like it.
- Try not to use it only when you leave the house. This one is surprising to a lot of parents and is not often thought about. Use the crate while you're home as well so they don't associate it with you leaving and end up not wanting to go in at all because they associate it with abandonment. This is why all the COVID puppies have separation anxiety. They were never left alone, *ever*! So when they get put in the crate, they panic. They are just not accustomed to being left or the feelings it brings. So do yourself and your dog the biggest favor and crate them even if you work from home. Trust me on this one!
- Do not put food and water in the crate with them if they are not fully potty trained yet. This one is just good housekeeping. I prefer never putting food and water in, but that's a preference. I just don't think it is necessary. We are just asking for accidents, and it's not fair to them since they may overindulge while you're gone and just not be able to hold it. They won't dehydrate while you're gone, I promise! As long as they wet their whistle once or twice a day, they are solid. Dogs are good at making sure they drink enough.

Now, some proper potty training expectations are in order! The following is more about potty training versus crate training, but you have to remember that your puppy is brand new at this. They have no idea what you are trying to teach them or how annoying it is to clean the carpets and the floor. They are at the mercy of their parents to teach them correctly and be consistent. If you aren't upholding your side of the bargain, this whole thing can crumble superfast.

Your puppy is an infant with no diaper. I know, what a nightmare! They simply do not have control of their bladder yet, and we can't expect them to. Just because your puppy can hold it in the crate for however many minutes you leave them in there, it does not mean they can do that outside the crate. Period. Many puppy parents use this example as an excuse for why they don't understand how their puppy had an accident outside of the crate after only a fraction of the time. These are apples to oranges. It is way easier to hold it in the crate than out and about.

I do not care how quickly one of your other dogs or the dog down the street was potty trained. Do not compare! Comparing is *so* detrimental. There are many variables and facets to this, and comparing is unfair. Comparing your dog's progress to others is as toxic as doing it to two different significant others, and we all know that never goes well! All dogs learn at different paces and have different struggles. Some clients will say, "I don't know, maybe it's because my dog is a [insert breed here]." This is such a fucking cop-out, and I hate it. Some breeds are known for being bad at potty training? That is ludicrous. If you follow a proper potty training protocol, the breed should not matter at all!

Sorry, but if there is an accident, it is *your* fault! I always tell my human clients that if there is an accident, the only face they should be shoving in the mess is their own! You are the one to be reprimanded and thrown in the crate. *You* are the parent! If you properly set up a consistent routine and understand the puppy's elimination habits, there should be few accidents, if any.

What does a proper routine look like for a puppy? Whenever your puppy comes out of the crate, they immediately go outside. No ifs, ands, or buts. If you can pick them up and carry them out, that is best! This is just until they're out of the extreme puppy stage. If your puppy gets distracted easily when you take them out, I suggest using a leash.

Next up in the potty training process is picking a phrase and sticking with it. Yes, everyone in the family needs to say the same thing! "Go do pee-pees," is my favorite. "Go potty" is common. The funniest one I ever heard from a client was "Do big business." Just pick something that rolls off the tongue naturally, and keep the entire family consistent.

Once outside, do not distract your puppy. If they get distracted by, well, pretty much anything, you should be quiet and hardly move or walk. Once they start to sniff, say your phrase in a monotone voice. This will refocus them on the task. Once again, if your puppy is easily excitable, try keeping them on leash in the beginning so you can easily refocus them and show them that playtime is after they go to the bathroom.

If you use a leash, try not to move around too much. Stay in one spot, and allow the puppy to sniff in the circumference around you. The more you walk, the more new smells you are introducing, which distracts them more! So keep it small, silly! Stop walking around so they can find the perfect spot. The perfect spot was way back in the beginning, but all the smells got them distracted. One circle of grass is more than enough for a little puppy.

Ah, finally, they're going outside! This is not a drill. This is a deer-in-headlights sort of situation. Do not do anything distracting, don't talk, and don't move until they are done going. Once they finish, you can start your excited praise. It should sound a little something like this: "Good girl, you did pee-pees! *Yes*, good job! Good pee-pees!" It is extremely important to repeat the phrase a few times after the act so they know what they did and will repeat it the next time they hear the phrase.

Now, the *most* important part. *Treats, treats, treats*! This is a must! Along with the praise, there must also be high-value food. Don't bother with the crunchy or soft-baked dog treats. If you want your dog potty trained properly and quickly—saving you both multiple headaches—go right to the fridge and grab some hot dogs or string cheese—anything dog-friendly and delicious that they don't usually get. Something that makes their eyes get wide when they get a whiff. Cold cuts can be a great option as well. There is nothing wrong with giving your dog people food (another ridiculous myth). We need pottying outside to be worth it for them and mark the correct behavior. We want a light bulb to go on and them to think, *AH! If I go outside, I get hot dog. If I go inside, I get nothing.* If they are not having this revelation, your house will be a wet and smelly place.

Okay, so now you want to go back inside. Your dog just peed, so you have thirty minutes before taking them back out again. We are going to follow a type of systematic desensitization and work up to more and more time between potty breaks to allow your dog to hold it for longer. But also try hard to not allow them to have an accident for the first two weeks.

I know that sounds impossible. But don't avoid attempting! If they don't have an accident at all for two weeks, it is highly unlikely they will after that. The brain will say, *Oh, we only go outside.* It is a psychological thing for them! I am not expecting zero accidents, but it is still worth the attempt.

Here is what the timeline should look like for brand-new puppies.

Every thirty minutes, they are back outside. Set a timer if you have to! Do this for two to three days. Once you can go a day or two without accidents, you can add fifteen minutes to your protocol. So, every forty-five minutes, they should go back out.

Continue to add fifteen minutes every few days. Once your timer goes off and you are outside for a decent amount of time, if your puppy does not go to the bathroom, you can go back inside—but only for five to ten minutes before heading back outside to try again. During those five to ten minutes, you are watching them like a hawk! I say again, *like a hawk*. Do not take your eyes off them!

Another important task you will have to master is identifying the signs that your puppy needs to go. Barking or whining seem to be the ones people expect the most, but these don't happen until they solidify that they go potty only outside and do not want to mess that up. So don't expect this in the beginning. (Also, before I forget, do *not* get a back doorbell for them to hit. They learn quickly to use that to go outside just for fun or to get attention. So fight the urge, unless you are into hearing a bell ring every five seconds.)

Sniffing and circling are the two most common signs. You have to watch carefully because this can last less than two seconds, and then boom, accident. So, if you see it and it is nearing the time for you to take them out again, get their attention as quickly as you can in a positive way, then get them outside. Standing and staring is another one, but this one is sometimes harder to identify, depending on the dog and their personality.

The best practice is to watch your dog's body language closely before they potty properly outside. What do they look and act like right before going? Some are calm, some are frantic, and some even get frustrated and may bite the leash or run around like they're crazy!

My favorite sign, which everyone forgets about because they think they're in the clear, is pausing during play and then, *plop*—having an accident. It happens so quickly that it should be a crime. Again, there's no one to be made at. Clean it up and move on. The goal is to watch your puppy closely during play, make sure they go potty before play, or stop them during play for a potty break. Then allow play to continue!

That brings us to the things to avoid while dealing with accidents.

Wee-Wee Pads

These are extremely confusing for all dogs of all ages. Having a wee-wee pad says to the dog that going in the house is okay. But it's not okay! If the goal is for the dog to go only outside, *we* have to be consistent. Clear is kind, and unclear is unkind. Wee-wee pads are never okay—not in the crate, not just in one room, not in an X-pen, and not by the back door. They will only further confuse your pup.

The *only* time it is okay is if you don't care if your dog goes in and out. Maybe you live in an apartment and don't mind that they go in and out. If you are choosing to use wee-wee pads, you are choosing to be okay with the fact that there may be misses on the pad and in other places. If you choose this lifestyle for your dog, you have to be okay with that. You notice I keep using the word *choosing* because it is a choice. You, not your dog, are choosing your dog's bathroom habits. So please, do not set them up to fail and not meet your expectations because of a lazy, selfish choice in the *now*. Getting a dog or puppy is a commitment. Meaning you need to do the necessary things when you are supposed to do them. Not months from now, when you are already frustrated and your dog has a routine. If you want a fully potty-trained dog, *no pads*. Period.

Story time! I have a new client. She and her husband are seventy-two and seventy-three years old. They just adopted a small three-year-old dog, but this pup lived in a crate his entire life and didn't have a puppyhood. The couple is struggling with potty training. When we first met, they had wee-wee pads down and were taking him out only five times a day. Of course he was going to go inside. This couple is so sweet, but they admitted to not thinking this through. She can't move fast at all to catch him if he is about to have an accident, so even after our first session, she did not pick up the pads because she did not want to clean up more messes.

I am telling this story because this couple is not unlike many other people. We cannot expect things to improve if we do not follow the necessary protocol and make changes to get there! We cannot expect our dogs to give us new behavior if we have not changed ours. Nothing against my sweet older couple. They're not unlike most. They just needed to change their mindset and help the dog succeed.

Shoving Your Dog's Face in Their Accident

This one is also a definite *no* and never okay under any circumstance. If you find an accident, clean it up and go about your business. Reprimanding will not fix the problem. Traditional dog training is lying to you. If you stick your toddler's face in their underwear if they have an accident while potty training, how do you think that would go? Do you think it would make the toddler more likely to go on the potty or just hide from you every time they had an accident due to fear and shame?

I think you know the answer to that one.

Again, if there is an accident, you probably weren't watching the puppy, missed a sign they had to go, or did not follow the protocol. If I find out you are doing this to your puppy, I am going to come over there next time and shove your face in it to see how you like it and if it changes your behavior! It's inappropriate and aggressive, and it doesn't fix anything. It just feeds your bullying ego in the moment because you don't want to be angry with yourself.

The same goes for "What did you do?" Instead of saying it to your dog, say that phrase to yourself in your head. Then clean up the mess, go on with your day, and try harder next time. Dogs may look ashamed or show they know they did wrong, but that doesn't mean this is the way to go. Yes, they are aware they had an accident most of the time, but that doesn't change the fact that *you* didn't take them out. They do not have thumbs. But they are still young and learning how to communicate what they need.

Fun fact: that look of shame and that look that implies that they know they did something wrong aren't always what we think they are. Some dogs don't know what they did, but you are yelling, so they go into fawning mode. If you do not know what fawning is, look it up. It's fascinating! It's the fourth fear response, and one no one talks about it. Fight, flight, freeze, and *fawn*. I fawn a lot because I dated a narcissist for eight years. It takes practice to stop and not fall back on that, but many humans do this, so look it up!

Anyway, dogs will avoid eye contact and look guilty. They are doing this to avoid a confrontation. Essentially, they are reading the room and trying to defuse. They know if they look guilty, the yelling will stop a lot sooner. So, just because they may look like they know they did wrong, don't be so sure. At the end of the day, we all mess up. Empathy and compassion go a long way. Just be a good dog parent! That's all.

Playing a Zone Defense

This is the best advice I can give any household that has more than two people living in it. Do *not* play a Zone Defense. This is man-to-man coverage! If there are multiple people in your home, someone needs to announce they are watching the puppy. If they need to go do something and can no longer watch the puppy, they need to *verbally* pass the buck to someone else before they leave the room. We all know what happens when you assume (ha ha), and the only one that suffers is the puppy.

Make a plan and tell your kids the deal. If no one is watching, then the puppy needs to go in the crate with an enrichment toy. So many parents struggle to get their kids on board with this, but you need to meet them halfway. Again, if you are always yelling at them to watch the puppy, nothing will change. Plus, they won't *want* to watch the puppy. So make it fun. Maybe a reward chart with stickers. Maybe the kid who watches the puppy with the fewest accidents for the week gets to pick dinner or dessert or choose the restaurant on Friday night. Make. It. Fun.

No, you are not bribing, and yes, I know *they* asked for a dog. I get it! But do you want this to change? Do you want them to *want* to help? Eventually, they won't need the rewards because they will find joy in doing these chores with puppy, and they'll bond more with puppy. And that leads to *wanting* to do nice things for puppy just because. It's all a process that eventually pans out, I promise!

Now for the part of potty training not based on protocol and consistency: potty training and anxiety.

Womp, womp!

It is extremely common for puppies and even older dogs to have accidents due to anxiety. Unfortunately, so many people think along the lines of *It's a dog. What do they have to be stressed about?*

Well, a lot, actually. Stress can be due to high separation anxiety and panic when left alone. This can be with a crate or with no crate. It can happen even in just a few minutes and even if someone is still home. Accidents can also be due to high excitement. Situations like meeting a new friend or you coming home from being gone. Even opening up the crate door and bending over them to pet or pick them up can cause stress.

It is important to note that these aren't accidents. These incidents do not mean your dog isn't potty trained. It means your dog is having a separate behavioral issue—separation anxiety, overstimulation, low impulse control, or nervousness—which results in stress pees. If you are dealing with either of these issues, take in this book in its entirety. You will start to understand and clearly see the differences. Do not reprimand your dog for stress pees. You will likely add to the stress and turn this into an OCD response.

Now, let's move on to combining potty training and crate training! It is a lot easier than you think. When potty training, it is important to use your puppy's crate to your advantage because it only aids your dog in the process. The crate can be looked at as your home base or a holding spot. You need this because you can't possibly watch your puppy twenty-four/seven. It isn't healthy for either party to expect that. It can also lead to codependency.

First quick tip and rule of thumb with puppies: try to not overwater your puppy. Many pups will drink, and drink, and drink just because the water is there and it is something to do. As long as they get a bunch when they eat their meals, you can restrict later in the evenings. If bedtime is ten p.m., I would stop water around six or seven p.m. Otherwise, you might be up multiple times at night, and you have to be okay with that. Limiting water isn't mean. It's just setting them up for success! Make sure they have access to water earlier on in the day. They will not dehydrate.

Should you use the crate for sleeping overnight? Some families absolutely need to, and some don't. You need to figure out what works best for your family. Unlike many trainers, I am pro dogs sleeping in bed. I know, I know. I should be in jail! But seriously, there isn't anything wrong with our dogs sleeping in bed with us. Plus, the pros outweigh the cons. If your puppy is a good, sound sleeper, is sleeping through the night, and is not getting up to potty, you can absolutely try them sleeping in bed at night. I have some clients who have their dogs in bed from day one and have zero issues, behaviorally or potty training-wise.

Now, if your dog is up consistently, is a light sleeper, is struggling with potty training, is anxious or high energy, and has a tough time settling, you will most likely want to do the crate at night as well. This doesn't have to be forever, but we want to avoid your puppy having accidents in the middle of the night without you knowing. We also don't want them waking you up to pee every time you roll over in your sleep. Most of the time, this is just a phase. But if it isn't, you can absolutely continue to use the crate for bedtime for the long haul if that works for your family and your dog loves their crate. You can have it in your room if that works for everyone involved. But if your puppy gets too worked up by being able to see you but not get to you, you may need to put puppy in another room where they are still comfortable but not distracted.

Although it is common for puppies to get worked up, and as long as you crate train properly, they should be okay with this eventually and start to whine or cry less and less, getting used to your new routine. It is important to keep your energy low once in the room with your puppy when it is time for bed so they can wind down and not get distracted by all your movement.

Like I said, some dogs wake up in the middle of the night and some sleep straight through from day one; it's truly the luck of the draw, like babies! There are lots of opinions on this. I believe there is an age range of puppies that cannot hold it throughout the entire night, and it is cruel for us to expect them to ignore it and go back to sleep. This age range is usually birth to four months old, sometimes six months old if you get them later in the game. If they are older, it could mean they did not have proper potty training and may need to start from scratch. Sometimes they might have bad habits from prior situations. Personality has a lot to do with it too! If they are easily excitable, watch your every move, and are hyper focused, they might wake up more easily in the night if they're in your room. If they do wake up, you need to respect the bark or cry and take them out to potty. But it is imperative to stay unemotional during this potty break. No excitement, petting, or playing. You need your pup to understand that this is only for potty purposes and you are returning to sleep. Four a.m. is definitely not time to play! (Unless you're into that sort of thing. And if you are, that's between you and your therapist! None of my business!)

But you must stay consistent with this, whatever you choose. As your puppy gets older, they should be able to hold it longer and longer, depending on your schedule. We need them to understand that there is no other value in waking up in the middle of the night, only to potty. This is crucial. As they get older and you know they can hold it longer, you can start to wean off responding to the whine or bark immediately to see if they go back to sleep or continue to carry on. If they do go back to sleep, then it's most likely their body clock waking them up. We can push past that by waiting them out. But if you think they really need to go, don't hesitate, please! Our dogs are extremely potty trained and love to sleep. So, if one of them is up in the middle of the night, it is only to go to the bathroom.

When waking up in the morning, your puppy will come out of the crate and go right outside immediately. Pick them up, if possible, to avoid them sniffing something while walking to the door and having an accident. Again, if they are holding it all night, that bladder is ready to burst. So you need to get them out ASAP! Also, try to keep your excitement super low. Your excitement can cause them to have an excited or submissive pee.

When they come back in after going potty, figure out what their go-to is. Some pups are still groggy in the morning, and some are raring to go! This will sort of set the tone for the day, but it is important to remember that every puppy is different, so don't get upset either way.

To best aid your pup and their potty training journey, create a loose schedule for the day, depending on your schedule. This can be helpful for families that have a lot going on. If there is a loose schedule, everyone can stay on a similar page because the expectations are listed. Keep in mind, puppies from eight weeks to about four months old can hold it in the house for only about thirty minutes, uncrated and not napping. So when they are not crated, you are on a time limit until they are crated again and in their home base.

Just like we discussed earlier in this chapter, start with a twenty-to-thirty-minute time frame and do a potty break. If they can go a whole day with no accidents on that schedule, add fifteen minutes the next day and keep increasing when they have no accidents. If you go outside at your time limit and they don't go, go back inside for five to ten minutes, then try again. Watch them like a hawk the whole time until they finally go to the bathroom. This is crucial. That's why I mention it twice!

You say you can't watch your puppy all day and have other things to do while you are home?

Welcome, nice to know you are still human! Use the crate during the day when you can't focus on your puppy 100 percent. Period. Do *not* feel bad. The crate is necessary to keep them out of trouble, safe, and from having an unnecessary accident. If you are cooking, cleaning, doing laundry, running up or downstairs for something, watching TV, eating dinner, working, being with the kids, helping with homework, etc., it is imperative to use the crate! It only benefits your puppy's resiliency and potty training while protecting your sanity. Just as you wouldn't leave an infant or toddler unattended, it needs to be the same for your puppy! By not using a crate, you are setting them up to fail and doing them a disservice.

Using the crate to your advantage and for scheduled potty breaks is great for all families, but it's even better if you work from home. If that's you, it's important to treat the situation as if you do not work from home. This is so your dog can get used to being in the crate for longer periods. The number of emails and texts I receive that say, "I need to go back to the office," hurt my heart. So it is best to have them ready for this change, God forbid it happens suddenly.

In the beginning, when your puppy is really little, you can do more breaks more often. But treat yourself like a dog walker. Keep a time limit on this break like anyone you would employ would do. This will help your pup learn what to expect from a workday at home with you! If you allow them to romp around while you work because you feel bad, I promise that it won't work out for either of you. Just like it is impossible for a new parent to work full-time with a baby or toddler at their heels, it will be impossible for you to work with a puppy barking for attention and getting into everything. This is also a setup for many accidents. You cannot watch for potty cues and work at the same time. You are not a superhero.

If you don't work from home, you may need to hire someone to come let your puppy out. If this is your situation, this is not where you should fall back on the X-pen with wee-wee pads because you feel bad. This will not get you the long-term results you are looking for. Spend the money on pet care now, and keep your sanity later down the line! It won't be forever and will be extra frequent only in the beginning.

For example, a nine-to-five schedule for a two-to-four-month-old puppy would include tons of enrichment and positive attention or exercise before you leave or pretend to leave at eight thirty a.m. The dog walker should come around ten to ten thirty a.m. for the first break, around noon to one p.m. for the second, and three to four p.m. for the third. You can add another visit in there if your puppy tends to have more separation anxiety or doesn't fully love their crate yet. The goal is for them to love it, not resent it!

Yes, this can be a little costly in the beginning, but again, it's only for a few months. As your puppy gets older, you can gradually extend the time between potty breaks. If you don't see any accidents in the crate and they are succeeding with their current crating and potty break schedule, you can start to slowly increase the amount of time they stay in there in between potty breaks.

Remember, slow and steady wins the race! If you let them out of the crate and there are no accidents, praise them and give them a treat. Let them know they did a great job holding it! And, as always, put a long-lasting frozen enrichment in the crate every time so they see the crate as a resource. It also exercises their minds, which means they can take a nice nap after. This is the way to the motherland!

Now, let me take some time to address common problems that might have popped up in your head.

What if you and your puppy had just been outside, then they came in and immediately had an accident? You'd probably yell, "We were *just* outside!" Instead of jumping to the conclusion that your puppy lives to make your life hell, let's talk about the actual possibilities. You may be dealing with a distracted or anxious dog. Unfortunately, this process will take a bit longer and require more consistency from you. Some dogs get easily spooked or distracted outside. They may find it hard to focus on a good place to go. Dogs need to feel safe before going to the bathroom. So, if they chronically wait until coming in to go potty and look kind of jumpy and wary outside—maybe standing frozen while sniffing with one paw up in the air—you most likely have a dog that feels secure enough to go only in the house.

Most of the time, we see this with poop rather than pee accidents. Pooping takes a lot more effort and keeps them in a stiff position for a longer period, so they can feel vulnerable and like sitting ducks. If you are dealing with this, you need to find a way to make outside less scary. You may need to change your tone when you are out there if you get frustrated easily by how long it is taking. You may be contributing to the problem if you are angry with them every time they are out there and feeling stressed. Instead, take them to one spot that might be less distracting or safer and more secluded.

You can also help them along with calm encouragement. Fence lines and tree lines seem to help dogs that struggle with this because they feel less vulnerable with their butts cornered and covered. If they put their butts in the corner, they can see out and around themselves properly. They need to see the three other sides of a potential attack in order to feel safe. Also, use extremely high-value treats. This can help your dog refocus on the task at hand and build some confidence.

Now, if your dog is just bouncing around and can't focus, keep yourself in one spot and just keep saying your potty phrase over and over in a monotone voice. No talking otherwise. Try to stay away from people, kids, other dogs, and any hustle and bustle. Your dog needs a place to go without distractions. During this time, they get only the circumference of the leash around you. The more you walk, the more new smells you introduce and the more distractions your dog will encounter. When they finally go, wait until they are done, then reward to the heavens! We need to show them that the quicker they go, the quicker they get this over-the-top reward.

In either of these situations—a dog not going when given the chance outside—be on them like white on rice when you come back in. You are not letting them out of your sight. If they are leashed and harnessed, just leave it on and let it drag. Maybe do some cue training for a few minutes, then go back outside and try again.

Now, let's say your dog is peeing or pooping in the crate. This one is wrong, and I feel for you! First things first—it's time to play detective!

Is your crate so big that your pup can go potty in one section and lie comfortably in a different spot entirely? You may need a divider to make it smaller.

Are they having an accident every time, or is it only when you are gone for too long? Is it that they can't make it that long? Or do they have separation anxiety and are too stressed to hold it? Does it happen the second you go to leave? Are they also showing other signs of stress, like drooling, screaming, and whining when you leave or when you come back? If it's the latter, it's most likely a separation anxiety issue. Dogs, especially puppies, cannot hold their bladder or bowel movements if they are stressed or scared. Head on over to Chapter 13 to learn more about combating separation anxiety!

If it does not seem like separation anxiety, you need to possibly make the crate smaller if it is too big or shorten your pup's time in the crate with a dog walker. Setting up a camera so you can watch back and identify the situation can be super helpful in figuring out the correct solution.

Ooh, one of my favorites! Some people say, "My puppy is stubborn." Others claim their puppy is spiteful! This is a misconception. Stubbornness and spitefulness do not exist in a dog's world. That would be to agree that dogs have prolonged thinking and can calculate maliciously for the future while thinking about the past. Which, let me reassure you, they cannot. Haven't you ever heard the phrase "Dogs live in the moment"? They live from moment to moment and learn only by association. They learn by how a situation makes them *feel*.

If you think your dog is being stubborn by not listening to you, there may be a few things going on that make you feel that way. They may have learned over time that when you say something specific, the boundary isn't held. So, the phrase has no real meaning—or, at least, not the meaning you intended. For example, when you say, "Come here!" when you want them to come inside, maybe they think it means, "If you don't come inside, I am going to come to chase you eventually." And they like the chase!

Or maybe they think it doesn't mean anything because the outcome is different every time. For example, you call them to come in, but they never worked on that cue with you—or at least not well enough for it to be solid. After a while, you just say it, and they absently ignore it because it has no meaning and you do nothing about it. You just let them come in when they are ready. Or the outcome isn't beneficial for them and doesn't meet their needs, so they ignore you to avoid it.

Here's another example. When you let them out in the morning, your dog knows you are going to put them in the crate and leave all day for work when they come back in. They are like, *nope*. And the longer they stay out there, the longer they have you home. So they avoid that horrible cue! Try to put yourself in their paws for a moment to truly grasp what is going on internally for them. When you do this, it is so much easier to empathize and keep our cool.

This is not stubbornness at all! That's avoiding something that doesn't meet their needs or is unfun to them. And you would do the same.

Look at a do-to list. We usually leave the least fun thing till last. When I clean the house, I clean the bathrooms last because 1) they're gross, and 2) I can't hear the TV while I do them. I am not stubborn because of this. I am just prioritizing my needs! As humans, we thrive on fun and enjoyment. I am sure that you, as a human, can understand that. If we get a task done quickly and do it well (because we enjoyed doing it), we get a dopamine hit, and that keeps us trucking along the to-do list.

Dogs are the same. They like doing *only* things that are fun to *them* and things that meet their needs. You have to figure out where you are hitting a wall and how it looks from your dog's point of view.

Read the second half of that last sentence again! This can help you figure out what you need to change for your dog so they'll be motivated on their own to do the thing you need done.

Another good example of this: I got off a training session last night with a woman client who lives alone with her rescue pup in NYC. Her best guy friend lives right downstairs, and his apartment has a backyard, so she and Chloe are down there two to three times a day. Lately, Chloe has been giving mom a hard time about going back upstairs at night. The mom told me she was being stubborn, which, of course I told Mom isn't possible, so instead, we broke it down. Couple of huge points. Kyle has the backyard, she likes him, and he has a dog she likes to play with. Mom does not have a backyard. When they go back upstairs, it's boring and time for bed. And after we discussed all of these facts, we also touched upon the fact that Mom might be more somber and/or releasing more stress hormones once upstairs, being that she is a single woman living in NYC alone and she may just be slightly more sad when she's no longer with her friend. I saw the wheels turning in Mom's head immediately. She was getting it! She was so focused on the power struggle that Chloe was giving her, she didn't realize all of these obvious reasons why a dog *wouldn't* want to leave somewhere.

So what did we come up with? Well, first off, do not engage in the power struggle. Do not get stern and more forceful. Put the ego aside, it cannot help her here. Change up the routine, and do not put the leash right back on her once she comes back inside Kyle's apartment because she will shut down. Have her come in, maybe Kyle can give her some love and do some fun cue training with her, and then Mom offers her some sort of high-value enrichment that she can show her and give her the second they get back inside their apartment door for Chloe to enjoy! The goal? Make going back upstairs more fun!

This is a great example of how to get curious instead of frustrated. In all tricky situations, we need to play detective and leave our own emotions out of it. This story leads up to my next favorite phrase to debunk when discussing this topic.

"My dog is spiteful and doesn't come in when I call them inside."

Well, duh! Yeah, similarly like Chloe, they know that when they come inside, the fun ends, you leave, you go back to work, you go to the kids, or they go back in the crate. Would you come back inside? This is not spite. This is a negative association due to continued unfun outcomes. If you want them to come inside, make coming inside more fun for them. It's easy. Just like with the kids! Do you want the kids to actively take the puppy out so there are no accidents? Make it fucking fun!

Now, to get back on topic, "spiteful" accidents are not spite. They are stress. (Don't roll your eyes at me!) Yes, our dogs experience stress *a lot*. Way more than humans want to admit because it would take away the ability to blame them for all the problems. If your dog goes the second you leave, it is stress!

I always tell this story, and it makes me laugh so much. When I came into John's life, my now mother-in-law was struggling with their Chiweenie, Chi Chi Bean. Her real name is Daisy Mae, but we all call her Chi Chi. I honestly couldn't tell you why, but it fits her! Anyway, she was *hyper*bonded to my mother-in-law. Nauseatingly so. Followed her everywhere. I think if John's mom got one of those baby-wearing sweatshirts, Chi Chi Bean would gladly climb inside and be carried all day long. People might mistake her for a newborn. Well, back in the day, if my mother-in-law went into her master bathroom and closed the door, Chi Chi would pee and poop outside the door immediately. My mother-in-law would come out a few minutes later furious!

When I came into the picture, I was able to explain that Chi Chi was so codependent on her that when the door was closed, she would go into fight or flight. She legitimately thought the world was ending. When they go into fight or flight, many dogs need to make themselves as light as possible so they can flee a situation if need be. This includes all their bodily fluids. (This includes throwing up too!) I know this sounds so dramatic, but it's 100 percent biological. They are not trying to make your life hell or piss you off. This is how their bodies biologically respond to this type of stress. And we have to help them!

If you do not help your dog become less codependent, don't be mad when they shit on your floor. For reference, Chi Chi no longer does this. She still follows my mother-in-law around, but it is so much better than it was. I can hold her at parties now without her using me to get to my mother-in-law. Yes, I have been physically used as a vehicle to get to her, and yes, we all know how sick she was for that! But she's so much calmer now, and I'm so proud of Lil' Bean.

The moral of the story: No, your dog is not spiteful or stubborn. Stop using that as a cop-out for why your dog doesn't listen to you! My ears bleed when I hear people say that. You have created a problem—probably accidentally—but that doesn't mean you don't have to take ownership. You need to remember that *you* are the parent. Children and dogs are products of their environments. If there is a problem going on similar to the ones above, it is a disconnect with your relationship, your dog is stressed, or the situation does not meet their needs and they simply do not like what you are asking them to do. Figure out what the problem is by putting your ego aside, and make room for your detective hat instead.

The next troubleshooting question is "Do they need to stay in the crate forever?"

No, of course not! As your puppy matures and becomes more accustomed to the rhythms of your home life, you'll begin to notice a beautiful thing—less dependence on the crate because they are maturing out of it and learning how to just be a part of the family without causing unintentional chaos.

This doesn't mean the crate becomes obsolete. Far from it. Gradually phasing out the crate as your puppy grows is more about shifting from strict necessity to a safety net and just keeping the crate familiar. It becomes that cozy, comfortable space your dog can return to any time they need security or peace. This transition is delicate; it's about reading your dog's cues and providing them with the freedom they've earned through consistent growth in behavior. When this stage is rushed, we usually see it backfire. So, just go at your dog's pace, and you'll be golden!

Now, maintaining good habits doesn't stop at the crate door. Continued reinforcement is key. Just as we don't forget our manners simply because we're not at the dinner table, puppies shouldn't forget their potty training because they're not in their crate. This means sticking to routines, rewarding and marking proper potty training behavior, and, yes, occasionally revisiting the crate during times of stress or upheaval to let them recoup in their safe space.

Remember, older dogs can have accidents too. Stress, sickness, and fear are all culprits when a dog has an accident out of nowhere. Don't immediately think your dog is regressing. Instead, play detective with compassion rather than getting all upset. Also, giving them a place to feel safe is not just about physical space; it's about the consistency and security you provide through your actions and expectations. Don't make your dog fearful of you or stop letting them out at their normal times just because they are older.

My three pups are thirteen, nine, and seven years old, and they go out on a schedule daily. And you bet your asses that I'm at the top of the stairs cheering them on to get them to go quicker in the dead of winter, which gets them so excited. It absolutely works! And yes, they get treats every time they come in.

Why? Because they are awesome fucking dogs, I love them, and who knows how much longer I'll be able to treat them and spoil them the way they deserve. Tomorrow is not guaranteed, and they deserve every ounce of happiness. I refuse to withhold treats and praise for fear of my dog not respecting me. Only insecurity speaks like that. Give respect, earn respect. Give love, receive love. That's the secret to all of this. Keep the trust solid and make training fun for both of you!

As we wrap up this chapter, it's important to reflect on the journey you and your puppy are embarking on together. It's a path filled with learning curves, accidents, triumphs, and, most importantly, a deepening bond between you and your dog. Remember, the essence of successful dog training lies in patience and consistency. Every puppy is unique, and what works for one may not work for another. It's about finding that perfect balance, understanding your puppy's needs, and adapting your approach accordingly. Your patience will be tested, but the rewards of a well-trained, happy, and secure dog are immeasurable. The crate, far from being a jail, becomes a tool of freedom—freedom from anxiety, mishaps, and insecurity for both of you. So you see, it is the opposite of jail!

This journey you're on is not just about potty training a dog; it's about building a relationship. It's about mutual respect, understanding, and love. As you turn the page on this chapter (both literally and figuratively), carry forward the lessons learned, the patience practiced, and the love shared.

Happy potty training!

Chapter 9:

Impulse Control

Low impulse control in dogs is best explained as a "See food, must eat" philosophy, a "Door's open, must escape" strategy, or a "Squirrel! Must chase" reaction. It's when our dogs act first and think later (or not at all), driven by their immediate desires and instincts rather than careful thought or obedience to cues.

Imagine a dog that spots a delicious treat on the table. Low impulse control means that, despite knowing better or having been told no, the dog's inner monologue quickly shifts from *I probably shouldn't* to *I definitely* am as they snatch the treat. This behavior is not limited to food; it extends to darting out open doors, jumping on guests, and tearing after moving objects without a care in the world, all without a pause to consider the consequences.

This behavior is *not* disobedience!

In essence, a dog with low impulse control is like an enthusiastic, lovable toddler who is constantly tempted by the world's sights, smells, and sounds and struggling to resist immediate gratification in favor of obedience or safety. It's a challenge for pet parents but also a doorway to many humorous, albeit sometimes frustrating, adventures in dog training.

What many people do not realize is that dogs are not born with impulse control (nor are children.) It *has* to be learned—and it can be encouraged and deliberately taught! This is why I always laugh when people say, "Don't worry, they'll calm down when they get older!"

Negative, Ghost Rider. They actually will not. Don't give that parent false hope and an excuse to tap out! That is why you see those older dogs that still go crazy when greeting guests or steal table food until the day they die. They never learned! It's up to us to help our dogs learn how to be patient and emotionally control their impulses. But we can do it in a fun way. It doesn't need to be agony!

In the world of our dogs, every day is an adventure filled with temptations and decisions. As pet parents, guiding them through the maze of impulse control is about not just teaching them manners but nurturing a bond built on trust and understanding.

Here's a deeper dive into common scenarios where our dogs' impulse control is put to the test and how we can help them navigate it with grace.

Dogs, much like us, face daily moments of temptation that test their self-control. From the tantalizing aroma of our dinner to the excitement of new visitors, these situations require them to navigate giving in to their desires versus doing what's expected of them. Understanding these moments helps us empathize with their struggle and provides a foundation for training.

The temptation of food is the hardest for my Oaklee! Imagine a struggle in which the mere sight or smell of food triggers an almost magnetic pull. Teaching them to resist this urge is about respecting personal boundaries and ensuring their safety and well-being. Also, imagine you were a stray. That urge to take food for survival may still hold strong even though you are safe now.

Then there is the excitement of greetings. Doors opening can signal the arrival of super-fun guests, turning our dogs into whirlwinds of enthusiasm. While their joy is infectious, guiding them toward calmer greetings ensures a pleasant experience for everyone. But the majority of the time, traditionally because of how we were raised, we are screaming, yelling, and plum frustrated instead of being helpful.

Leash reactivity—reacting strongly to the sight of another dog or person while on a leash—can spark a range of reactions, from curiosity and excitement to defensive barking and vulnerability. Or all of the above! Understanding this behavior is key to managing and eventually reducing such reactions.

Overzealous play is when dogs often forget their strength and manners in the heat of play, especially with other dogs or children. Teaching them to approach and play gently is crucial for safe and enjoyable interactions, but some dogs have a tough time with this due to overexcitement. It is on us to help them learn what it *feels* like when they are going to the dark side of overstimulation so they can make the choice to pull back and decompress.

Patience and duration, meaning the challenge of maintaining cues or remaining calm under excitement, tests their ability to control impulses over time, a skill vital for the overall emotional health of all dogs.

So, how do we get our dogs to settle the fuck down? Seems impossible, I know, but it's easier than you think. You just need to be dedicated to the process.

Building a foundation for impulse control starts with small, manageable steps, focusing on success at each level before introducing more complex challenges. This approach not only enhances learning but also strengthens your dog's confidence and trust in you, which is absolutely what we want! I like to imagine steps or a ladder, with every new level of intensity being another step or rung upward! But until they master the previous level, we cannot expect a different result for anything higher and get upset. Expectations need to be realistic, or we will all fail.

We start off simple. Begin with basic tasks that your dog can easily succeed at, gradually increasing the difficulty as they show readiness for more. Simultaneously, try to minimize distractions. Our goal is to create a calm training environment by reducing background noise and activity, allowing your dog to focus fully on the task at hand.

For example, let's say a family member is in the kitchen opening up a plastic bag while you are trying to teach your dog the wait cue. This is super unhelpful, as your dog will most likely lose concentration. I mean, it's a plastic bag. It could be treats! Of course they are going to break away from training.

Using high-value rewards is an absolute must. Capture your dog's attention and motivation with treats they find irresistible. This makes the training process both effective and enjoyable. You need to use something that trumps the family member opening that bag in the kitchen.

Here is a huge tip: training treats will absolutely not cut it. Your dog will ditch you every time! It needs to be some sort of human food, like string cheese, hot dogs, cold cuts, etc.

And along with your yummy treats, you absolutely need positive reinforcement and a great attitude. Encourage and praise your dog for every little win, however small. But encourage and praise them when they are frustrated and fail too. When you're helping a kid with math homework, are you going to badger them and expect them to love math if they get a problem wrong?

No. We should be encouraging kids to keep going because failure is a part of life. So is getting back up after a fail. They need a boost, and so do our dogs! Fostering a positive association with training sessions is so important. We do not want them to leave the situation thinking, *God, that was awful!* We want them to want more and not to stop.

Another key is being consistent and clear.

What in the world does that mean?

Only. Say. The. Cue. Once.

Then wait. I mean it! Only say it once. Obviously, first make sure your dog is paying attention. Eye contact is necessary before saying the cue. Then make sure you are loud and clear. To clarify, you are not angry, and you don't use a harsh tone, which is what many people think they need to do to achieve this goal. Instead, you use a monotone and are just loud enough to be heard over any chaos.

Consistency means ensuring your dog understands what's asked of them without confusion or frustration. When you say the cue only once, your dog is forced to figure out what you just said and what you are looking for. And they'll remember it instead of the charade some dogs do when you pull out a treat. They never learned the words for or action required by a cue, so they just throw every trick they know at you—sit, down, paw, high five, roll over. And there you are, confused because you didn't ask for anything yet.

When you say it once, they learn to listen and retain it! They'll learn to wait for a cue rather than perform out of panic. What is the point of working on cues if your dog doesn't know what you are asking for?

The next component to this is crucial: "You cannot combat anxiety with discipline!"

Do you know who said that?

Me. It was me! It is one of my favorite personal quotes so far because it is so simple and so true. We know that anxiety or excitement cannot be addressed through discipline alone. Instead, empathy and tailored strategies provide the pathway to improving impulse control in high-stress situations.

If you are experiencing a panic attack and someone tells you that everything is fine and to calm down, don't you wanna just punch them right in the face a little bit? It's insulting because if you could calm down, you would. If everything were fine, you wouldn't be freaking out!

We do this to our dogs all the time by saying, "It's okay! Calm down!" And your dog is like, *No, it's not damn well fine. I am freaking out! And you sound angry, so I feel even more unsafe right now.*

Empathy in a moment of freak-out, even if we don't understand the freak-out, is the only way to teach impulse control. Your dog is having a tough time. You don't get to argue with them or use the excuse that they are stubborn. That is minimizing their struggles and making it seem like they are choosing to be a pain in the ass. Dogs are naturally eager to please, so I frickin' hate when *stubborn* is thrown around constantly to describe dogs that haven't been helped at all. Do you think they *want* to annoy you and inconvenience you? Definitely not.

"But why can't I just make them do a cue and hold it to calm them down?" Many people ask me this question. Let's go through an example to better understand why discipline will not help improve your dog's impulse control issues surrounding stress.

Let's say your dog absolutely goes bonkers at the door when your parents come over because she loves them so much. Some trainers will have you make her *stay* on her *place*, which is a bed not in the same room as the front door. This means she can't see who it is at the door. Whenever you try this, she refuses to stay in her place because she wants to go see her grandparents. She is shaking with excitement and simply cannot do what you are asking of her. She breaks every time you step out of the room to open up the door.

This is not disobedience or stubbornness. Of course you are frustrated because she knew how to respond to these cues when you practiced. But now the difference is that her favorite people are at the door. What you're asking for is too much for her to handle. She does not have the emotional impulse control to handle that yet. Grandma and Grandpa are too high on the scale of excitement. So, by forcing her to stay in her place and not allowing her to see the door, you're making the situation worse. She will get more and more worked up as time goes on. Once she gets over to them, she will be at level ten of excitement. She'll be losing her mind and probably injure someone or jump accidentally. You end up getting this super-excited dog instead of the "calm and desensitized" dogs these trainers are promising.

I have two better options. I usually suggest that my clients do a combo of both options while focusing more on the second one. That's because more natural, normal, authentic training works better than just cues to achieve a goal in an unnatural situation. But I like to talk about both.

The first technique is practicing "Wait at the door." The goal is to sit your dog seven to ten feet away from the front door, but they need to be where they can see who is standing in the doorway once it's opened. They cannot be in a different room or trying to crane their head around to see. This will absolutely break them from their *sit.*

Find that perfect spot, usually right in the middle of a hallway or arch, or even where the floor changes, like from tile to carpet. These spots are best because they visually help the dog pop back to the same spot every time versus inching up closer to the door. Have your dog sit in that spot and tell them to *wait.* (Hopefully, your dog has already learned this.) Your goal is to slowly take one step back at a time until you get to that door.

Start out by taking one step back. Then pause and take one step forward. Say, "*Yes*! Good wait!" and give lots of treats. Keep adding one step each time. You will see as you go farther toward the door that your dog's threshold may get pushed. You may see some shaking, feet tapping, or restlessness, or your dog may just break from the sit altogether. When you see restlessness, take it slow and maybe repeat that number of steps a few more times before adding more so your dog can get better at waiting before you move to the next level of stress.

You are going to eventually get to the door, touch the knob, and go back to your dog. Next time, do the same thing, but now play with the doorknob without opening the door, then go back to them. Next time, do the same thing, open the door just a little bit, close it, and go back to them. Next time, do the same thing, but bring the door open ⅛ of the way, shut it, then go back to them. You will continue this process in tiny steps until the door is wide open. Then you can shut it and go back to your dog without them breaking from their *sit.*

Anytime your dog breaks out of their *sit*, it is okay! It's normal. They *need* to fail to understand how this works, but you need to have a positive aura and give them the emotional boost they need to keep going and succeed. When your dog breaks, just say, "Eh-eh," and lure them right back to their original spot with a treat and start again! They will eventually understand that the longer they take to calm down, the longer it takes to get the yummy food.

Now, if your dog wants nothing to do with this exercise and is awkwardly walking away, maybe they're uncomfortable or your food is not of high enough value. Make them want to work on this and help them. If they are having a tough time, take a break. This should not be figured out in one session, especially if your dog is a young puppy. But that uncomfortable awkwardness does happen. Do *not* force them. You will drive them further away from wanting to do it. Change it up so they are more comfortable, or switch your location. If another dog is around, remove them, as this can contribute to weirdness.

Once your puppy has the empty front door down, you are going to transition to someone standing at it when you finally open it.

Gasp!

I know your dog is gonna lose it, and that's kind of the point! *Expect it!* If your dog is a door darter, use a long line and let it drag. Safety first! When you start this, you always need to start with the lowest level of distraction and work your way up. This means you need to start with the least exciting person in the house and then go up the ladder of exciting people. The least exciting person always gets a little bit offended by this title. But hey, there is only so much I can do!

Absolutely do *not* start with the most exciting people. It's too much stress on your dog and just plain torture for everyone involved. If you do that, you will cause your dog to fail over and over again. They will get discouraged about the whole training in general and won't want to participate in the future.

When you practice this, allow your dog to see who it is. That way, they're aware and aren't wondering, *Excitement or fear?* while they're trying to focus. They need the whole picture to properly calm down. When they finally see that person and break from their *sit*, immediately close the door in the person's face (sorry!), say, "Eh-eh," and lure your dog right back to that spot. Remember, we are not mad or frustrated!

Yes, it will take them a little bit to come away from the door. If you need to use a leash to help you help them, do it. But you are not using the leash to manhandle them or correct them. It is just to help them come away with consistent pressure away from the door. The more they practice, the better they get at this part.

They eventually understand that the quicker they get their shit together, the sooner they get to see that person. Remember to have patience! Your dog is trying, I promise. Think of how hard it is on you when you're learning something new from someone who sounds annoyed, irritated, and inconvenienced. Not a good feeling, right?

Keep closing the door on your door person every time your dog breaks before the "okay" that is the release. The release should not happen until your door person has slowly come into the house and the door is closed. Make sure the person stays quiet and does not make eye contact with the dog. Once you say, "Okay," the door person needs to get down on one knee to encourage no jumping from your dog. They should have treats on them too!

Now, that technique definitely takes a lot of time and energy. Oh, and if I haven't mentioned it yet, patience! It is something the entire family needs to work at and be on board with. The one downfall is that a lot of pet parents do not want to do this every single time a guest comes over. And for sure, we all have guests and family members who do not listen for shit! So, because life is life, there is another alternative. This is why I said in the beginning that this is the better, more authentic option. Honestly, it is more doable and realistic, and it doesn't take as long. But these techniques work even better if you do the previous technique first with just you and get your dog comfortable with the front door. Desensitize them to it, then proceed with the next technique!

The next option is the method of manifesting the behavior you want to see in a normal, natural situation!

For example, pretend that you or someone else is coming home from work. Again, use a leash to help you control the situation if your dog is a typical jumper. I prefer most dogs to be wearing a front-clip harness during this so they don't choke themselves and no one accidentally leash-pops or tugs them all over the place.

You or the person comes in calmly and immediately gets on the dog's level with high-value treats. Keep the treat in the palm and let the dog only nibble at it instead of eating the whole thing right away. This will keep your dog's focus and simultaneously calm them. While treating them, encourage them with a soft voice and continuously pet them without riling them up. Nice, calm pets. This encourages the dog to stay on the ground and not jump up because they are immediately getting everything they are looking for. This way, they feel loved, are getting the attention they're craving, and are being treated with a high-value reward. They are getting everything they could want in that moment.

This method calms them way faster because we are forcing the brain to focus on two awesome things at once—food and attention. It helps the brain not say, *OMG, they're home! I need all the pets and eye contact and love. Love me, love me, love me*!

This happens from an early age mostly because so many trainers and unqualified advice-givers tell people to ignore a dog until they calm down, saying, "Don't give attention until you see good behavior."

What happens when you do this to a child? They start to feel unloved, insecure, and like they need to try *harder* to get the attention they are seeking—even if it's trying harder to get attention in a negative way. Any attention is good attention. And do you really want to tell your dog that you love them only when they behave? Sounds pretty douchey on paper, right? So stop ignoring your dog when they are having a hard time. It's torture, and you are most likely making it worse.

Also, it doesn't work.

Now, everyone's first question is, "Do I need to get down on my knee every single time I come in the door now?"

Yes, consistently, for two to three weeks. After a little bit, you will start to wean off bending down and getting on their level. Instead, you will start coming in and bend over immediately with treats, still giving lots of pets. After another week or so, you can wean off bending over all the way and come in more normally, but you are still doing the treats and calm love and pets. The dog will start to realize that whenever anyone comes in, they get great food and love—and there is no reason to jump. They will be more patient because they know it is coming. After all, you have been consistent.

This doesn't happen overnight. It takes some time. So, my humans, just be patient! Once they do well with that and change their OCD response to the door opening, you can also wean off the treats each time and just give love. I promise this is so worth it! This technique changes door greetings for life.

Both strategies require patience and consistency but lead to a dog that can manage their impulses even in the most exciting of times. You need to remember that impulse-control training is not a destination but a journey, one that varies from one dog to another. Celebrate the small victories, learn from the setbacks, and remember that every moment of training strengthens the bond between you and your dog. And isn't that the whole point? As you continue on this path, you'll find that the lessons of patience, understanding, and mutual respect are invaluable. They transform challenges into opportunities for growth and connection.

In the chapters to come, we'll explore specific training techniques, share success stories, and offer insights to help you and your dog navigate the wonderful, sometimes chaotic, but always rewarding journey of building impulse control. Together, let's turn those impulsive moments into teaching opportunities filled with love, laughter, and learning.

Take a deep breath. They can only learn as well as you teach!

Chapter 10:
The Eighth-Month Mark

A lot of you are probably like, "What in the hell is the eighth-month mark? And why is there an entire chapter on it?"

I understand the confusion. Before getting my certification in behavior, I had no idea this was even a thing. I would say 50 percent of dogs experience this, and their parents call me distraught and about to have a mental breakdown. They say, "My dog woke up one day and was so reactive out of nowhere."

If this has happened to you, I'm sorry. If you have a young puppy, listen up so you can prepare! Because of all of these calls and case studies, I felt the urge to do some personal snooping about the time frame and all the random behaviors these dogs were showing.

This is all about understanding this developmental leap. As we journey through the fascinating world of dog training and behavior, we encounter various milestones that mark significant phases in our dogs' lives. One such pivotal period is the dreaded eighth-month mark. This is when many pet parents observe a sudden and rapid increase in reactivity or other intense changes in their dog's behavior.

It is, unfortunately, due to the onset of maturity. For larger-breed dogs, you can expect this change around eight to ten months of age. For small-breed dogs, we can see this change as early as six months! The smaller pups don't grow as long, and because they are little, I believe they come into maturity quicker due to the need to protect themselves. Napoleon complex, if you will!

Regardless of when this takes place, our dogs undergo a profound transformation as they transition from puppyhood into adolescence. This part kind of sucks, point blank! This period is akin to the teenage years in humans, characterized by hormonal changes, increased independence, and, yes, unfortunately—a fair share of mood swings. It's a time when dogs start testing boundaries and exploring their environment with newfound curiosity and, often, a dash of recklessness. But the biggest and most problematic change we see is the awareness that the world can be a scary place. Dogs have a lot of thoughts about this scary place at this stage, whereas before, they were more of a happy-go-lucky puppy.

I always equate this to little kids. (I know—shocker.) But if you can remember when you were little, running around naked was kind of just what you did for a few years without any real worry about it. You didn't care who saw you. Then, usually around the age of five or six, you became aware of how you looked, how people saw you, and how you saw yourself. Someone seeing you running around naked would be embarrassing, and you would feel exposed. If you have kids in your life and you've seen this, you know what this looks like and what I am talking about.

This is the exact feeling our dogs get during this eighth-month mark. On a walk—a walk they have taken every day since the beginning—they all of a sudden feel vulnerable and uncomfortable when they see a neighbor from afar. This is when the alert barking starts or the less noticeable freezing comes into play. Maybe you have a random worker come do some work on your house, and now your dog is fear barking, backing up, and growling. They have never cared about random guests prior to this, and now you are mortified.

The emergence of reactivity during this developmental phase can perplex and frustrate even the most seasoned dog parents. Several factors contribute to this sudden shift in behavior. Hormonal changes are usually first. As dogs approach maturity, hormonal fluctuations can significantly impact their emotional and behavioral state, leading to increased sensitivity and reactivity to their surroundings. This is why I am all for neutering and spaying when dogs are young. The rule we had at the shelter was four months or four pounds! The majority of the time, that is how old your dog should be or how much they should weigh when you're thinking about whether it's safe or not.

Now, I think giant-breed dogs are the only exception to this guideline. These are your Great Danes, Saint Bernards, Newfoundlands, etc. They grow bigger over a longer period of time than even large-breed dogs, like Labs. So I give them a bit longer before I suggest spaying or neutering. But I feel that the longer they have the "goods," the more time we are giving behavioral issues to rear their ugly heads. Many people say it will stunt their growth, but I care more about behavior than what they look like. Now, if stunted growth were to cause a dog pain or produce a health issue, sure. But I have never seen that happen or read any studies on it. Overall, I want all of our dogs to be as healthy as possible, but I do feel that waiting cannot only be detrimental to their behavioral health. So we have to weigh the pros and cons. For me, behavioral health comes first.

I know this topic is controversial. I am *not* a vet, but I always urge people to do their research and think things through with their common sense. I also find it strange that spay-and-neuter clinics charge a fraction of the cost while a regular vet practice charges a large sum of money for a procedure that lasts forty-five minutes for females and a whopping twenty minutes, *tops*, for males. The majority of the time, vets also tell you to wait until your dog is over a year old, even though spay-and-neuter clinics wait until four months or four pounds. When you use common sense, the idea that the bigger the dog, the more anesthesia it takes and the more money it costs might pop into your head and never leave, as it did with me.

American health care systems are messed up, so it is important to do your due diligence and come at this properly, with all the info. So again, ask your vet first, but also follow up with your own research and thought process. Also, find yourself a good vet who tells you all the necessary information and side effects without pushing products, procedures, and meds on you. You need a vet who is on your team, listens to you, and connects with your dog. Amazing vets are a dime a dozen. Never stop trying to find the perfect one, and never settle!

What was I saying? Oh yes, hormones! An intact male dog—one who still has the goods—can smell a female dog in heat from up to five miles away. So picture your one-year-old male pup just trying to relax at home, but he *can't* because there is a female close by that his body is telling him to go impregnate! I mean, talk about torture! And he can't explain to you what is going on in his head. You just think he is acting out, tearing shit up, barking, and being agitated for no reason. Maybe he is even having accidents in the house all of a sudden when, in fact, it is all biological and makes perfect sense.

The behavior we see from male dogs is similar to what we see in female dogs before, during, and after they go into heat. Going into heat means they are going through their menstrual cycle, which can last two to four weeks. Yes, two to four *weeks*! They are frantic and overstimulated, can become extremely territorial of their belongings, and tend to not want to be touched by anyone, especially male dogs. This can alter your dog's personality and attachment styles forever. For my females, I feel like it hardens them and changes them over the long term. Honestly, it breaks my heart.

Story time! (You know I'm chock-full of them.) So, I had a client back in the day who had two dogs. The older one was a male who was probably around ten years old. He was pretty much a happy dummy, but he was still intact. They then brought a female puppy in. If I remember correctly, they had her from around eight to ten weeks old, and everything was great! They did not get her spayed. When she was around eight to ten months old, she went into heat (shocker), and her brother tried to mount her. She corrected him. She didn't harm him other than hurting his pride, but it was rough. My clients told me that the female was never the same after that. I met her shortly after that incident, and I just felt horrible for her. It was like that experience brought up all the stress, anxiety, and stranger danger lurking under the surface, and it just got worse and worse. She never trusted her brother again and started to associate all of the world's scary things with him. If someone in the apartment complex walked by the window or the doorbell rang, she would redirect on him. Many times, she made contact. Stitches were needed here and there.

The first time I met her, I couldn't get within twenty feet of her. It seemed like at the moment she was mounted, her brain went into permanent fight-or-flight mode. With intense behavioral modification and medications, we made decent improvement. Thank God her family loves her so much and does everything in their power to keep her safe, but I always wonder what her life would have been like if they'd both been neutered and spayed and that mounting situation had never happened.

So my point is, the smallest, most insignificant moment to you could be life-changing for your dog.

Here's another fun anecdote. Many people wonder when their dog will lift their leg to pee. Can you guess when that might be?

Bingo—around the eighth-month mark!

Why?

Because that insecurity is coming into play as they come into sexual maturity. Want to know why they even lift their leg?

The higher the stream, the bigger the dog. So they try to get a high stream on a wall or a tree so that when the next dog comes up, they can see how high it was and potentially be threatened by the first dog's size. Yes, it is like meatheads fighting over who's got the bigger muscles at the Jersey Shore.

When my Oaklee, the most gentle giant, was brought up to New Jersey from South Carolina, he was still intact. He was a stray. So, who knows how many babies he has down there! *Ugh*!

Anyway, when he is home with his sisters and even his boy cousin, he pees like a girl. We like to go into Red Bank. It's a small city in Monmouth County, New Jersey, but it's still busy. Since it's close to the ocean, there are many beautiful sights and restaurants. If we go there, he immediately lifts his leg to pee on the first thing he smells another dog's pee on. His brain is telling him to be the biggest pup there and intimidate the rest. He does this even though he is the most docile pup ever and his emotional regulation and correction with other dogs is primo! He is the least insecure dog around other dogs, and even *he* does this. It makes me laugh. *Men*!

Hormones aside, the eighth-month mark is all about testing boundaries, which is extremely common during this time. With adolescence comes a natural desire to explore and challenge rules and boundaries, and this leads to behaviors that may seem reactive or disobedient. Like when your dog won't come inside even though they know the come cue. Again, this is not stubbornness. This is them exploring the world and having their own feelings, wants, and needs about certain situations. These feelings are now overriding your demands—the demands they used to greet with that "Here I come with a smile on my face" attitude. So I get why this is confusing and frustrating for the majority of parents. But these are the growing pains of having a dog or toddler.

It is also important to remember that they are unaware of *why* you are demanding what you are asking for and how this refusal affects you negatively. "Come" just doesn't meet their needs at that moment, and they do not understand how irritating this can be for you. Try to keep that in mind the next time you want to lose it!

What's the old saying? "You get more flies with honey than with vinegar"? Yeah, that's it! This means you should be nicer to people because when you are nice, you are more likely to win others over. When you are bitter and sour, you tend to push others away, or they become more resistant. This is the same for dogs! They do not like being forced into anything. So, while you deal with this super-fun change, remember to avoid the power struggle at all costs! You will not win this battle. Remind your dog about what's fun about listening, and motivate them like you did back in the day when they were a malleable little pup. Make them *want* to come to you! If your attitude is "You listen to me when I talk to you!" start waving your white flag now because you are already a loser.

Lack of experience also has a lot to do with this. Despite their physical growth, eight-month-old dogs are still learning about the world. Hell, they haven't even experienced all four seasons yet! Without sufficient positive experiences to draw from, they may react fearfully or aggressively to new situations. This means they are highly susceptible to PTSD.

Some people think it is extreme when I say this because we're talking about dogs. How can dogs have PTSD? Well, it is extremely similar to how humans experience it. They can accrue chronic anxiety, hypervigilance, and avoidance of certain people, places, noises, or situations. They can have intense and dangerous sleep disturbances, which leads to grumpy pups during the day. They can have an intense fear of being alone, to the point of breaking out of crates, ripping off molding, tearing holes in walls, and jumping out of windows. Yes, I have worked with dogs that have ended up on the roof due to such horrible fear and separation anxiety. They can also experience severe depression and grieve the loss of a loved one. Dogs are so emotional and complex, but many humans pass them off as "just dogs," thinking they should behave one way or the highway.

They deserve more!

So, how do we navigate the eighth-month mark? Understanding the underlying causes of this sudden reactivity is the first step toward addressing it. There are some strategies that can help both you and your dog navigate this super-fun developmental leap. Consistent training and socialization are extremely helpful. Continue with consistent, positive reinforcement training to reinforce that life is not as scary as they think, and provide opportunities for socialization to build confidence. But here is the kicker: this *needs* to be in moderation! Socialization does not mean heading to the dog park or going for daily strolls on the boardwalk.

Why?

Because you cannot control anyone else in this situation. At all. You are at the mercy of everyone else, like that dog at the dog park who isn't actually dog friendly. That person at the beach who's running toward you, screaming for their off-leash dog to come back. The off-leash dog barreling toward your dog! That person who thinks all dogs love them, so they keep coming closer with their hand extended for your dog to sniff. That random thunderstorm you had no idea was in the forecast. That loud motorcycle that went by at the park.

See where I am going with this? These are all *terrifying* to a dog struggling at the eighth-month mark. It's our job to continue working with them while, first and foremost, protecting them at all costs. Do not put them in situations that they cannot handle and you cannot control. There are too many variables! There will be so much time for all that stuff later down the line. But while they are trying to figure this stage out is not the time.

The next thing you need is tons of patience and understanding. Recognize that this phase is just as challenging for your dog as it is for you.

Real talk for a second. Do you actually think they are enjoying themselves during their hard moments? I hope you are answering truthfully. Try to approach setbacks with empathy and patience, offering support and guidance as your dog learns to navigate their emotions.

It's the same with our toddlers. I recently just went through a *rough* time with JJ. Like to the point of questioning if I was a good mom or not. He was so angry and resistant to pretty much everything we were asking him to do, and we would immediately get frustrated. He felt it and wouldn't budge. After a few weeks, I had to reevaluate. So I sat down and really thought about it from the dog-training aspect, and I reminded myself that you get more flies with honey. So, instead of joining in his chaos with frustration and pushback, I got relatable and then curious.

I said, "I remember being your age and not wanting to go to school too. Can you tell me what you are feeling and why you don't want to go?"

We'd chat a bit, and then I'd say, "How about we make brushing our teeth fun this morning, and then Mommy will sing the Olaf song the whole way to school?"

Boom. Teeth brushed and in the car.

Now, obviously, you can't have this type of talk with a dog that is refusing to walk or get in their crate, but we can make the things they are resistant to more enjoyable. First, we can keep our damn cool. Second, we can have fun with it. Get back to basics! Become relatable. Think, *I probably also wouldn't want to get in the crate. Hmm.*

I believe this is the only way to get out of both scenarios alive.

Next, you need a semistructured routine.

What in the hell does that mean?

Maintaining a structured daily routine can provide a sense of security and predictability. A consistent schedule for meals, walks, and training can help mitigate anxiety and reactivity. Now, I am saying a *semi*structured routine for a specific reason. I feel it can be detrimental to do the same routine daily and never leave things to chance.

Why?

Because I prefer our dogs to be a little more bombproof. A little more go-with-the-flow, if you will, and a little less panicky if something is slightly off. When our schedule is exactly the same all the time and we step one toe out of line, our dogs are like, *No, we don't do that!* and then they panic. This isn't healthy. My dogs eat when I get up. The time is different every day, but it is usually the first thing I do unless the kids need something immediately.

Dinner is a different story. They get fed any time between six and nine p.m., and they go with it. This works for us because our life is a little chaotic. I can't always be around at six p.m. to feed them. I would hate for Oaklee to be stressed about eating an hour late because it would engage old anxiety. I also don't want to feed that pang of anxiety I'd have over getting home at a specific time to avoid causing them stress.

My parents feed their dogs at exactly 5:30 p.m. every night, and Gatsby gives you the stare-down at 5:29 p.m. It's terrifying but also kind of impressive. But I don't think this aids him, his anxiety, or my parents. If they are out, they get worried if we arrive late to feed the dogs dinner for them. And there I am, thinking, *I know damn well you guys didn't care this much if Nikki* [my sister] *and I were hungry when we were younger!*

Sometimes, variety can be super beneficial for dogs, especially if their behavior tends to be more OCD oriented. So routine is good when you both benefit. But if you find your dog cannot recover when there are little changes or hiccups, this is something to start slowly switching up so they can learn to deal with life's uncertainties! Just like with kids, you can't control every outcome. We have to prepare them for that and help them *deal* with it so they have the ability to recover. That is our job!

Now, moving on to the next tip for the eighth-month mark: seek out professional assistance immediately. You should do this before you hit this point. In fact, if you see any hint of reactivity, fear, or anxiety before the eighth-month mark, you should already be working with a behavioral consultant. Do not play around with this. This is not a joke! These feelings can change your dog for life. The second you see a change in your dog leading up to or during this time, you should find someone to help! This is not a "It could be a phase, let's wait it out" or a "Let's google it and do it ourselves to save money" situation. Both of these options can be extremely detrimental and dangerous. Plus, they can cost you more down the line. I'm talking money and sanity, my friends.

Last but not least, focus on the bond and embrace the journey. Strengthen your bond through activities that both you and your dog enjoy. Whether it's a game of fetch, a peaceful hike, or simply quiet time together, these moments of connection can provide a calming anchor for your dog during turbulent times. But remember to always meet *their* needs! Don't make them walk if they hate walking and it brings you both grief. If they like a good cuddle, cuddle. Do what makes you both happy. This sometimes includes losing ideas or specific visions in your head that you had when you got your dog—like going for long walks on the beach. Visions can change, and that's okay. Embrace it! We can always table certain ideas and visions, then eventually come back to them after we figure out what the problem is for your pup. There is so much time for change!

To wrap it all up, the eighth-month mark is a significant milestone in your dog's life, marking the transition from puppyhood to adolescence. While it may bring challenges, it also offers a unique opportunity to deepen your understanding of your dog and strengthen your bond. By approaching this phase with empathy, patience, and a commitment to ongoing training and socialization, you can help your dog navigate the complexities of growing up with confidence and grace. It is normal for your dog to change during this time! Try not to panic. Remember, every dog's journey is unique, and the path to maturity is filled with learning opportunities for both of you. Embrace the challenges, celebrate the victories, and cherish the journey you're on together. With the right support and guidance, your dog will emerge from this phase a more confident, well-adjusted, and loving companion. And you'll be one of those beloved former clients I have who forgets how bad the beginning was because the *now* is so good!

Remember, they're only eight months old! There is so much time.

Chapter 11:
Reactivity

What better way to follow up that eighth-month mark than by flowing right into reactivity!

Now, I think we can all agree that nobody *wants* a reactive dog. But, unfortunately, it happens—a lot! Figuring out why your dog has become reactive will help us fix the problem at its root. There are a myriad of reasons why our dogs can become reactive, but it is important to go over the types first.

As I explained earlier, there are two different types of dogs: smarty-pants dogs and happy dummies.

A lot of people get a little offended at first when I say their dog is a happy dummy. But honestly, I say it with the utmost affection and envy! It's a *good* thing! What you need to understand is that the happy dummies have the best lives possible. This way of thinking is preferred and so much more enjoyable for the dog. These are the typical therapy dogs that don't care about anything, Elevator music is playing most of the time, and they're just happy to be here. Kids can jump all over them, people can pet them anywhere, and they tend to be overly friendly, seeking out any and all people. They're chill and just go with the flow! They are usually really social dogs that don't seem to skip a beat if a routine changes. They'll greet a burglar with a smile and a tail wag. A.k.a., marshmallow for brains. Which, I swear, I mean with all the respect and love in the world.

My dogs Oaklee and Tishi are happy dummies, through and through. I think if the term were in the dictionary, they'd be pictured next to the definition with their big smiles. As long as they're with John and me and there is food, they'd be happy to be homeless and live in a car. These dogs live the life, truly. I myself am jealous of this. They're so easygoing and are so much happier for it. It is a much more peaceful life.

Now, for the smarty-pants dogs. This is our dog Pudge. She is so intelligent that it's painful! If we were living in a car and homeless, she'd be losing her mind! She'd have a thousand questions and problems, and she would not give a fuck about the food we had to offer her. If you are dealing with reactivity, intense fear, or overstimulation, you most likely are dealing with a smarty-pants pup. My condolences to you! It is not for the weak. These are the intelligent, hyperfocused dogs that watch your every move, sleep with one eye open, and are one step ahead of you. They know what you're gonna do before you even move. These are emotionally advanced dogs, and they wear their hearts on their sleeves. Their advanced emotions are in a different ballpark than our happy dummy dogs' emotions are.

This can happen just from birth when being hyperfocused and anxious is just how they came into the world. Or maybe things changed for them around that eighth-month mark.

It is important to mention that sometimes, on a rare occasion, we can have a dog that's both and merges the two. That would be the mix of a happy dummy and a smarty-pants. These dogs are goofy and happy-go-lucky when they feel safe, but they still have the tendency to be reactive and anxious in certain situations. I'll give better examples of this later, but let's dive super deep into smarty-pants dogs so you can fully understand all the ways they could end up with reactivity. Because our goal is to identify what might have happened to get us to this point of reactivity. And if you don't have a reactive dog, you'll want to fully understand what to avoid!

Let's start with the most common situation, which is a dog that's a smarty-pants from birth. The culprit is usually poor breeding. A lot of dogs from breeders struggle with inbreeding and the behavioral effect of that. Unfortunately, many purebred dogs, especially in my area in New Jersey, are puppy mill dogs. So many people are surprised when I tell them that the puppy they got from the Amish is actually extremely inbred. They argue with me and say how nice the people were and how clean the barn they were brought to was. This is most likely false, and they were lied to. These breeders have a massive barn, swarming with filth and dogs in crates, that's miles away from that quaint little barn.

Now, how can this be? Well, the biggest culprit where I live is the Amish population in Pennsylvania, but New York State is decently bad too.

Listen, I am not here to bash the Amish by any means. They make kick-ass food. I am not trying to be stereotypical and say they all do this, but it is extremely common.

You're probably asking, "Aren't there laws in place to stop this?"

Unfortunately, no. Our animal laws, even in New Jersey, are currently garbage, and many of the laws that do exist aren't enforced. The laws pretty much say you can treat dogs like livestock. The Amish are farmers and have a lot of livestock, so they are doing what they have done for years. No one is stopping them or putting in the effort to bust them.

There are also many rumors that breeders like this pay off law enforcement to turn a blind eye. I would *hate* to think this is true. But, unfortunately, I tend to be on the naive side with stuff like this. I just can't fathom someone doing that, but not everyone cares about animals, and not everyone is a decent person who follows the law.

What about the AKC? That's the American Kennel Club. They decide which breeds are purebreds, establish rules on showing dogs, identify which bloodlines are pure and acceptable, and determine who is allowed to do what.

It all comes down to verifying bloodlines, keeping the bloodlines strong for showing, promoting aesthetics, and other ridiculous motives. They don't care about health and long-term effects.

Want to get real? Let's get real!

For example, Doberman pinschers may suffer from hip dysplasia, bloat, blood clot disorders, or the big killer—dilated cardiomyopathy, a disease that can cause heart failure. This is already a serious issue in the breed. Around 60 percent of Dobermans are thought to be affected by heart disease. This year, that number is projected to reach 70 percent. By 2039, 100 percent of Dobermans may be affected by or be carriers of this disease.[1] By 2039! That is only fifteen years away! To be clear, one of the nastier side effects of this disease is that it doesn't always present symptoms in time to treat it. Sometimes, the dogs just drop dead. I know—it is absolutely horrible.

The only way to fix this and save the breed is outcrossing. Outcrossing is the mating of two unrelated dogs. Some breeders define outcrossing as the breeding of two dogs with no common ancestors in a four-generation pedigree. But the AKC would not call these outcrossing puppies "pure," which is just ridiculous. So let's just kill off the entire breed altogether?

Cool. Smart. These are the rules of the AKC. That's why when people go to show me their AKC paperwork, I puke in my mouth. They do not matter. Nobody cares! All I care about is if your dog is happy, healthy, and not gonna drop dead because of a genetic disease that could have been avoided!

So, what does this look like for our everyday purebred dogs like puppy mill and pet store dogs? Well, no one is going to prove that the bloodline is what they say it is. All the breeder needs to do is present papers and say the dog is registered as an AKC-certified purebred, and most buyers are pleased. Ridiculously pleased, in fact! But they never think of how fragile the whole thing is. How easily breeders lie to parents.

---

1. Doberman Preservation Project (homepage), accessed April 19, 2024, https://www.dobermanpreservationproject.com/

Your dog could be the product of two dogs that should not have been making puppies together for obvious reasons. Like brother and sister, dad and daughter. Even just close cousins is not a good way to go. There is a lot of irresponsible breeding going on, and we can't prove it. With all these intact dogs all around each other, how do we know who impregnated who? Half the time, the breeders themselves don't even know. (Again, I am talking about irresponsible breeders.)

Then there are those people who think they got a purebred, but something seems a little off. So they do a DNA test and find out their dog is a mix. Those clients always have a good laugh at themselves afterward. Well, most of the time, anyway. Anytime it happens, the client will contact the breeder, who claims those tests are never right.

So, what can you do? I'll tell you what you can do. Stop buying from pet stores and puppy mills. End of story. Super simple. Just stop doing it!

Now, I have to give some of you the benefit of the doubt. Some of you try to make sure you're buying from a reputable breeder. Puppy mill breeders are good at hiding the fact that they're selling puppy mill dogs. Many of the people I speak to, even my own clients, say that when they picked up their new puppy, the conditions were so poor that they felt like they rescued them.

I'm sorry, but no. I get it, but no. It is not a rescue. All they did was support more puppy mill breeding. Now, if they called the police and took the dog without paying, then yeah, I'd say they rescued the dog. But if they paid the breeder, they did nothing but buy a genetic mess and support this horrible process.

These breeders will never stop until we stop. Everyone needs to stop supporting and buying from them. It is so simple! People would rather give $4,000 to a horrible person who is making a personal gain off of forcing dogs to have sex and get pregnant than adopt a puppy from the shelter for $600. All because they want "pure" for aesthetic reasons. As if this will save them from needing me down the line.

If your dog has genetic trauma and issues due to breeding, you bet your ass you are going to be paying way more than just $4,000. The majority of it will be on training and trying to help your dog function like a happy dummy. It is so ass backward that it hurts my brain. As humans, we are our own worst enemies.

I also want to make it clear that dogs that are a genetic mess deserve love too. They deserve it no less than a rescue does. The love and devotion are the same, but we do need to draw the line somewhere. Stop buying from them, and report them to your local government. It is the nicest thing you can do for those poor breeder mama dogs, whose nipples are down to the floor and who can't walk because they're never out of a crate. That is who you are helping when you say enough is enough! My poor old Tishi, she walks like she's bent at the hips, ready to take a pee, all the time. That is just how her frame is now because she was used for breeding, left outside in a crate. For years!

Okay, end rant. Sorry, but there will probably be a few more of those. If you can't tell, I do not support breeding and humans making profit off of their dogs. I find it super nauseating.

Now, let's get back on track.

What is genetic trauma? These are experiences in lineages that are passed down epigenetically. This is best explained through examples. It is important to mention that genetic trauma can be present in any puppy. I just tend to see it in a lot of puppy mill and pet store dogs due to how they were made, whelped, and treated during puppyhood. Behaviorally, they usually don't have a shot if they have an ounce of advanced intelligence or sensitivity to scary situations.

But let's say Mom is a puppy mill mama. She's stuck in a crate, abused, neglected, scared, and trying to survive. The stress that she is experiencing can get passed down to her puppies. It can happen even before the pregnancy. Meaning if she was in an abusive or stressful situation before she was even pregnant, that can also get passed down to her babies through epigenetics.

This can also happen to stray mamas because their conditions are also super poor. Some of them are fighting for their lives to survive out there. It gets passed down.

This is why it is frowned upon for breeders to use for breeding any dogs that have any behavioral issues. But again, there is no one enforcing this rule. Many people meet the mom and dad when they pick up their new puppy and tell me how nasty the parents were acting or how reactive or fearful they were. If that is the case, there's a fifty/fifty shot of seeing the same behavior in the puppy.

This still blows my mind a little bit, but I wasn't good in chemistry and science. But it makes sense. Still, I find it fascinating that this can happen to just one puppy in a litter, just a few, or none. It is a gamble. Just like how each human baby is different even though genetic siblings come from the same parents. My two boys are dramatically different! They are currently two and four years old and have wildly different demeanors and personalities. Just the same, littermate puppies can have extremely different personalities.

Story time! I had a cute young couple come to me with their older puppy, which, if I remember correctly, wasn't even a year yet and had already gone through three aversive trainers. Sigh. He was an Aussie shepherd who was eight weeks old when my client went to pick him up. The breeder was a vet tech at a vet's office. Shame on her because she should have known better! She is what we call a "backyard breeder." No papers, no experience, but she probably thought, *Hmm, let me breed my reactive female Aussie with a local Aussie male and make some quick money*. Disgusting.

My client met the mom. She was not friendly and was indeed extremely reactive. Again, shame on that vet tech, who made her poor, fearful dog go through getting pregnant, being pregnant, and dealing with the stress of losing her puppies. Yes, this is traumatic for a lot of mama dogs that do not have the temperament for breeding.

When my client picked him up, he was petrified. He screamed and cried. He also paced and was stressed from the beginning. She got him in the car, and he calmed a bit in her arms, but then he puked the whole forty-five minutes home. My client's husband was away on a business trip and came home two days later. She was holding the puppy when he came in. The dog took one look at this man and immediately peed and pooped all over my client. Then he jumped out of her arms and put himself in a corner, continuously shrieking and peeing all over the place.

He was nine weeks old. *Nine fucking weeks old*! That is the best way to describe what bad genetics can do to a dog. It is torture. These dogs don't have a shot in hell. Sadly, they're set up to fail before they even come into the world. My heart breaks for dogs like this. We can make improvements and make life more manageable and less scary, but this poor Aussie will never know the bliss that Oaklee and Tishi enjoy daily. They don't have a care in the world. That poor dog knows if someone farts down the street. It's no way to live, and it could have been easily avoided.

Okay, end rant number two in this chapter! Sorry, but I am just ridiculously passionate about reactivity, and I can't help but go off.

Now, let's get into what we are dealing with here. It is a lack of innate coping skills for recovering or bouncing back, which makes them more susceptible to emotional trauma. These dogs constantly feel like they are in fight or flight. The cause can be excitement, fear, or both at the same time.

Let's say you take your dog for a walk and they see something that scares them. You just know that's it for them. They're going to be frazzled the entire walk, pulling you home or just continuously barking into the void at nothing until they get home to their safe space and work it out. This is what low coping skills and the inability to recover look like.

As stated in the previous chapter, the eighth-month mark is like a recollection of an incident from when they were younger. Remember that PTSD we spoke about? Sometimes there's an underlying story to it. Sometimes we don't know what that story is because we adopted them later in life. I had one client whose puppy got attacked at the dog park. He seemed to be okay, But once he hit ten months, he didn't want any other dogs near him. You have to keep in mind that some of that stuff comes back, and we don't get to say, "But you were fine!" These are all things to be aware of and watch for.

To clarify the difference between both types of dog, the happy dummies sort of let this trauma or stressful incident just fall away as if nothing happened. They easily shake it off, recover, and self-regulate. The smarty-pants dogs, on the other hand, definitely hold on to that trauma and mark it as PTSD. They associate the scenario, how it played out, how it felt, and what the outcome was. This can pop up down the road and affect them later in life.

Now we are going to get into the beyond. What can happen after birth to contribute to this lovely reactivity? Let's go over trauma in puppyhood. Here are a few common things that I consistently hear from clients:

Their puppy was attacked by another dog.

Their puppy was taken from Mom and siblings before twelve weeks.

Their puppy was on a stressful transport, like a truck or plane. I can't tell you how many times I ask, "Where did your puppy come from? What was the situation?" Usually, it was a transport of some sort with a scary situation. Anything more than a two-hour transport on a truck or just a plane ride in general can be traumatic.

Their puppy bounced around from home to home. We see this quite a bit with rescues. They get minimal interaction and are over-crated and confined when they're young. Some families just don't know what to expect when getting a puppy. They get overwhelmed, so the dog is in the crate almost twenty hours a day. This hinders their socialization and confidence at a young age.

Their puppy was neglected or abused. This is the worst. Neglect is when someone does not treat a dog correctly but is unaware that what they are doing is wrong. It's not intentional abuse. This mostly comes down to being uneducated. Abuse is knowing well and good that what you are doing is mean and horrible.

So, any of these examples above could give a puppy some trauma!

Another variable that can contribute to a dog's reactivity down the line is a lack of socialization due to illness or injury. Many clients have come to me with puppies that survived parvo. That's the really bad puppy virus that, more times than not, kills puppies under four months of age and even older dogs with compromised immune systems. When I hear of a puppy that survived this disease, it is pretty much a miracle! Parvo pups are not allowed to do anything—no socialization, no exercise, no walking around, and no affection. It is highly contagious, so they are quarantined and exiled immediately. It's heartbreaking. And even more so because they don't get the love and affection they require because caretakers need to be all gowned and masked up to not spread it to other dogs. I think this is why many parents get a little nervous when their vet says not to socialize a young puppy with any other dogs before the puppy has their shots. They're so scared their dog will pick up parvo that they literally don't let them outside to see the world. This can also hinder a dog.

Something to keep in mind is that parvo is normally common only in really dirty, dog-infested areas and among dogs that are not vaccinated for parvo. If you are walking your puppy down the street in a clean, safe neighborhood, you can ease your nerves a bit. We all want to keep our dogs as healthy as possible, but this is sometimes out of our control. Just keep this in mind and adjust your behavioral expectations if your dog does experience illness or injury at an early age or even later in life.

Next up, we have trauma in adulthood. This is usually during or after the eighth-month mark. This can be anything that feels scary or negative to your dog! It could be the smallest, quickest moment. Their entire psyche is so fragile that sometimes it's astonishing. This could be an incident at the dog park or day care. Or it could be something sneaking up on them or popping up out of nowhere. I call that the "back alley dog/incident." An example is when you are walking your dog down your street, and another dog or person just pops up from behind a car or down a sidewalk in an apartment complex. Sometimes, we don't hear these things coming, and neither do our dogs. But this sudden presence from out of nowhere spooks the crap out of your dog. Because your dog was not expecting it and it's so close to them, they go into a deep fear response. When this happens, a dog may no longer trust certain areas or situations. They may get scared of a scenario that looks similar to the traumatic moment. They may no longer trust going for walks at all. Maybe they won't even walk with the person who was holding the leash during that scary time because of that associative learning. This situation is similar to when a dog contracts an illness. We can't always avoid or control it.

We will go over ways to be prepared and help them learn to recover later in this chapter.

The majority of the time, when a dog is dog reactive, it is because they had a scuffle or scary moment with another dog at one time. This can be a random dog on the street that got out of their house, a dog at day care that they once trusted, or a dog sibling at home. I have a client dog, poor thing, who used to play with his dog friend at the beach consistently. I believe it was a few times a week. My client is a cute little midsize hound mix, and his friend was a little Boston terrier. The Boston terrier apparently was a tennis ball guarder, but for whatever reason, his parent thought it was a good idea to bring the tennis ball to the beach. My poor client didn't even like playing fetch, but the other dog was playing with the ball, and it unfortunately went under my client's legs. He was just standing there, minding his own business, and the Boston terrier attacked him even though they were besties. Multiple bites just because the ball was close to him! After that incident, my poor client was petrified of other dogs because he had no idea what happened. He also didn't want to go to the beach anymore. We could not explain to him that his friend was having a hard moment guarding and that he didn't do anything to deserve that. We couldn't tell him that not all dogs will do this to him. We couldn't tell him that the beach was not the common denominator. So it took us some time to undo that one unfortunate moment.

Loud noises are another terrible culprit when it comes to triggering reactivity and anxiety. Those noises can come from large trucks, sirens, fireworks, motorcycles, construction, and smoke alarms. Anything that scares a dog. Many dogs have a hard time recovering from this. I'm working with one dog right now that will not leave the house because they live near a huge construction site that's been going on for months. She's losing her mind.

These sudden sounds are so random, and they cannot find any direct cause for them. So their overall anxiety goes up when the sounds are more likely to happen. Dogs may run for a safe place when you cook because they are anticipating the smoke alarm. They may be super reactive at the door during a specific time of day because they are anticipating the mail or an Amazon truck. They may pace around and bark at nothing because they feel a thunderstorm coming. These are all things that can spike a dog's anxiety and fear, but it is hard to account for them or avoid them.

Next, and probably the most detrimental, is aversive training or high-stress, emotional situations that are constant. As we discussed in previous chapters, aversive training is anything that involves prong collars or shock collars and any techniques that rely on correction-based, punitive, or fear-based training. This is the training that says, "Do what I say right now, or else." These methods can scar dogs emotionally for a long time because they use pain, discomfort, and fear to make the dogs stop feeling, needing, or wanting something. That makes for a more agitated, reactive, anxious dog.

This is similar to the effect of physically and emotionally abusive relationships. It's like having a family member or significant other who is randomly triggered or takes things out on you. You may feel like you are walking on eggshells constantly, and this can do a lot of damage mentally, especially for young children.

Remember that fawning response I spoke about earlier? This is similar for dogs when their parents use a shock collar or physical correction. When I was at someone's house once, one of the other guests was playing excitedly with their dog. They were both having a great time running around together, and the dog was jumping up and being silly. The parent took the remote to the shock collar and zapped her out of nowhere. She screamed and ran away.

The dog didn't go near the guest she had been playing with for the rest of the night, and she was shaking in her crate. She didn't understand why she was shocked. No one used a cue to give her a chance to do better, to know that a correction was coming, or to do anything specific that her parent needed from her because no one except the playful guest was engaging with her. That parent took a friendly, happy dog and suppressed her into an anxious mess, making her fearful of people for no reason.

Aversive training can leave some of the largest wounds on dogs, and the crazy thing is, those wounds are avoidable. Aversive training is a *choice* the human makes. Humans can keep acting like their choice isn't horrible, but I believe it bites us in the ass eventually, one way or another. It is time to choose better and advocate for our dogs. A little later on, we will discuss how to undo this trauma.

Next is intense, consistent emotional stress in the home. Usually, this is unintentional and not directed at the dog. This can be a nasty divorce or domestic violence situation, the death of a beloved family member, a new baby, someone moving out, someone slowly dying from an illness in the home, or even a big move—any big change that the dog was unprepared emotionally for. Our happy dummies are usually resilient against these changes. But smarty-pants dogs are so much more susceptible to anxiety and trauma because they tend to be unable to let these experiences roll off their backs and be unaffected.

So many dogs I've worked with become reactive, depressed, or anxious when someone passes away. It is so sad. Dogs often do not get the opportunity to grieve the loss of someone or another family pet. This is why, as a family, we want our dogs to pass away in our home, if possible.

We had a blind puppy named Opal. She was amazing but had something wrong in her brain. She was born blind, so there was most likely a malformation. We could not stop her seizures and had to let her go at a year and two months old. It was devastating. Our amazing vet, Dr. Samantha Mammen, and her fabulous vet tech, Danielle Rullo, came to our home to let her cross over. This allowed Oaklee to lie with his sister while this happened so he could understand and grieve. We did this purposely. I wanted him to be able to process and be there to feel it happen. So many of my clients have dogs that are depressed and have abandonment issues because they did not process a loss. Types of stress like this can change a dog forever unless we step in and give them the opportunity to process. Now, I know this is not always possible, but if you can do it, try to make it happen for your dog.

Let's head back to injury and illness. It's extremely important to consider your dog's health at all times, but even more so when we see reactivity or sudden changes in behavior. Many dogs are good at hiding pain and discomfort. Some have an extremely high pain tolerance and won't cry or whine like others do. They may tense up, clam up, and lash out instead. This is usually the number-one thing I talk to clients about, especially if something comes out of nowhere. Did anything change with the dog physically or health-wise? Because we do have to take that into account. There could be something going on that is directly contributing to the change in behavior.

I always use the following example because I want everyone to see how black and white a situation can be, even when we just don't know or our eyes are just not open to that possibility.

I trained a dog out in California. Mom and Dad came to me because he started guarding his food quite severely *out of nowhere*. They unfortunately googled first and used aversive, fear-based tactics that made it much worse. Once we started, I told them he needed to see the vet first because I thought something was up. Lo and behold, he had ruptured his eardrum and needed three surgeries. He went through a rough time and was in immense pain while also being challenged while eating every day.

If our dogs are ill and in pain, we cannot hold them accountable if they are struggling physically or mentally. So, injury and illness are always something to consider before resorting to training. Dogs will exhibit reactivity to protect themselves because they may think they are in fight or flight. This is because they physically are at a deficit even though we're not trying to hurt them. But in this state, they are more likely to perceive normal human behavior as a threat. They are vulnerable, and we all know that vulnerable individuals can struggle to appropriately perceive reality. If you're unsure, ask your vet to look for hidden causes of pain or discomfort. This can be life-saving.

That wraps up all the things to watch out for if your dog becomes reactive out of nowhere, along with things to avoid so you do not get a reactive dog down the line.

To move forward and have success, the main thing I need my human clients to understand is that we cannot fix or avoid reactivity without empathy. If you cannot empathize with what your dog is experiencing or has experienced in the past, this will not work. It's time to just get on board and realize that your dog is not being naughty. You have to believe your dog is doing the best they can, just like we're all doing the best we can with what we know. But here you are, trying to better yourself for your dog. They will gravitate toward you so much more quickly when you use the techniques I will soon share with you.

We have to understand that something significant is going on in their brains in these moments of stress. We are not seeing and feeling what they are seeing and feeling. Until we can agree with that, lose the notion that they are being bad, and take our emotions out of the equation, we cannot expect change. So buckle up and get on board!

The million-dollar question is, What is reactivity? Understanding it is half the battle. It's when dogs become aroused by common stimuli. They may lunge, bark, and growl. They may become so preoccupied with what is triggering them that they can be difficult to control and move out of a situation. They may even accidentally injure a loved one during this time of stress. I will say this until the day I die: there are no bad dogs. Even the most dangerous dogs are usually this way due to intense fear. That is why I do not call them aggressive. They can have aggressive tendencies, but I will never use that word to describe a dog. It is unfair!

In my almost ten years of doing this and dealing with many mentally ill and abused dogs, I have seen only two truly aggressive dogs. I believe something was wrong in their brains from birth. Again, it wasn't because either of them was a bad dog. It was that something was not right with them. The point is that dogs aren't born just wanting to bite people and other dogs. They all have a drive to be social and loved, like humans do. So, if your dog has a kinship with you or a bond with someone, that means they can do this. They may just be fearful of other people and have a lot of trust issues. This is intense fear versus aggression.

So stop calling your dog (or other people's dogs) aggressive! Dogs make noise. They bark and tell you how they feel if they are uncomfortable, if you let them. This does not mean they are aggressive. That word gets thrown around so much, and I can't take it! If your dog air snaps at someone, they are not aggressive. They showed restraint by not making contact. I assure you, dogs could land so many more bites than they do. They make a conscious decision not to make contact. They are way quicker than we are. An air snap is just a warning. If someone creepy asked your young kid for a hug and they said, "No, thank you," would you be upset or proud that they were able to identify something was off and had the confidence to speak their needs? Really think about that!

Yeah, as a parent, it may be uncomfortable to have to deal with that awkwardness with the creepy person, but how great is it to see your kid empowered to say no? In today's world, we need strong kids who know what is right and wrong and who have the freedom to say no to things that make them feel uncomfortable. I see so many parents, to kids and dogs, forcing them to show love or affection toward people. Why? I believe as parents we want our kids and dogs to be seen as wonderful little individuals to be proud of, and in turn, we forget that that is not why they were put on this earth. They are not here as a trophy. If your kids or dogs are saying no to affection or interaction with someone or something, *listen to them*. This is an important skill all kids need to learn. Do not shut off the part of their brain that keeps them from danger and makes them a people pleaser.

Kids deserve a say in who they hug and so do our fucking dogs. Someone has creepy, weird, abrasive vibes? Your dog gets to say no. But they can't verbally speak it, and you, as the parent, don't always step in or notice the subtle cues that mean "Leave me alone." So they have to handle it the only way they know how—with a growl, an air snap, or a bark! How else would you like them to communicate? Our dogs and our children should never have to appease people or avoid awkwardness just to avoid creepy people getting their feelings hurt, ever! And they definitely shouldn't have to do something just to avoid embarrassing you with their choice to not do something just because someone asked them to. It's not about you! Get used to awkwardness. Get used to discomfort. It's good for you! You don't owe anyone anything, and neither do they. *No* is a full sentence.

So why do dogs go bonkers in certain situations? Why does it seem like they can't even hear us?

It is called the red zone. That is the term a lot of people use when we're describing severely reactive dogs. The red zone is an extremely heightened state of alertness and intense emotions. When they're in it, dogs slip into survival mode. I describe it as having horse blinders on. They can't hear or see you. It's similar to us when we are in a dangerous situation and can feel parts of our brain switch off so the survival parts can focus. Dogs in this situation are experiencing such intense fear and terror that they are now in fight or flight.

Here is some science for all you nerds! Impulses travel at lightning speed through the limbic system to the hypothalamus, which then fully activates the fight-or-flight response via the pituitary gland and endocrine system. Because of this response, dogs will not be able to tap into the part of the brain that holds on to the ability to listen and all they have learned from you during training. Their cortisol is through the roof at this point, making it impossible for them to hear anything else going on. These are the moments when we get frustrated as pet parents, thinking they're being spiteful or stubborn and choosing to embarrass us on purpose. And I hope that by now, you are catching on and know that this is just not the case!

For safety purposes, your dog's brain has tuned you out. Only the trigger matters. I always enjoy using the following example because I think it is extremely comparable and helps humans understand what is going on for their dogs.

If you were held at gunpoint, would you be able to look away from the gun? Would you be able to focus on something else other than the person holding the thing that could kill you?

Most likely not. Even If somebody you trust deeply told you to look away, you still probably couldn't do it.

This is when we are in fight or flight. Our brains shut down. I'll use my own example of this. Ugh, so embarrassing. Last year, I was home alone with the boys. John was away, and I swear this shit *only* happens when he's not home. I am rolling my eyes so hard right now. Well, at three a.m., our Ring siren started going off. I immediately panicked out of a dead sleep. I looked at my phone, and it said, "Motion in Garage." But my stupid fight-or-flight brain read, "Garage door open," and my worst fear was realized. I thought the boys and I were goners.

But do you know what I did? I came out of my room, which is right at the top of the stairs that lead to the front door and connect to more stairs that lead to the garage door, and I stood there. Just stood there. Well, I called 911, of course, but they took a *long*-ass time to answer. So I stood there for probably close to ten minutes, just frozen. I had no idea what to do. I didn't even grab a knife or anything to protect myself. How pathetic.

Anyway, once the cops got there, I calmed down a bit, and they checked the basement and garage. The door was still locked, so no one had come in. A cardboard box had fallen off another cardboard box in the garage and triggered the alarm with motion. So it was an overreaction on my part. If I had only been thinking clearly, I would have noticed what my phone was actually saying and saved myself a lot of trouble and anxiety. And for anyone wondering, none of my three dogs did *anything*. Oaklee came out with me, jumped on the couch, and fell back asleep as the alarm blared. Nice, right?

So, the point I am trying to make is that all our common sense and even reading abilities are altered when we're in fight or flight. How can we expect dogs, who cannot explain to us what they are feeling or understand logic, to be able to listen to cues while they are feeling super threatened?

We can't.

We have to work on them not stepping into fight or flight. That is a huge part of fixing it.

Okay, so now it is time to learn how to fix this shit!

First things first—proper equipment. This is first not because it is most important but because it is so simple that people think it is insignificant and doesn't matter. But it makes all the difference: if you want to fix this problem, your dog cannot be wearing anything that causes pain or discomfort. Period. Using pain will make this problem worse.

I prefer using harnesses on dogs. I never think it's appropriate to walk a dog on just a regular collar, martingale collar, or slip lead. Not only are they unsafe, but they can be detrimental to your dog's throat. We do not want to collapse their trachea. But this can happen simply when too much pressure is put on that area of your dog's neck. If your dog pulls or has any type of leash reactivity, they should be on a front-clip harness. My favorite is the Easy Walk made by PetSafe. The trick is double-clipping your leash clip to the D-ring on the harness and the D-ring to your dog's regular collar. (Yes, they need to wear a collar as well.) This harness fits properly on the majority of dogs. But some dogs are weirdly shaped, and it just doesn't sit right. So we have to figure out something else. But this harness works for 95 percent of my clients.

Why do we want a front-clip harness? It makes a dog feel less reactive right off the bat because we're not engaging the freedom reflex. When this reflex is engaged by a pulling sensation from the back, it makes them want to grip the ground and move forward. This can be any collar or harness that pulls from the back. We condition this reflex at an early age by pulling our puppies all over the place on a leash instead of talking to them and verbally encouraging them to follow us. So, if we can eliminate engaging that reflex, we can reduce reactivity quite a bit just by switching to a front-clip harness. So simple!

The next bit of hardware we need to discuss is the type of leash you are using. I prefer a regular, flat, nylon leash around six feet long. I don't suggest leather or rope leashes. I find they're extremely hard to hold on to and difficult to wrap around your hand for better control if you're trying to get a better grip. The leather ones just kind of slip, and the rope ones hurt your hands and give you rug burn. What we definitely don't want are retractable and bungee leashes. These are super dangerous. The retractable is more so than the bungee. I feel that the bungee is more dangerous for the human because your dog thinks they can pull you farther, and it encourages them to lunge. This can pull your shoulder out of your socket or injure you if you are not prepared. The retractables can break, snap back at you, wrap you and your dog up, give you horrible rugburn, and ultimately teach your dog to not stay close to you. Do yourself a favor and throw that retractable in the trash, please and thank you!

One other important thing you absolutely need is a treat pouch. It is necessary, and you will need high-value treats when working on reducing reactivity. There are no ifs, ands, or buts about it. This is a must. A ziplock bag in your pocket is not going to work. You will fail because you are going to be fumbling with the ziplock bag while also trying to hold on to your super-reactive dog's leash. You need a treat pouch clipped around your waist, where your treats are easily accessible.

If you have been remotely paying attention, I'm sure you have also concluded that high-value rewards are necessary! Again, a nonnegotiable. For most of my past training, I used hot dogs. If you're gonna go with the hot dogs, I suggest Nathan's all-beef skinless dogs cut into tiny pieces.

Cut them up like you would for a toddler. They don't need to be big. I've recently switched to Nathan's turkey hot dogs. This is because I was recently diagnosed with an alpha-gal allergy. This means I am now allergic to pork and red meat—all mammalian meat. Yes, it is as horrible as it sounds!

Unfortunately, I was bitten by a tick that had previously bitten a deer. It still had the sugar from the deer on it, and when it bit me, that sugar from the deer went into my bloodstream. My body identified it as an allergen and attacked. So, now I have to watch what I'm using with my hands because if I ingest mammalian meat, I could go into anaphylactic shock. Yep, super fun! Thankfully, my dog clients don't seem to mind the downgrade to turkey too much. But if your dog is picky, go for the real hot dogs. But choose the all-beef ones. They tend to have way less fat and nasty stuff in them than the pork ones do. String cheese is also a great option—low moisture, cut into tiny pieces. Cold cuts can be a game changer for some dogs, but try to get the low-sodium ones.

Many parents are hesitant to use these high-value options, but if your dog is struggling in fight or flight, you need something to bring them out of it. These options seem to get dogs over the hump when they're fixated. Nonperishable high-value treats that your dog will love are the Stewart freeze-dried liver treats. Those are fabulous. They come in huge chunks, and I get the big tub on Amazon. Even the pickiest of dogs seem to like the liver treats!

Now, this is not the time for crunchy, cardboard treats or soft-baked training treats. Remember back to when you were held at gunpoint. What food is more likely to get you to not mind the gun day after day? A burrito or a filet mignon? Go with the good stuff if you want to help this process along quickly.

Now that you have all your supplies and are set up for success, let's dive into the life-changing method. This isn't the quickest thing to understand, so I am going to use examples to explain it thoroughly. Just stick with me!

As discussed in previous chapters, a dog's mental abilities are on par with a three-year-old human's. So this means your dog is always at a two-year-old learning age, no matter how smart, how silly, or how old they are. They're always, till the day they die, a three-year-old in terms of how they think. Again, just because they're intelligent and on that smarty-pants level, it does not mean the way they learn has changed. It just means their emotions are more advanced and intense. We want to always keep that in mind.

Would you ever yell at a toddler for being fearful of a thunderstorm? Really think about this. If a three-year-old heard thunder and lightning and started to panic, scream, and cry, would you ever deal with that situation by yelling at them for how they are acting? I am praying the answer is no because that would be crappy, and you shouldn't have kids. I use this example because this happened last summer with my three-year-old. In the summer, we spent a lot of time in my parents' house. There was at least one thunderstorm every weekend. It was horrible, and JJ was freaking out. He had never cared about storms before, but he was at an age when he was starting to realize what was going on, and negative emotions were coming into play. Thankfully, John and my dad (his two favorite people) sat with him in these big, comfy chairs in front of the big window at the front of my parents' house. They explained that thunder can be a little scary but that we don't have to worry if we are inside. And they had ice pops together while they watched the storm. John and my dad got excited about the thunder and showed him a good time even though it could be super scary for a little kid. After two or three times, JJ started to get excited about a storm and thoroughly enjoyed that time with them. They changed something scary into a fun bonding experience between them all. Honestly, it was beautiful, and I am so grateful that the men in my life were able to normalize my son's fear instead of telling him to stop crying, be a man, and get over it. I know that's a memory he will keep with him forever.

Now, why did I tell you this adorable story? Because that story is the whole enchilada—the whole thing, the whole method. This is going to be the method you're going to use with your dog. I like to start off by using that story because it's easier for people to empathize with it and understand. It helps them get on board. This is because I need pet parents to mentally do away with all the bullshit they have heard for *years*. Like, "Don't praise bad behavior!"

When John and my dad sat with my son, having ice pops and enjoying a thunderstorm together, were they praising his bad behavior? Or were they helping him normalize his feelings, self-regulate, and create new, positive emotions and feelings related to the thunderstorm? So, the rule of thumb is, if it is not how we would handle it with a kid, why would we insist on doing it with our dogs?

Seriously. Think about that, and don't tell me because kids are kids, and dogs are dogs. If that is your response, reread the beginning of this book, do us all a favor, and stop getting dogs. They deserve better. They deserve more. They deserve to be treated like we treat our kids.

Now, if you treat dogs and kids in the old-school way, it's because of the backward, outdated parenting and training methods that have been passed down from generation to generation for hundreds of years. It ends here. We're going to undo all of that. YOU are going to end the generational trickle of terrible dog training!

I also want to take a quick second to say that if this was how you were raised—with old-school, fear-based parenting—I am sorry that happened to you. You also deserved better. You deserved to have someone let you feel your feelings instead of forcing you to shut them up. The truth is, your feelings made those adults uncomfortable. When anyone tells someone to stop feeling something, it is because that emotion is uncomfortable for them. Watching you experience it made them even more uncomfortable, so they had to shut it down. They forgot what it felt like when that was done to them when they were kids. And the generational curse continues until you decide to break it.

Now it is time to heal yourself by healing your dog (or your own kids). Gentle parenting isn't weak. It's teaching someone how to control their feelings and not bottle them up, while keeping your own emotions out of it. The same applies to our dogs. We are helping them communicate appropriately while staying in control and making good choices. We can allow them to say they don't like something and respect it without engaging in a power struggle rooted in our not wanting to be disobeyed. We cannot make anyone *not* feel something. Feelings just don't just go away. They lurk beneath the surface, just waiting for an opportunity to rear its ugly head and unload.

This is what happens to our little boys. They get told to toughen up and stop crying. These little boys grow up to be insensitive, angry, bottled-up fathers and husbands who unload on anyone, at any time. And then we have other people judging them and making them feel worse, as if this is not a product of our how society works.

If you are denying that generational curses and the differences between how men and women are typically raised have anything to do with dog training, you are sadly mistaken. Women claim that men are power hungry, aggressive, insecure, and insensitive when all we see in Disney movies is the princess needing to be saved by the prince. We idolize men who are tough and cutthroat. We want a man to be jealous and fight for us. But when they do it and take it too far because they never learned how to control it, they're monsters. We expect our men to be tough and save us, but God forbid they show that they are having a hard time. Women don't want weak men. That's what our little boys have heard since day one, and we wonder why they are so hardened and angry. If you want your knight in shining armor, you have to be a safe place for him too. If we want our men to grow up showing compassion, patience, and empathy for our dogs and children, it starts when they are kids.

This is something I wanted to touch on in this book, but it was hard to find the right place. When we discuss men in rescue or men in dog training, we find that there are not a lot of men in rescue because of a lack of empathy.

Also, a high percentage of men in dog training are toxic and aggressive. We *need* this to change. We need parents to show their young boys how to be compassionate and empathetic by leading by example, not by ordering them to do so. Men get a bad rap in this industry, and unfortunately, it is not without cause. I am not here to tell men to be better and get their shit together. I am here to tell all my readers that they didn't just learn it from nowhere. They learned it from their families and their idols.

Now, just because that is true, it doesn't mean we continue to train in a crappy way. Everyone in the world has the right to feel their trauma and their issues, but they also have a duty to others to figure it out and heal. No one else should bear a cross because you went through something horrible. Your ass better be actively working that shit out to better yourself and your family. No forever pity parties here!

So, if we want the future of animal rights, welfare, and training to be bright, we have no choice but to change how we parent. When we show compassion, children learn compassion. When we give them room for emotion and feeling, they teach others to do the same. Our kids are sponges and want to do good in this world. We have to give them the platform to do so! For any men reading—if this happened to you, if you were raised to toughen up and bury it deep, I'm so sorry. You don't have to do that anymore. You can be a compassionate, emotional, sensitive parent now and still be a badass. You just need to choose it for yourself, your dog, and your family!

This is why it is so easy to compare kids and dogs! Dog training is learned just like parenting is. It is remembered in the brain. "Monkey see, monkey do" is a saying for a reason. It is time to teach ourselves and our children how animals should be treated at all times, no matter what—even when they make mistakes and bad choices.

You are still a good pet parent even though you made bad choices in the past. You still love your kid when they make a bad choice. But if you don't say or show that you still love them, they can't believe something that's never proven to them. A bad parent is someone who knows they can do better and chooses not to. I am going to give you all the tools. Now it's time for you to do the damn thing!

Okay, third emotional rant over. Back to our originally scheduled programming! Back to your dog's reactivity.

I have a few questions I need you to answer before moving forward.

What is the goal for your dog?

What is the mission?

Is it to get your dog to do ________? (fill in the blank)

What do you want out of this training?

The majority of the time, people will say, "I want my dog to listen to me!" Or "I want my dog to stop barking."

No, that is not what you want, and this is part of the problem. Either you are unclear about the mission or the mission does not make sense. In reality, what you *really* want is for your dog to like the thing they currently hate. Right? If we break it down and take our own ego out of it, it becomes much clearer and more doable. If your dog hates other dogs, you want your dog to like other dogs, right? Or at least you want them to not despise them. So that's your goal! How much easier does getting your dog to like something sound compared to getting your dog to listen to you?

It's way easier to do, I promise.

So, in order for this to happen, there can be *no* yelling, corrections (verbal or physical), or negativity while working on reactivity. This is why we don't use aversive training. If a dog *hears* a sharp "*No*!" and *feels* a leash pop every single time they *see* another dog, they associate all those things *with* the dog or trigger. There are no fuzzy feelings here. Why would we expect our dogs to not react poorly if we are yelling and correcting them? Your dog is thinking, *Okay, screw that dog. I don't want to see that dog anymore. I don't like the situation. I want to be gone from this. Mom turns on me every time another dog comes around.* That's because they think the dog is the thing that brought on the pain because, prior to that, everything was fine. They were just walking along with you, enjoying themselves, and then *bam*!

This type of training is just so backward and does not check out. It is why millions of dogs will continue to struggle with reactivity until the day they die.

So, what *do* we do? What is the right way to do this?

All right, I am about to change your life. It's simple, and it's way more fun. Are you ready?

The second you see the trigger, you need to get excited and praise your dog. Yes, I said *praise your dog*! You are so excited the entire time. And you need to become a human Pez dispenser with those treats. And no, your dog doesn't need to behave or do anything to get the treats. You're shoveling treats into their mouth, saying, "Yes, good boy!" over and over and over again while they are barking, lunging, and growling. They are in the throes of reactivity, and you are praising and treating them. You need to do this until you're out of the scenario or the trigger is gone.

Let's get two things straight. No, I am not insane, and no, you are not praising bad behavior.

What did we learn already? For a dog, barking, lunging, and growling are just ways to show *fear*. That's an emotion, not a behavior. Your dog will not think you are praising them for their reactivity. That is not how they learn! If you are having these thoughts, you have to retrain your brain to undo all the old-school thoughts. If it helps, instead of lunging and barking, I want you to picture screaming and crying, like a scared toddler does. This will help you normalize it and realize it is not aggression.

By praising the presence of your dog's trigger, you're turning your dog's negative association with that trigger into a positive one.

Let's use the example we touched on in Chapter 1: barking at the mail carrier. So many families suffer from this. First, your dog hears or sees the mail person and *feels* insecure, protective, fearful, and uncomfortable. Usually, there is also a glass door or window in the way, which will engage barrier frustration. This behavior is triggered by any object that a dog feels is a barrier that's keeping them from something they want to get to. Essentially, you can have the friendliest dog, but they could be reactive behind a gate, fence, window, door, or leash! This is common. The moral of the story is that barriers ignite emotions that would not exist if the barrier weren't there. So we have to take that into account as well. Anyway, your dog is feeling all these things—they bark, lunge, and growl. Then what happens?

The mail person goes away! Your dog wins the battle every day. They have no idea that the mail person doesn't break into the house because their job is to simply bring the mail and leave.

When a dog is losing it at the window, we immediately start yelling: "*No*! Go lay down! Leave it! *Enough*!" We never take a moment to realize how this negativity affects our dog's association with the mailman. We are just so uncomfortable, annoyed, irritated, and inconvenienced by their emotions that we try to shut them down as quickly as possible.

Does this sound similar to the analogy I made earlier in this chapter? When we yell and reprimand, the yelling and reprimanding are attached to the thing that changed—*not* to their behavior. So we're reinforcing that the mail person sucks. And what is our mission? To get our dog to *like* the mail person. See the problem here?

The dog will think that every time the mail person comes, the people they love yell at them. Everything was fine before the mail person showed up. So, to change this up and fix the association, we need to say, "Yes, the mail person is here, and they are great!" We throw a party by being so excited, with treats and love everywhere. When we do this, the dog eventually starts to think, *Oh, I kind of like the mail person now*. And that's your goal—to get them to like the arrival of the mail person.

When we change the association, the barking, lunging, and growling will fade away on their own. We won't be stuffing those feelings in Pandora's box. We are healing the fear, letting it float away, and attaching more positive feelings.

I want your dog to *love* the mailman! I have a couple of clients whose mailmen have figured this out. They leave a treat with the mail as a peace offering, and it works perfectly. *Genius*! After a few times, the dog is like, *Hmm, this ain't so bad. I kinda like this person!*

Some of these mail carriers have gotten the idea of counterconditioning!

Now, I want to make another point super clear: if you choose to praise and treat just by waiting for good behavior, you will get nowhere. Again, this is not how dogs learn. If you wait for them to be calm, the trigger is most likely gone, and you are marking and praising nothing. Their brains may still be looking for the trigger, so they are stiff and quiet, but they aren't acknowledging anything you are trying to do. You can't praise and mark calm like that. Dogs do not register that at all. I know that rewarding your dog when they are in the throes of insanity goes against everything you know, but you just need to remember the mission: get my dog to like the mail carrier. And then execute! I hope this example makes the method a tad more clear and relatable.

Now, let's get back to reactivity on leash because I think the majority of people struggle with that.

The goal is to always have your dog under threshold. What is being *over* threshold? Imagine you have a favorite video game you play on the easiest level, and you feel calm and in control. But if someone changes the game to the hardest level, it might become too difficult for you to handle. You'd feel stressed or upset. For a dog that's reactive on a leash, being over threshold is like playing that game on the hardest level. When a dog is under threshold, they're calm and comfortable. They're able to listen to you, follow cues, and self-regulate, just like you playing the game on the easiest level. But certain things, like seeing another dog, can make the situation much harder for them, like switching the game to a much harder level. When this happens and the dog becomes over threshold, they are too stressed or excited to listen. It's similar to how you'd struggle to keep up with the game on the hardest setting. The dog might bark, lunge, or act out because the situation is just too much for them to handle calmly.

The goal in training is to help them stay under threshold more often, making their experiences more like playing the game on an easier level, where they feel in control and relaxed, but to eventually reduce the threshold distance over time. Baby steps are key!

When you are out for a walk, begin the praising and treating, as explained above. Even if your dog is over threshold, the goal is to create some space so they can get back under. But we are *not* making a U-turn or hiding. If your dog is losing it, you're still praising and treating even though you probably feel ridiculous. It does not matter. You may not get through to them in that specific moment when they're over threshold. But eventually, they'll start to come down the ladder of intensity. I use the ladder a lot. Think of it as zero to ten. Ten is when you're in the red zone and over threshold. But you need to keep in mind that the more you do this technique, the quicker your dog will come down the ladder successfully.

This doesn't happen overnight. You may get frustrated and embarrassed the first couple of times because you are not used to it. That is okay! Give yourself a little grace. This is a big change for both of you, but if you pay close attention to your dog during this time, you will quickly see the little differences. I know this can be tough because there are a lot of emotional layers to this for humans as well. Just try not to care too much about the looks you may be getting from your neighbors or anybody out and about. It does not matter. What does matter is that you put all your energy and thoughts into your dog. Because if you cared as much about the situation with your dog as you do about what people think about you, you'd be halfway home by now. So tune that part out the best you can because the quicker you get through it, the fewer times you will be embarrassed! It's math! Don't be your own worst enemy here.

Now, why are we not making U-turns and avoiding a dog's triggers? So many trainers still come after me for this one because they are cue-based trainers who teach management. Their notion is that the second the dog is over threshold, the situation is too much and you should retreat. They also think that keeping a dog over threshold for any period of time is harmful. But this situation is not that black and white. Every dog experiences reactivity and being over threshold differently. Some studies say that when a dog shows any bit of vocalization or physical stress when seeing a trigger, they're over threshold. I work with some dogs that could see another dog a football field away and lose their minds. If we went by this notion only, we would never make any progress. How can I get a dog to see that there isn't a threat without proving it to them by getting closer and without something bad happening?

So, the answer to this is simple: I do not do management or maintenance training. I use systematic desensitization and counterconditioning. Our goal here is to finally get our dogs over the hump of reactivity, not run from the things that set them off. That's like trying to avoid and hide my kids from thunderstorms. It would be impossible and fucking stressful. Is that the kind of life you want with your dog? Because I could almost guarantee that every reactive dog would think, *I would like to not feel this way anymore when I see ______.* So, no. I do not avoid triggers because I believe it is a disservice to our dogs. They deserve a reactive-free life.

Also, for clarification, we are around a dog's triggers for mere seconds before their reaction starts. We are not making dogs stand in front of the thing that stresses them out for long periods of time. That would be torture. We are going to keep moving without running away and work our way up to longer situations, but we absolutely go at their pace!

It's extremely important to add that if a dog's reactivity and anxiety are significantly high, I do not do any type of training like this until we find a way to bring down their stress. That is a hard rule for me. I will not put a dog through something they cannot handle. We are often dealing with dogs that have chemical imbalances due to past trauma or birth, so they need pharmaceuticals for a short period to help them through. We can use medication and antianxiety supplements to our advantage to create positive associations in positive behavior modification. They are just another tool in our toolbox. If you are dealing with a dog that has intense reactivity and aggression issues with other dogs, strangers, kids, or babies, *do not* use any of these methods without the guidance of a certified behavioral consultant or vet behaviorist. You can do way more harm than good. If this sounds like your dog, please read Chapter 13 on anxiety to learn how pharmaceuticals are sometimes a necessity for certain dogs.

Another reason I do not tell my clients to run away is that if we retreat the second we see the trigger, we are agreeing with the dog's fear. We are saying, "Yes, this *is* scary, and we *should* flee!" We want to avoid this at all costs. Again, not running away does not mean keeping dogs over threshold for long periods. You should never be standing still and making your dog continuously watch their trigger. No way! Always keep moving forward however you can. For example, if you are walking down your street on the left-hand side and see a dog walking toward you with their parent on the same side, I am not telling you to just continue walking straight without creating space. Here is exactly what you should do:

- Size up the scene. If the scene is unsafe, absolutely turn around and get out of there. But try to be as nonchalant as possible with your dog. We do not want them to think you left because of the trigger. Distract them and keep calm. They will sense urgency out of nowhere and identify the change. An unsafe scene would be an off-leash dog, unruly children you do not trust, a person acting strangely, etc.
- If the scene is safe, create space if you need to. This could mean crossing the street, but do not make a beeline. Be nonchalant and take your time. You can zigzag slowly, all while praising, treating, and getting excited.
- Make sure you don't get tense in general, including with the leash. Dogs can feel the difference. They are just trotting along and enjoying themselves when, all of a sudden, you get tense and wrap up on the leash to keep them close to you. Many times, your dog is

bucking back and forth like a bronco and immediately smells your cortisol rise. Take your time and slowly wrap up on the leash. Try not to rev the engine! It's just a normal day in the neighborhood. You don't want to agree that the trigger is stressful.

- Continue walking forward, even when your dog sees the trigger. It will be gone soon! Situations like this usually last only a few seconds as long as the other person also keeps moving along. Keep praising, treating, and getting excited! Do not stop.
- If you feel your dog is having a hard time moving forward, try to move in front of your dog and walk backward. That way, you and your dog are now face-to-face, and you are pulling them along with you with gentle, continuous pressure on the leash (not tugging or leash-popping them). Not only is this physically easier for humans, but dogs are more likely to see and hear you when you are in front of them versus on the opposite side of the trigger and adjacent to them. If you are clumsy and not good at walking backwards, please be super careful or do not try this method!
- Keep praising and treating until the trigger is gone. Get excited right afterward so they know it was a good thing and that they are amazing!

One of the main things I have learned is that when we use this process, we are allowing our dogs to feel their feelings and get over them in *their own time*. They get to realize, *Oh, that wasn't that bad! I've been kind of overreacting every time I see a dog. I came out of that situation unharmed.* By doing it this way, they get to feel and learn. When we run away, we shut it down. We don't engage at all, so nothing can change. The dog will continue to stay dysregulated when seeing the trigger from afar. But with my method, they get to conclude that the trigger isn't as bad as they originally thought.

Now, walking past a trigger in a "ship in the night, face-on" situation isn't my go-to training scenario, but it happens consistently in everyday life and is pretty unavoidable. So I wanted to touch on that first. My preferred method is exactly what I do at my farm, where the reactive dog walks behind the trigger without any additional stress. I manipulate it all in the dog's favor. It's simple to work on this if you have a friend or family member who has a dog like my Oaklee. They need to be extremely calm and indifferent to dogs, but friendly. This is not the time for the overexcited, jumping, dog-friendly dog. That can sometimes be as bad as another reactive dog! If you can find one, his method calls for a happy dummy pup that can just coexist.

I come out and get to know the dog first. Sometimes, they love people and hate dogs, and sometimes they hate both. So we take our time if we need to. But the goal is for me to be able to hold the dog's leash and walk them safely while they feel comfortable as well. Once the dog has sniffed around the farm, seen the goats and pig, gotten to know me, and has just relaxed in the new environment, we prepare for Oaklee to come outside. While I get him from inside the house, my client takes their dog behind both of our F-150s. Having two big-ass trucks helps because this way, the dog does not see Oaklee until I want them to see Oaklee.

Once I have him, we find a way to switch dogs. I want the dog client's parent to walk Oaklee down the long driveway, away from the garage, where my dog client is with me behind the trucks. The dog client will be about ten to twenty feet from Oaklee once he starts to fork off away from the house and walk away. I do this on purpose. I want my dog client to be as close as possible to Oaklee, as quickly as possible. In fact, the majority of the time, I have the dog client's nose to Oaklee's butt within five to ten seconds.

Some dog parents look at me like I am delusional when I explain this process beforehand, like they're wondering, *Are you sure about this?*

Yes, I am.

Why?

Because 90 percent of the time, the client's dog will flip out in the first five seconds. But they realize that I am allowing them to walk toward Oaklee instead of pulling them away, that Oaklee couldn't care less and is not looking at them, and that they're getting tons of praise, treats, and love.

Then they soften almost immediately. Instead of being terrified, they switch to confused and curious. Which I think you would agree are better emotions!

About 10 percent of dogs continue to carry on barking, lunging, and growling. But the intensity definitely lowers the closer they get to Oaklee. They still may look like they want to nip Oaklee's butt or tail. I am watching the dog the entire time to see what their body posture is telling me. Are they looking for a nibble, or are they just desperate for a sniff of his butt? It is 100 percent my job to know the difference and figure it out. For the tougher cases, John helps me out by walking Oaklee backward so he can see the dog head-on and tell me what their face is doing and whether to pull back or not.

Just because this group of clients does not give us the same behavior as the 90 percent, it does not mean the training session was for nothing. On the contrary, they get to leave that day having a positive interaction close to another dog that didn't end poorly for them in any way. It is the first step to recovery, and we have to start somewhere. Depending on the dog's daily anxiety and other behavioral issues, we will definitely discuss some sort of solution for anxiety relief during the training process!

You have to remember that this is only 10 percent of dogs, and maybe less. The other 90 percent succeed beautifully. Those are good numbers, and it doesn't take me ten sessions to get the dog close to Oaklee.

Half of them will pull toward Oaklee, get within five feet, and look at me like, *Wait. I've never been this close. What do I do now?* They aren't even looking at Oaklee. They are trying to figure out how to get to the side of him instead of behind. They are too nervous to sniff but do not want to have a problem or pick a fight, so they just look more awkward than anything.

We usually see some displacement behaviors and regulation markers, like shaking off (the dog looks like they're shaking water off, but they're not wet), yawning (when they are clearly not tired), jumping up on the handler, and sniffing the ground. These are all signs that a dog is stressed but trying hard to calm down, which is amazing! They are using other parts of the brain and coming out of fight or flight.

The other half always crack me up, mostly because of the parents' response. This group of dogs will carry on for maybe one to three seconds and then just silently pull toward Oaklee. They'll get right up to Oaklee's butt, take a sniff, and then come right back to me because I am cheering like a cheerleader, and they are so damn happy and proud of themselves. They go back for more sniffs and eventually walk shoulder to shoulder with Oaklee.

The parents look at me like, *What the actual fuck just happened?* I just laugh because, honestly, it's funny. I proceed to tell them that we just needed to give the dog a chance to think different thoughts!

It's not always perfect like that, but I'd say 45 percent is a pretty decent percentage! Also, another awkward 45 percent eventually get there too. They just need another time or two to get comfortable. Those are usually the ones that never got proper socialization as babies and just seriously have no idea how to socialize successfully. The remaining 10 percent need more time and adjustment. We may need to adjust meds first, so we always come up with a plan to move forward and improve.

Anytime I do this method, I cut it off before the dog becomes too stressed for too long. If I am dealing with the 10 percent, I let them get close to Oaklee's butt two to three times. But if I see no markers of stress or intensity going down, I call it and bring Oaklee back inside immediately.

For the other two groups, I keep an eye on them and how they are doing during the walk. Some love Oaklee, and we get to them seeing each other face-to-face and having some interaction. They may even make some play attempts, like a play bow. But other times, they just coexist. I usually never have Oaklee outside longer than fifteen to twenty minutes. The goal is to cut it off, short and sweet, before the dog becomes overexcited or overwhelmed by these new feelings. Baby steps! I always say that everyone's famous last words are "Let's just keep going a little longer. They're doing so well!" If someone says this, stop immediately. I am not joking. I want your dog to *want* Oaklee to come back.

Now, let's touch on the main reason I do it this way. You may have noticed that Oaklee always leads in front, never turning around to look at the dog. Also, I never have them socialize face-to-face unless they can walk side by side with no weirdness at all for more than ten minutes. This is extremely important! It is the only reason why this works so well.

Somewhere along the line, we adopted the notion that asking, "Hey, is your dog friendly?" and immediately bringing the two dogs face-to-face out of nowhere is the proper way to socialize. When I see videos of this or watch it in person, I cringe so hard. It makes my skin crawl because that's just waiting for something to go wrong. We are asking for one or both dogs to become uncomfortable. It is just such an unnatural way for them to greet each other, and it sets them up to fail. Even if they are curious and want to go smell that other dog, they are also simultaneously having other emotions, like fear and protective emotions. It's not all rainbows and sunshine up there all the time. Even the friendliest of dogs still have these thoughts. This is how all creatures survive. Multiple emotions battle each other all at once, from second to second, with dogs wanting to be social and friendly while also making sure they are on guard and don't get hurt.

So, these two dogs see each other. We bring them together within seconds, and we don't let them get used to just being in each other's presence. When they meet face-to-face, one or both dogs might get stiff but will most likely have upward, stiff tail wags. Then they both go for the butt sniff. This is the pivotal point. When they make that motion, when they look like yin and yang as they're sniffing butts at the same time, they are exposing the jugular vein. That is the part of the neck that, if bitten, is easily fatal because the dog can bleed out quickly. So, in the animal kingdom, animals usually do whatever it takes to avoid this. When they feel threatened and are exposing the vein, the brain can trigger the release of adrenaline (epinephrine), a key hormone and neurotransmitter involved in the body's acute stress response. This response is part of the sympathetic nervous system's activation, often referred to as the fight-or-flight response, which prepares the body to either confront or flee potential danger. When that adrenaline hits, we often see a scuffle between the dogs. Or one of them may give the other a correction, letting them know to back off. So many parents get so confused because they don't understand why their dog is acting like this, and more so, why their dog looks excited to meet and then acts that way. Simple: they did not have enough time to process the situation, regulate, and make sound choices. They are forever *toddlers*! You have to make the right decisions for them to avoid a meltdown.

The next time someone asks you if your dog is friendly, you can instead say, "Yes, but can we do a pair walk side by side first? They usually do better with that than immediately going face-to-face." And then you parallel walk and follow your dog's lead. Only when they look ready and interested should they get closer while they continue walking.

Throw the whole face-to-face, stagnant butt sniff out the window. We are done with that! Any time you are doing a dog meet going forward, make sure your dog has another option or activity than just staring at that other dog. Let them sniff, let them walk, let them eat food, talk to them. They should be relaxed and at least five minutes in before they are super close. These interactions should never be rushed, especially if you don't even know the person.

Just because someone asks if your dog is friendly, it does *not* mean you have to prove it or let the dogs meet. You can simply say, "No, thank you." That doesn't say anything about you and your dog. You don't owe people anything. First and foremost, protect your dog at all costs. One small, insignificant moment can unfortunately scar them for life, so treat this with tender love and care. And take your damn time. I say it again because I know so many people struggle with this: You don't owe anyone anything. Just keep walking! There is no rush. Your dog will thank you later.

Oh, and for my female readers who struggle with not wanting to offend anyone or disappoint people, remember this and tattoo it across your forehead: "No" is a full sentence.

Raise of hands: who doesn't yet have a reactive dog and would like to avoid it at all costs? Thankfully, now you know exactly what to do when you are already in it. Now, let's go over how to avoid it altogether. Because I am sure that as I've gone through this entire chapter so far, you were like, *Um, how do I not experience any of the things you are saying? This sounds horrible!*

I feel you. Nobody wants a reactive dog, so we start at the beginning!

Ah, puppies! They're like sponges in cute, fluffy bodies, soaking up every bit of the world around them. It's during this golden period of puppyhood that we've got a prime opportunity to steer them away from the path of reactivity and toward being well-adjusted, happy-go-lucky pups.

So, how do we do this? Let's dive into the nitty-gritty of preventing reactivity in puppies.

First off, socialization is your new best friend. And I'm not just talking about letting your pup sniff the neighbor's dog through the fence. That usually doesn't go great either. Proper socialization means exposing your little one to a variety of sights, sounds, people, and other animals in a positive and controlled manner. Think of it as throwing the coolest, most diverse party ever, where the guests range from the mailman to the vacuum cleaner, and the dress code includes everything from hats to umbrellas.

The key? Keeping these experiences positive and short. Rule of thumb: if you can't control the outcome, don't do it. A treat here, a happy voice there, and voilà! You're building a puppy who sees the world as a fun place, not a scary one. You can't be silent. You have to show your dog a good time.

If I was with my kids at an amusement park and there was suddenly a scary clown (let's face it, all clowns are super creepy), I would not take my kids and run back the other way or just let the clown silently creep the kids out as we walked by. I would talk to the kids the whole time, like, *Wow, look at that creepy clown. How funny is that? He's just pretending! His job is to scare you. How silly! Let's just keep walking if you don't want to say hi!*

Talk them through it! You are the angel on their shoulder, talking them through hard times. Their brains already have the devil's words down pat. We need to be the voice of reason and confidence!

Next on the agenda, but slightly a repeat from our puppy chapters, are bite inhibition, how to handle rejection, and how to recover.

Teaching your pup the art of a soft mouth is crucial. Play biting is how they learn to control the strength of their bite, and it's important for them to understand that human skin is off-limits for those sharp little teeth. So are other dogs! Engage in play, but the moment those teeth touch skin too hard, the game stops. It's like saying, "Whoops! Party foul!" in dog language. This not only teaches your dog self-control but also helps them manage their excitement and impulses, which is a big deal in the world of preventing reactivity.

When they are young, they may take it too far with other dogs, kids, or people, and the immediate response might not be a good one. They may get the bejesus scared out of them when an older dog corrects them loudly or sharply. We want dogs to be able to work this out, but we also want to set them up for success. If your puppy hasn't napped, been stimulated, or been exercised appropriately, do not let them loose in the room with the older grumpy dog that will have nothing but a nasty response to give them when they attempt to get attention or play. If this happens consistently, this puppy might feel like all other dogs act this way and then be reactive and fearful moving forward. Or how about bigger men with sunglasses and beards? This spooks little dogs quite a bit, but we want to desensitize them and set them up for success. This means lots of praise and treats from you and the person who might look a little scary to the average dog while everyone stays super positive. Puppies are super malleable, but we need to catch them early and try not to overdo it.

Let's not forget about teaching them to love their alone time. Yes, separation anxiety is a real thing and can lead to a whole host of reactive behaviors. Start early by giving your puppy short, sweet breaks from human interaction and encouraging them to enjoy some quality time with their toys or a nice chew. This isn't about ignoring them; it's about teaching them that being alone is just another part of their awesome puppy life.

Being alone is okay and normal. It's also sometimes super helpful for regulation. When we help them identify how they feel and how much better they feel after they rest, many dogs will start to gravitate toward separating themselves on purpose because they *know* it feels good.

Pudge was properly crate trained, and even though she had no real dog mom from two weeks on, we did a solid job with her. She's small, and my kids are toddlers. If you don't know, toddlers are *insane*. Love them, but dear God, they are crazy. Pudge will sleep happily in our bed with the door open all day rather than on the couch where the kids are because she is thinking, *Why in the world would I put myself through that stress?* She sees the value in some distance during the kids' crazier times and comes out when they are eating and more relaxed. She is so smart, it's crazy! She is not depressed or feeling unloved. She created this lifestyle and knows how to ensure that she lives her life how she wants without putting herself through nonsense. She amazes me! Also, because she was properly crate trained she does not experience separation anxiety and is not a Velcro dog that is attached to me, needing to be out in the chaos with me and the kids.

When we talk about avoiding reactivity, we should also cover fear periods. Puppies go through these like teenagers go through mood swings. It's during these times that your pup might be afraid of a leaf that danced too close to their paw. It's crucial to handle these periods with patience and positivity. Don't force them to face their fears head-on during this time; instead, offer gentle encouragement and lots of treats for bravery, even if it's just a tiny step forward. This is the time to tread lightly and be as empathetic as possible.

Lastly, remember that your reaction to the world around you impacts your pup more than you might think. Maybe even more so than their original emotion about it. If you tense up every time another dog walks by, guess who's picking up on that? Your puppy. Be a model of calm confidence, and your puppy will follow suit, thinking, *If my human isn't worried about the giant hairdryer in the sky, then neither am I!* Be the calm you want to see from your dog!

In the grand scheme of things, avoiding reactivity in puppies is about more than just training; it's about setting the stage for a lifetime of curiosity, confidence, and cool, collected canine behavior. By focusing on socialization, bite inhibition, alone time, fear periods, and your own reactions, you're not just training your puppy. You're teaching them how to navigate the world with grace and gusto. And honestly, is there anything cooler than that?

Truly, there is not!

Chapter 12:
Resource Guarding

As if there should be anything scarier and more inconvenient than reactivity, we have resource guarding. I'm sorry, this is just how the cookie crumbles!

Resource guarding is a term that might sound like something out of a medieval history book, where knights defend their castles against invaders. But no, we're talking about our dogs just trying to figure out that what's theirs is theirs. And they're not too keen on sharing, thank you very much. Whether it's a juicy bone, their favorite squeaky toy, or even a spot on the couch, dogs that exhibit resource-guarding behaviors are essentially saying, "Back off. This is mine!"

So, what exactly is resource guarding? Imagine you're enjoying the world's most delicious slice of pizza. You turn around for a second, and someone tries to snatch it from your plate. Your likely reaction? Protect that fucking pizza! That's resource guarding in a nutshell. But for dogs, it's when our canine companions react (sometimes a bit too enthusiastically) to keep a valuable resource they believe is under threat. This behavior can range from a subtle side-eye, which is silent communication, to more overt actions, like growling or snapping. It's their way of putting up a DO NOT DISTURB sign.

While it might seem alarming, remember that guarding resources is as natural for dogs as scrolling through our phones is for us. It's hardwired into their DNA to protect what they believe is crucial for their survival. But just like we learn to share and secure our belongings in a socially acceptable way, our dogs can learn too.

It is also important to mention the emotional component of this. Many pet parents immediately feel a lot of negative emotions when their dog guards from them. We immediately get offended and say, "How dare they guard from me?"

Then the need to create a power struggle and demand respect floods in. "Drop it *now*! You think you are going to treat *me* this way?" we say. Then we switch over to fear and concern, asking, "What just happened? Where did that come from? How could this have happened to *my* dog?"

It is so normal to feel all of these things. How we were raised lends to all of this, but it is time to wave the white flag and surrender.

By this, I don't mean to let your dog do whatever the hell they want, hoard everything, and be nasty whenever they feel like it. I mean, wave the white flag and surrender to the process. By doing so, you will need to check the emotions at the door. Just like in Chapter 11, your emotions don't matter here. They are not helpful, and they will not fix the problem. They will likely make it worse. We'll touch on this a little more later as we go, but I wanted you all to understand that these are real and normal emotions to have. But it is time to check them at the door so you can successfully get on the other side of resource guarding with all your fingers still attached!

So, who are the usual suspects when it comes to resource guarding? While it might be tempting to think it's just the smarty-pants, brainy, always-on types that are plotting their next move like chess masters, any dog can decide to start guarding. Yes, even the happy dummy who seems more interested in chasing their tail than anything else. The common thread among guarders? A deep feeling of insecurity or a struggle to manage those big, overwhelming emotions.

Let's go diving into the psyche of our dogs to reveal the tapestry of factors that could trigger resource guarding. This is a behavior as complex as it is common. Just like humans inherit traits from their parents, dogs, too, come wired with predispositions, with some breeds or individuals more naturally inclined to guard their precious possessions. This instinct can be further shaped by their life experiences; a dog that had to compete for every morsel (like a stray) or toy in the past might understandably view the world as a place where nothing comes without a fight.

Stress, too, plays a significant role in this behavioral tapestry. An anxious dog, overwhelmed by the unpredictability of their environment, might find solace in controlling the few constants in their life, such as food, enrichment, toys, furniture, or even people. But it's not just psychological factors at play. Physical needs left unmet—be it from hunger, lack of stimulation, or even pain—can exacerbate guarding tendencies. Moreover, dogs are astute learners, and those who've discovered that guarding ensures their treasures remain untouched are likely to employ this strategy time and again. This complex blend of genetics, learned behavior, stress, unmet needs, and past experiences crafts the unique behavioral landscape each dog navigates, with resource guarding being one path many choose to tread.

So why do dogs guard? It boils down to one word: value. Dogs place value on resources in two ways:

- Inherent value: Some things are just naturally valuable to dogs, like food. Survival instinct kicks in, making these items worth protecting.
- Added value: This is where we come in. The way we react to certain items can increase their value in a dog's eyes. Ever made a big fuss about getting a sock back? Congratulations, you've just added value to that insignificant sock.

Understanding this psychology is key to addressing resource guarding. By managing how we react and what value we assign to objects, we can start to change our dog's perception of what needs guarding.

Science!

Let's take food, for example, which has a high inherent value to dogs as it's essential for survival. Most dogs naturally protect their meals, but how we interact with them during meal times can amplify this guarding behavior. If you've ever hovered over your dog while they eat, perhaps trying to train them to accept your presence, you might unintentionally signal that their food is at risk, inadvertently heightening their need to guard it.

The same goes for putting your hands in your dog's bowl while they are eating. The world needs to *stop* doing this! This is usually the first gateway to serious guarding. Some dogs are super submissive and just do not have a guarding bone in their bodies, but a high percentage will eventually get there if you keep probing them. They may *look* fine with it for a little bit when they are young, but as they get a bit older, they think, *They are always touching my food. This feels odd, and I am a little stressed. I hope this stops soon.* So you keep going with this, thinking you are doing an excellent job of desensitizing your dog. Then they get a bit older, and out of nowhere, they are thinking, *Stop touching my fucking food!* Then they growl at you. Now *you* are pissed when they're the one who should be furious.

If your dog came up and put their nose or paws on your plate even one time while you were eating, you would immediately reprimand them and make it clear that it is your food and that when you are eating, you would like space. But what is the number-one advice trainers give? Put your hands in your puppy's food so they are comfortable with you touching it whenever you want.

Stop! This is creating guarders left and right. It happens over time, not overnight. But it will seem overnight because dogs silence their stress until they can no longer take it. We demand respect that we refuse to give. By doing so, we are creating a hostile environment for our dogs. They do not understand that you are trying to desensitize them to you being able to handle their food. They just see you touching it, and it makes them think that their food is more valuable than they originally thought because you want it too!

On the flip side, consider a tennis ball that becomes a coveted treasure not because of its inherent value but because of the added value we've unknowingly assigned to it. Imagine a scenario where every time your dog picks up a tennis ball, it turns into a high-energy game of chase. Your dog learns that this ball is not just fun but a key player in the most exciting game in town. Thus, the tennis ball's value skyrockets, and so does your dog's motivation to guard it from anyone who might steal it away, including other pets or even you.

Similarly, a piece of stolen contraband, like a sock, a bra, or underwear, can gain monumental value in the eyes of your dog if every time they snatch it, it results in a dramatic, attention-filled episode of keep-away. The sock itself is mundane, but the reaction it elicits turns it into a prize worth defending.

This is especially true for dogs that are not getting their needs met daily and thrive on negative attention. They take this item knowing the response it will get them. They want the chase. It fills their cup up, but then we, as parents, get emotional and angry. We corner them, maybe under the table or in the corner of the room, and they feel trapped. Most of all, they don't want to be in trouble. They only wanted your attention. Yikes, the plan has backfired, and they now feel threatened. Now their brain switches into fear, protection, and guarding mode. You'll probably hear a low growl, see the whites of their eyes, and maybe even get an air snap in your direction.

By recognizing these dynamics of inherent and added value, you can modify your behavior to reduce the likelihood of resource guarding. This is something you should practice from the very second you bring home a puppy because guarding can start almost immediately if you do not play your cards right. To have a guarding-free life with your dog, your dog needs to fully trust you, have their needs and resources met consistently, and be given proper boundaries with empathy and mutual respect from humans and other pets. Let us dive into these!

Building trust between you and your dog is fundamental to preventing resource guarding. Trust is established through consistent, positive interactions, ensuring your dog feels safe and understood. For example, when you feed your dog, make it a calm and positive experience. You can be in the same room with them while they eat, you can walk around, or you can talk to them gently—all without trying to touch their food. This shows your dog that your presence is not a threat to their resources, which reinforces trust because you never take it.

The off time you do need to grab the bowl—because maybe something is dangerous in there—they won't even bat an eye. The off time you touch them while they are eating, they won't think anything of it. The off time your grandkid wanders into the kitchen and gets too close, your dog will just be confused and look around or not care at all instead of thinking their food is in real danger.

The moral of the story: Guarders are created and provoked. They are not born intense and solid.

Responding to your dog's signals is just as important as building trust with physical objects of value. Giving them space when they show signs of wanting to be alone further builds a trusting relationship. For instance, let's say your dog is asleep on the couch when you sit down and start to pet them. They give you a small growl. Parents usually either reprimand their dog for growling or continue petting and ignore the growl to desensitize them to it. But imagine if humans did this to each other. I am laughing because we do this as humans. We constantly fail to respect each other's boundaries, even when they are properly explained.

Let's say your significant other likes to wake up by cuddling you, but you don't like it. You don't like being woken up before it is necessary, and it scares you awake every time they do it. You have told them this over and over again, but they just keep doing it anyway. It goes from you explaining it calmly, to you feeling uncomfortable and unheard, to you feeling angry and disrespected. Your partner says it's how they show love. It's their love language, and they feel they should be able to express themselves and you should just learn to like it. Otherwise, you are being ungrateful. But the truth is, showing someone love isn't about you and how it makes you feel. True love is about making that person feel loved in the way *they* like to feel loved. Otherwise, it is just selfish and an excuse to do whatever you want and not respect other people's boundaries. After your partner does this consistently, regardless of your clear communication, you may not feel safe around them. You even don't want to tell them anything intimate or even be near them.

This is what drives relationships apart the most—not respecting each other's boundaries and not feeling like the other can be trusted with your head, heart, or body.

I am hoping this analogy helps you make sense of our guarding dogs! For example, your dog is asleep on the couch. You wake them up out of a dead sleep, so they say, "Please stop." Then you get angry.

You get *angry*. How crazy is that?

But as humans, we are easily offended when we don't get to do exactly what we want to do when we want to do it.

What if that was my husband, and he was enjoying his nap? And I woke him up so suddenly, just because? Kinda rude! Imagine that I was mad that he didn't appreciate that! It sounds more crazy when it is human to human, and that's the problem. Our dogs still count even though they are dogs. We have to think about this and what is in our brains. You pet your dog, and they don't like it right now. Are they allowed to tell you they don't want it?

If you say no, stop getting dogs. That is not love. Unlike being a dictator, who prioritizes power and control, you cannot impose or command genuine love and respect. Are you a dictator, or are you an empathetic, unconditionally loving parent?

If you want to build trust with your dog, you need to allow them to communicate clearly. When you do this consistently, you get to know your dog's likes and dislikes well, which brings down their daily stress. Over time, they may seek out behaviors they once did not like, like being petted, sleeping with you or snuggling, giving kisses, and going belly up. If we allow them to communicate freely without reprimand, they will always give us a warning.

Many parents come to me and say their dog is unpredictable. Truthfully, they are wrong. Dogs will *always* tell us what they are thinking and feeling from the beginning. But if we train out the warning signs, what are they left with? Dogs came into this world with two things: their bark and their bite. Humans reprimand the bark and then are confused when they get the bite. It's ridiculous. Stop reprimanding the growl, the bark, the look, and the teeth being shown. Instead of saying, "They shouldn't be growling at me!" maybe you should get more curious and ask, "Why are they growling at me?"

Our Chihuahua, Pudgalina, has been super vocal from the beginning, but she is also super honest about how she is feeling. We have mastered all her vocalizations and what they mean. When she wants to play, her tail is floppy and going a mile a minute. She shoves the toy or her snout into us, pauses, and then bounces back and forth, wanting to be roughed up. And she runs around. But there is a playful growl and bark combo in there. We have learned this is different from her "fuck off" growl. We will hear this at night if we are getting settled for bed and go to adjust her when she does not want to be touched. Sometimes, we can adjust her with zero response. She likes it because we snuggle her up by the pillows. But there are just some nights when she wants to stay by our feet and does not want to be physically manipulated. Now, this doesn't mean I just leave her and not get myself comfortable. Instead, I calmly and kindly ask her to move, and she does it. On. Her. Own. And because I asked nicely, she felt like it was her choice. I didn't demand, and I didn't force. This builds trust between us. She feels she can let me know to please not touch her, and we respect it. Then we give her the choice to move herself. No harm done.

The key is checking your ego at the door and not getting offended by something that someone else wants or does not want. Just like humans, dogs have emotions, likes, and dislikes, and they should feel safe enough to voice them without retribution. We are far, far away from that as a society, but it sounds nice!

Human example: A grandparent getting mad and offended that their child has asked them not to kiss their brand-new newborn on the lips, to avoid them getting sick. As a grandparent, if you get *mad* at this, this is a *you* problem. This is a huge topic going on with family dynamics because up until now, it feels like setting boundaries was taboo and dramatic when it is just a simple *Please don't do that.* Your child asking you not to kiss their child is not a slight on you. It is to save their own child from sickness. Do not make this about you. We all have the right to set a boundary without someone getting butthurt. Yes, even our dogs!

Another huge way to avoid resource guarding altogether is making sure you are meeting your dog's needs and resources consistently! Ensuring your dog's needs—such as hunger, thirst, exercise, and play—are met on a consistent basis is crucial. For instance, if your dog knows they will receive regular meals, they are less likely to guard their food aggressively. Similarly, providing consistent access to toys and personal space can prevent the guarding of these resources. An example is having a routine in which your dog gets exercise, mentally or physically, at the same time each day. This helps reduce anxiety and the need to guard toys as a resource because your dog is mentally and physically satisfied.

A great example of this is what I call the famous holiday surprise. It happens so consistently on holidays like Christmas because there are always gifts and a lovely dinner with fancy food. Family members like to bring the dog's gift as well now. The majority of the time, it is a bright and shiny new toy or treat—something the dog never gets, maybe ever. Usually, it is some sort of large animal bone, rawhide, or fun squeaky toy. With this new, exciting thing, mixed with the overstimulation and stress of a holiday with tons of guests in the house, their dog sibling, a kid in the home, or even you can make one small move too close to that new object, and you can have a guarding incident on your hands.

Why?

If this dog had enrichment toys or bones more often, they would have been unfazed because they would know, from experience, that no one is going to take this from them. We will touch on this in more detail later in the chapter, but many parents restrict or take away toys, enrichment, and bones to eliminate guarding once they see a spark—especially between dog siblings. This makes it so much worse.

You cannot eliminate guarding. That's like trying to eliminate joy or anger. Guarding stems from insecurity, and until the insecurity is softened, it will move from thing to thing. The second there is something even remotely interesting, a dog will jump all over it and defend it from all the others. If toys and bones are around consistently, they won't care if someone picks one up because the same thing is two feet away from them.

If you have already eliminated something from your home because your dogs guard them from each other or you, please do not go right home and give all the toys and bones back. You need a trained professional to help you go about this properly and successfully. Guarding can be extremely dangerous, and we want to tread cautiously with dogs that are intense in this area so no one gets hurt.

The other piece to the puzzle is setting proper boundaries. This is true in any relationship. Like Brené Brown says, "Clear is kind. Unclear is unkind."[2] We can't read minds, and our dogs definitely can't. Establishing clear and consistent boundaries with empathy is essential. This means teaching your dog what is acceptable and what is not in a gentle but firm manner.

For example, let's say your dog loves to play fetch but has a hard time dropping the ball for you to throw. You do not want a game of chase, so you ask them for a drop and make it clear that you will not be chasing them to get the ball back. To play, they need to drop it willingly. You are calm, cool, and collected the whole time. You are just waiting patiently. You are not frustrated and demanding the ball.

2. Brené Brown, *Dare to Lead* (Manhattan, NY: Random House, 2018).

What is the fun in that? It is *their* playtime, and they are obviously having a hard time losing control of the ball. Makes sense. Give them the time to figure it out and process those feelings. This sets a boundary and does so in a way that respects their feelings and provides a positive outcome, helping build mutual respect and understanding. All family members must follow the same rules to maintain consistency. This is especially true for things that the dog is definitely not allowed to do—like go on the furniture.

Let's say Mom feels it's a big no-no for the dog to be on the couch. She just doesn't like it or want it. The whole family agrees, but when Mom isn't home, Dad lets the dog come and snuggle on the couch.

Who gets in trouble here?

The dog. Dad is not being consistent, and the dog may think that rule doesn't exist, so they jump up on the couch in front of Mom, not thinking anything of it. Mom gets angry and frustrated, thinking her dog is deliberately not listening anymore. But in reality, Dad is getting him in trouble by being dishonest and setting the dog up to fail. Hold the boundary! And if you don't like the boundary, get a new wife! Nobody made you marry someone who doesn't like dogs on the couch! That's usually first-date conversation, right? So this one's on you, Dad!

Last but not least, to avoid resource guarding altogether, you must foster mutual respect among household members. Mutual respect involves teaching both your dog and any other pets or humans in the household to respect each other's space and belongings. An example of fostering mutual respect is supervising interactions between your dog and other pets, especially during feeding times or when toys are involved, to ensure that no one is invading the other's space or resources.

When we adopted Tishi in 2020, she had to learn how Oaklee and Pudge function throughout the day, what they like, and what they dislike. She learned quickly not to go near Pudge or look at her when she has a bully stick. Oaklee doesn't mind sharing at all. In fact, they have such a trust and mutual respect for each other that if he finds an old yak bone and is chomping, she'll wait a respectful five feet away and just wait for him to finish. I have seen him notice her, keep chewing for a little bit, slow down, and then toss it to her, letting her know it's her turn. She'll pick it up, lie right next to him, and start chomping. He'll stay and just pass out next to her. It is so sweet, and I just love watching their relationship. It is a "what's mine is yours and what's yours is mine" type of situation, and they do it so subtly.

Back in 2018, though, we had our blind puppy, Opal Marie. Opal was born blind and didn't know anything of it. She was happy and oblivious as a clam. She adored Oaklee, and he basically raised her. Their relationship was similar to the relationship between Tishi and Opal, but Opal was way more obsessed with Oaklee and needed him a lot more because of her disability. She was only eight weeks when she came home. Opal and Pudge were different. Pudge was *not* a fan. Pudge did not understand why Opal smacked into walls randomly, pounced all over the place, had no self-awareness, and, most of all, never respected Pudge's "fuck off" signals. I am laughing while I am writing this. Opal was such a fucking amazing dog and was just so blind and dopey. She had us laughing all the time. I miss her so much! Ugh. The world can be cruel sometimes.

Opal wanted to be Pudge's best frickin' friend, but if Pudge could have spoken, she would have said, "*You can't sit with me*!" We often referred to her as Regina George. In 2019, I was so damn pregnant with JJ that I did not see a situation unfolding right in front of me. Pudge really only likes bully sticks, and she would have her bully a lot longer than Opal did since Opal was a bigger dog. Pudge liked to take her time. Well, Opal would finish hers and bop around the couch area, not realizing how uncomfortable Pudge was getting with her bully stick so close. One day, I realized what was going on only when I saw Pudge spot Opal across the room as Opal was coming in toward her. Pudge got low and beady-eyed, then started to show teeth. To figure out where this was coming from, I started to observe and see what had unfolded.

And I realized it was all my fault. I'd put too much pressure on Pudge to be nice to her disabled sister with something so high value, and I had expected Opal to realize what was going on when she literally couldn't frickin' see. Pregnancy does crazy shit to you!

So we switched things up. Any time Pudge had a bully stick, I would be there, monitoring. I would let Pudge know I had her back and that I would make sure Opal didn't take it or come too close. I praised her and treated her, letting her know that when Opal came into the picture, she got more good things. I also reset the boundary for Opal. I would give her enrichment somewhere farther away, and if she started to migrate over, I would say, "Go rest," which means, "Go relax on your bed for a bit." It worked great. If there was a time I couldn't monitor, I would put Pudge in our room with the door closed. Easy peasy!

This is the same for humans. This means teaching children not to disturb the dog while eating or sleeping. Children do not go into the dog's crate or on their beds. Children do not get to climb all over the dog, ever. These are hard boundaries, and in my professional opinion, they are nonnegotiable. It is never necessary for your kid to play on your dog or get in the dog's food bowl or crate. They have their own food, their own bed, and their own toys. Parents allow this for two reasons: they think it's cute and funny, or they are lazy and don't feel like setting that boundary. This is *so* unbelievably dangerous.

Story time! A family I work with came to me last year, distraught. Their sweet five-year-old Lab/hound mix had bitten their eighteen-month-old daughter in the face twice. Once we got down to the nitty-gritty and I was able to figure out how we got to this place, I was not shocked.

They had been letting their daughter play in the dog's food bowl since she was old enough to crawl. They thought it was adorable that she'd play in the food and pretend to eat like a dog. All the while, their dog was on the couch, watching her do this straight fucking faced. The dog watched her every time, stiff and unblinking. They took this to mean the dog didn't care and didn't mind. Well, one day, the dog was eating, and the daughter hobbled over. The dog turned right around and air snapped at her. The daughter did not acknowledge this as anything because she was a baby, so she kept going. That was when the bite happened.

Who gets in trouble and who gets hurt? The dog and the kid. All of that should have been avoided. Now, this family wasn't just being careless. I love this family! They are in the bucket of a few of my favorite clients. Both daughter and dog are loved beyond words. They just didn't know any better. They were uneducated.

We see tons of videos of kids doing funny things like that or crawling all over the dog, and it's just seen as this normal thing. When we have animals and kids living under the same roof, these boundaries and rules are not a suggestion, they are mandatory. Your kids and you should be held to the same standards and boundaries as your dog. You don't want your dog to steal food out of your kid's hand? Well, your kid shouldn't touch dog food or enrichment. You don't want your dog to play with your toddler's stuffed animals? Then your kid should not touch your dog's toys either. You don't want your dog to jump all over your kids? Make sure your kids do not rile up the dog and jump all over them.

Mutual respect helps create a harmonious living environment where resource guarding is less likely to develop because everyone's boundaries are acknowledged and maintained. The random times things go wrong will not be dangerous because your dog's stress will not be nearing its threshold of tolerance.

By focusing on these four areas, you lay a strong foundation from the beginning for a relationship with your dog that is based on trust, respect, and understanding, significantly reducing the likelihood of resource-guarding behaviors. This shift in our approach can gradually alter our dog's perception, helping them learn that the world is not full of items that require guarding but rather a safe place where their resources are secure and plentiful. Science and psychology working hand in hand pave the way toward understanding and reshaping our dogs' guarding behaviors and transforming potential conflicts into opportunities for trust and reassurance.

But what if you have never seen the signs of guarding before? I tend to forget that ordinary people don't see the crazy shit I see or know the crazy shit I know! I'm so deep in the hole of dog behavior that I forget what it feels like to not be aware of this stuff or talk about it every single day. It is exhausting, I'll admit it. But I do love it! So let's dive into what it looks like.

Understanding the body language of a dog prone to resource guarding is crucial in preventing situations from escalating. Before a dog resorts to growling or snapping, they exhibit several warning signs that, if recognized early, can allow for timely intervention. These signs include a stiff body, a possessive stance over an item, whale eyes, a low growl, ears pinned back, and a fearful expression. They may switch to baring teeth or snarling if the situation continues without any intervention. Acknowledging these signals is the first step in creating a safer environment for the dog and those around them. If you see any or all of these signs, immediately stop what you are doing and start talking nicely to them. Say, "Good girl! Yes, you are a good girl." Honestly, say anything as long as it is sweet and nonthreatening. We have to defuse the situation!

Now, let's say you are already in the thick of it. Your dog is a full-blown guarder. Guarding is an everyday occurrence, or things look like they're headed that way. We have to go over a few important things first.

In addressing the issue of resource guarding, there are several key strategies we must employ regardless of the specific item or resource your dog is guarding. First and foremost, working with resource guarding can be complex and potentially dangerous. It is important to have a thorough understanding of animal behavior and appropriate training techniques before attempting to modify resource-guarding behavior.

Additionally, it is recommended that you seek guidance from a certified behavior consultant or veterinary behaviorist to ensure the safety of both the animal and the handler. The information provided in any response related to resource guarding is for educational purposes only and should not be considered as a substitute for hands-on professional assistance. It's crucial to manage the environment effectively to ensure safety for all involved, creating a setting where no one is at risk of getting hurt. You should *not* be DIYing this. Period. There are so many subtle layers of guarding that this absolutely needs guidance from a behavioral consultant or vet behaviorist, from start to finish. Have I made myself perfectly clear? You should not read this chapter and think you are capable of fixing your dog's resource guarding without professional help! Got it? Okay, good!

Okay, now we'll go over the dos and don'ts. I know I have beaten this one to death, but I don't care. I also want to explain a bit more.

- *Never* reprimand. Never correct your dog for showing warning signs, as these are not acts of dominance. They are important communication efforts. By not listening to the communication and demanding respect, you are the one being dominant, and this ain't a good look. Don't do it. Instead, praise them when they communicate clearly, and let them know they can trust you.
- *Never* take things out of your dog's mouth. Demonstrating to your dog that you have no intention of taking the guarded item away helps build trust. It's essential to convey to your dog that your presence, and the presence of what they value, results in positive outcomes—more resources and affection rather than less. Depending on the object, figure out a way for your dog to drop it on their own, without a trade and without a cue. We want them to lose interest *on their own.* More on how to do this for each specific type of guarding is coming up.
- *Never* trade. It's important to avoid the common pitfalls that can exacerbate the problem. Trading can seem like the best and simplest idea at the time, but it can lead to increased anxiety and guarding behavior. If your toddler won't take a bath, but you offer an M&M,

they will eventually realize that an increased tantrum at bath time can get them better resources each time. Pretty soon, you'll need to be offering a whole banana sundae just to get washed up.

- Instead, we want to make it clear that the object is not that valuable and not that big a deal. Act nonchalantly. If there is anything you take away from this chapter, I hope it is this. The second you realize that your dog has something, do not react. Act as if you do not see it. Or, if you do see it, act like it's no big deal. No staring, no gasping, no reprimanding, no using cues, no asking them to drop it, no chasing, and no trying to trick them. You need to act like you do not see them or care. More on this later.
- *Never* eliminate. By eliminating the valued object, like a bone or a toy, you are putting it on a higher pedestal, making a problem more likely to occur if that object accidentally shows up. This can be dangerous because other pets or humans will not expect the item to be there, thinking it was previously eliminated. They don't even realize they might be walking into a land mine. Instead, keep the object, but create a plan for your family so your dog can enjoy it safely without the risk of anyone else getting hurt. Protocols can be put into place to ensure nothing bad will happen. Then you can move away from management and into more normalcy.

Now we are going to get into the specific types of guarding. The rest of this chapter will discuss food, enrichment, stolen contraband, toys, furniture, and people and the affection they give.

Food Guarding from Humans

First, what is the dog's history with food? Are they older and this just started? Or have they been doing this since they were a baby because they came from a horrible situation where they had to fight for food to survive? Is the stress of a new baby and a lack of resources provoking this? Figuring out the *why* is the most important part because it will influence the behavioral modification.

Next, we need to pinpoint their threshold. Will they react unless left alone? Or can you be in the room but not be allowed to walk by too closely?

The first small piece of advice that can make a big difference is just changing the position of their food bowl or picking a calmer room where they feel safer. Dog bowls are usually positioned right at the edge of a room, so the dog is facing the wall while eating. This does not bode well for a dog that is feeling uncomfortable and vulnerable. Fix it so your dog can see the whole room instead, then respect all communication they give you. This is *not* an obedience training session by any means. You are not asking them to sit, look, back up, leave it, or stop eating. The only thing they need to do is keep eating and eat all the additional high-value food you will be throwing their way. They get love, praise, and better food than what they are already eating when you are around their food. You are rewarding and praising them even when they are reacting and having negative emotions! Your only goal is to get them to trust you and like you being around their food.

Food Guarding from Other Animals

If your dog is food guarding from other pets, is your dog properly correcting your other pet? Does the punishment fit the crime? Does your other pet listen? These are huge questions because if your dog is correcting the other dog properly and the other dog is just not respecting their boundaries, it's way more of a respect issue for the other dog than it is guarding. We need to make sure that the other dog isn't the issue first. If you do have a dog guarding from other pets that are simply in the vicinity, you need to reduce the stress the guarding dog is experiencing on a daily basis. Next, does your dog's setup need to change? Can you change where they eat, create peace and quiet, have a less busy feeding time, or keep them farther away from the other dog while monitoring in the middle?

Next is an important question that many people do not ask or even think is a problem: Are their eating habits increasing their guarding and anxiety around food? Examples include grazing, not finishing meals, eating meals that are too big, etc. These are usually a huge gateway drug for pet-on-pet guarding. Your dog is well aware that their food is a major resource. They know that is how they survive, but the portion you gave was too big. They eat half, and now the rest is just sitting there all day long as your other dog walks by it over and over again. The stress is building day after day. If your dog is a grazer and a guarder, start here to fix it. Grazing should never happen under any circumstance. It can be dangerous and a catalyst for other behavioral issues and anxiety.

Now, on the flip side, you need to make sure you are giving enough food. If they are hungry—better known as *hangry* (hungry and angry)—in these situations, amping up the food can be a huge game changer. You can't expect a dog not to guard if the resources are not being provided. They think there isn't enough food!

The last part is working on the scenario in which you are most likely seeing the guarding take place. Many exercises can reduce the guarding and negative emotions your dog is feeling while keeping everyone safe and content. A professional trainer can tell you exactly what to do and when to do it. Doing this on your own only puts both pets at risk. That is exactly why I am not going into detail about the exercises and exactly what to do.

Guarding of Enrichment Items

This behavior, whether guarding from humans or other pets, calls for a nuanced approach. Many times in this book, I've said that enrichment might be one of the most important things your dog needs. This fact does not change just because they are having big feelings about it. Previous interactions—such as taking items away and eliminating or reprimanding the dog—can influence current behavior and increase it. It's vital to make the dog feel safe and respected without demanding they relinquish the item. Introducing better resources and praise when near their possessions can alter their perception of human proximity.

Similar principles apply when addressing guarding against other pets, focusing on safety, controlled environments, and positive associations with shared spaces and resources. Giving high-value enrichment on a more consistent basis—along with proper safety precautions and calm, encouraging human monitoring—is a one-way ticket to success. Use leashes, crates, and gates because safety is always number one. Never force the pets to get closer together, ever. Let them go at their own pace! If one or more of the pets or people seem stressed or uncomfortable, end the session, and end it on a positive note. Talk to your behavioral consultant about a game plan for when and how to work with your dog, what to use, where to do it, and how often. That way, you'll be sure that you are doing the right thing for your family's dynamic.

Guarding Stolen Contraband

I love talking about this one because the solution makes people think I am insane until they do it. Then their jaws are on the floor. It's so much fun and so simple! Dealing with stolen contraband, like shoes and tissues, requires us to ignore the behavior to avoid reinforcing it with negative attention. If a dog is seeking attention, a lack of response often leads to them losing interest in the item. If the item poses no danger or can't be swallowed—like a tissue, a paper towel, shoes, and socks—allowing the behavior can sometimes be a strategic choice to avoid escalating guarding behavior.

If a dog takes a paper towel and just tears it up and walks away, who cares? Stop gasping, grabbing for, and assigning value to things that are not a big deal. If your dog takes things and historically does not eat them or destroy them, do nothing. If they grab your shoe and wait for you to respond, do nothing! Continue watching TV or making dinner. They don't eat the shoe, so the only thing making the shoe valuable is you. Player #2, do *not* enter the chat! Ignore it, and your dog will come and show you, like, *Hey! I have a shoe! Don't you see me?* You'll continue to not care, and they will eventually lose interest and drop it all on their own.

But it is important to note that if your dog is doing this, they are looking for a need to be met, and you should still meet that need even though they stole something. Just make the contraband unrelated to the need being met by switching up the scenery like we discussed in Chapter 5.

However, dangerous items that your dog will swallow necessitate calm, distraction-based interventions so you can safely recover the item without confrontation. Never corner or trick your dog. They will never trust you again after that! Let's face it. Your dog is smarter than you! Even though you are nervous that they will get injured, you should still give no big emotion or response to this. I know how hard this is, but you *need* to try! If you do not think this is something your dog will swallow immediately, wait fifteen to thirty seconds, and leave the room.

Yes, leave the room. They will most likely follow. Once we can let a little time pass, they will be thinking more about what you're doing than guarding that item. If you know this will not distract or interest your dog, ask them to go for a walk or do something fun! But do something to break up the scenery so they don't think they get a walk for stealing your car keys. You can even pretend to go to the bathroom first.

The next bit is the kicker. If it's not dangerous, let them eat it. This includes tissue, paper, paper towels, and even socks and shoes that might not be important. They are looking for a response, so a casualty here and there will aid in the bigger battle! All of those items are replaceable. But if your dog takes things you don't want to replace, put out older versions you don't care about, like old shoes.

However, if it is something super dangerous—scissors, a knife, a razor, an earring, or anything that can cause obstruction or an internal puncture—

stay calm, go to the fridge for something *good*, and throw little pieces all over the place. But never get too close to your dog. *Act natural*! Do not freak out or look like all you want to do is get that item from them. Once they drop the item and go for the food, do not jump on it because, after that, they will never drop a valued item around you ever again.

The main takeaway when it comes to stolen contraband is that if they are doing this, they are looking for negative attention and to have one or more needs met. That is the first place to start. Do not ignore an unmet need just because you are pissed they guarded from you! That is everyone's biggest mistake in these situations.

Guarding Toys

Toys are the most common objects that pet parents eliminate to stop guarding. Don't do this. Toys have value only if the dog finds them enjoyable. Otherwise, they are not nutritionally based or inherently valuable. Reducing toy guarding involves creating a safe space away from busy areas where the dog can play. Don't directly interact with or clean the toys in their presence. This approach, coupled with nonchalant praise, can reduce guarding behaviors.

Pick a nontraffic area in your house to keep the toys so the dog feels the toys are safe even when they aren't in the same room. When they play, don't show too much interest or make eye contact. If your dog doesn't like movement around their toys, walk outside their threshold and toss treats every so often to reinforce that playing around you is a good thing.

Now, guarding toys with other animals can be a bit trickier. Give each dog or pet ample time to safely play with their favorite toys alone. Eventually, use boundaries like baby gates so both dogs can see each other playing once they lower intensity overall. Only do this with humans in between to negate gate fighting. Also, praise them and engage in the toy with them if they allow to build confidence and trust in the other animal.

Furniture Guarding

This is another one of my favorites. It might be because I find it ridiculously rude to remove a dog from the couch or not allow dogs on the furniture at all. This phenomenon often stems from a dog's perception of furniture as a valuable territory or a resource that warrants protection, especially in spaces where they feel particularly comfortable or secure.

Furniture guarding is learned. If they are never dominantly forced to move, they will have no problem sharing furniture space because this has never been deemed that big of a resource, so it is not at risk. To mitigate furniture guarding, start by identifying the situations that provoke the behavior. Is it confined to a particular piece of furniture, or does it occur in any spot they choose to lie or stand? Assess whether the guarding is directed toward all humans and pets or if it's selective. Understanding the dog's threshold—how close someone can get before the dog reacts—is crucial. Rather than removing access to the guarded spot, which can increase anxiety and add more value to the spot, focus on associating your approach with positive outcomes. This could involve offering treats, praising, or engaging in a favorite play activity whenever you or another pet approach the area. This promotes a positive association with the presence of others. It's important to maintain a dynamic, nonthreatening presence while avoiding direct stares and not lingering too closely, which could escalate the guarding behavior.

Let's say any time you approach your bed at night, your dog gets tense and growly. Incorporating enrichment activities can help redirect your dog's focus and reduce reliance on the furniture as a source of security. Have a frozen marrow bone ready every night when you go to bed. You can kindly lure your dog to a bed on the floor or maybe move them out of your spot in the bed and coax them down more by the foot. By consistently reinforcing positive interactions and respecting your dog's comfort levels, you can gradually reduce furniture-guarding behaviors, fostering a more relaxed and trusting environment for everyone in the household.

Rule of thumb: anytime you want a dog to adjust themselves while in an already super-comfortable position, make it worth their while and make it feel like it was their choice to move. They'll do it gladly more and more.

And I am sure many of you noticed that I said nothing about eliminating them from the spot or furniture. The phrase "They need to earn being on the furniture" makes me want to puke. Stop removing dogs from furniture because they are having a hard time. It does not fix the problem. It will only increase both the guarding and the power struggle you have created.

Now, what if they guard furniture from other pets? Safety first: leashes ensure that no one gets hurt and we have total control. Dogs don't always realize they can retreat or create more space. We have to be prepared to help them with this. This requires tons of praising and counterconditioning while your dog is under threshold. Remember to keep sessions short and sweet. And, like always, if someone is too stressed by the activities, shut it down positively and try again later. You can always use enrichment as a distraction if they don't guard their enrichment from the other pet as well!

When you have dogs guarding furniture from other pets, you have to monitor them when they are around each other and that furniture. You cannot train only some of the time. Manipulate the situations to work in your favor. When you can't watch them, they have to be separated or not in a position to guard from one another until you are present and attentive.

Guarding People

Distinguishing between guarding and insecurity or reactivity due to the handler's behavior is essential. In the home, reframing situations where the dog feels they lose attention or resources during certain interactions can shift their perspective toward positive outcomes. For example, if your dog *finally* has alone time with you on the couch at night, when you are both relaxed, they are getting unconditional love. They feel so safe, but your ten-year-old, who is constantly needing you throughout the day, comes in to say goodnight. What do you think your dog is thinking?

OMG, get out of here already! You had her all day. It's my turn!

They patiently waited all day for their time with you, and this kid does not quit. So they growl at your kid. Again, these are valid emotions for a dog that does not feel like their cup is filled. Another human sibling might even say, "Can you go away already so I can have five minutes with Mom alone?" This dog is guarding their affection and time with this particular person, not solely the couch.

Understanding and addressing the triggers of guarding behavior, especially when directed toward family members, is vital for a harmonious household. We have to be ready for this with empathy and understanding to turn it around. Kids or other pets get growled at the most. Significant others are second on the list. These individuals are seen as resource takers. Dogs start to associate a feeling with a person coming toward them on the couch. They're thinking, When my brother approaches, he always takes Mom's attention away. Get him out of here!

So, what do we do? We take a resource taker and turn them into a resource giver! So simple. This kid, pet, or partner should only bring better things when they approach. This can be manipulated and made a part of the daily routine to quickly turn this around! We are going to change the dog's thought to *Now when my brother approaches, I get so much love from my person. They bring me good food, and everyone cheers for me!*

There can be many layers to this behavior, and it's not always that black or white. Sometimes, other things in the family dynamic need to be fixed, especially when we are dealing with children. This could be the dog's lack of trust in that child. This is usually due to a lack of predictability and boundaries, so we need to fix that everywhere, not just in the situation with the couch at night before bed. So again, I urge you, if you are dealing with this, you need a trained professional like myself to pick this apart for you so it can be fixed appropriately and safely. Doing some of these exercises could make things worse if the reason is not what you think it is!

We are going to finish off this chapter by briefly touching on pharmaceuticals and antianxiety supplements. While behavior modification techniques can be effective in reducing resource-guarding behavior, pharmaceutical interventions may also be necessary in some cases, in conjunction with behavior modification. Psychopharmaceuticals should be recommended by a behaviorist or a behavior consultant and prescribed by your vet. They are not a band-aid or long-term solution. They are simply another amazing tool in our toolbox, and they work in conjunction with all the exercises we discussed throughout this chapter.

When I have a client whose dog's guarding is severe, I usually have to suggest that they speak to their vet about medication because there is most likely a chemical imbalance going on. This can be due to trauma or genetics. It is extremely common and, thankfully, fixable. Chemical imbalances cannot be fixed with just behavioral modification or a positive attitude. They need medication to help balance out everything going on in the brain. The medication helps a dog function properly and make sound decisions. If your dog's chemical imbalance makes them think they are in danger when they simply walk into the room where their toy is, they are feeling and seeing something that is not real. Their brain is not seeing the situation properly or logically, thus making them make a bad choice. But to them, it is *so real.* This is where the intense empathy comes in. We don't see it. We don't feel it. But we *need* to believe it is real for them.

I will talk about all the options and what they entail in the next chapter, but I wanted to briefly touch here on the fact that many dogs need pharmaceutical help when they are guarding, and I promise it is okay! It is not the end of the world. Your dog is not broken or damaged. People have hard times like this too, and they just need a little help. Meds in this category should never be forever. Just like with behavior modification, our goal is to fix it for good so you are not training for the rest of your dog's life. Let's fix the issue at the root and do our due diligence for our dogs so they can succeed and get to the other side of this once and for all!

Chapter 13:
Anxiety

So, who *doesn't* have anxiety? Raise of hands.

Nobody?

Okay, yeah. That's what I thought. Not only is our human society going through an epidemic of mental health issues and anxiety, but so are our dogs! Anxiety in dogs is as complex and varied as the personalities of the dogs themselves. It's a shadow that can follow our dogs from puppyhood to their golden years, manifesting in ways that are as unique as they are. But fear not, dear friends, for understanding is the first step on the path to relief. Let's unwrap the layers of anxiety, revealing its many faces and how we can help our dogs navigate their anxious moments.

Separation Anxiety

Separation anxiety is one of the most tedious and unfun things to work on in behavioral dog training! The heartache of parting is not ours alone; our dogs feel it too. Imagine the pang of watching your best friend walk out the door, not knowing if or when they'll return. That's separation anxiety for you—marked by a chorus of howls, drooling, pure panic, the remodeling of couches, and the unintended indoor "accidents." Our task is to teach them that solitude is not forever and reunion is always on the horizon.

But *how*?

Separation anxiety is so stressful for everyone involved, and because you are not physically there with your dog while they are freaking out and panicking, you can't help them. So you feel helpless. I feel you on this, way more than I'd like to admit.

When we adopted Oaklee in 2018, he just fit right into the family. He was more of a happy dummy, go-with-the-flow kind of dog, coexisted with other dogs, and left Pudge alone. It just seemed perfect. We left him home, uncrated because he was so ridiculously chill and was already potty trained.

First two weeks, no issues. He did only one thing, which, to this day, I find hysterical. He would take John's shoes and place them on the couch next to him properly, like the left and right shoes lined up, respectively. I thought John was being rude as hell and leaving his shoes on the couch because I thought there was no way a dog could do this.

Other than that, we didn't see much anxiety. He was just a big mush who had definitely been mentally and physically abused and wanted lots of love. But he was pretty lazy and relaxed a lot!

One day, we got home a little later than expected from work. John and I got our wires crossed about who would be home first, and we wound up being out of the house for six hours instead of four.

We came home to a *destroyed* house.

It looked like we'd been robbed! The blinds on the windows were cut in half, my island chairs were in the living room, and my couch was in the kitchen. Pee and poop everywhere.

No, I am not exaggerating.

For about six months after that, we couldn't leave without him having a panic attack. It was so stressful. We felt chained to the house because we didn't want him to feel any distress. We went through four crates. He broke the first three with his nose and his body weight, which I would watch in amazement on the camera. To this day, I think he was born without normal pain receptors. He ate a hole in the door of the fourth crate, stuck his head through, and got stuck. It took us forty-five minutes and a lot of butter and tears to get him out. It shook me to my core to think about what might have happened if we hadn't come home when we did.

Thankfully, I can now say that after a bunch of behavioral work, he is able to be uncrated and left in my bedroom with his siblings for eight hours with no issue at all.

I am telling you this story because, to this day, Oaklee is still the worst separation anxiety case I have ever dealt with. It changed me for life as a dog trainer. I always say if Oaklee can do it, so can your dog. But we need to do what's best for your dog specifically! This, yet again, should not be a DIY project to save some money. It can be dangerous and leave you in a worse-off place than when you started. So please, for all that is good in the world, contact a professional who is certified by the International Association of Animal Behavioral Consultants (IAABC)!

Now, let's dive in! Separation anxiety is more than just a few whimpers when you grab your keys. It's a profound distress that grips some dogs when they're left alone. It's as if their world crumbles every time you step out, leaving them in a state of panic and fear because they think you may never return again. I will delve into the heart of separation anxiety, guiding you through how to understand and compassionately address this condition so you can hopefully get on the other side of this!

First, we must learn to recognize the signs of separation anxiety: destructive behavior, accidents, incessant barking, attempts to escape, shaking, drooling, and even self-harm. These are not acts of rebellion but cries for help from a pet terrified of solitude.

We need to create a plan to reduce this anxiety over being left and abandoned—a perfect plan for your dog and your family's lifestyle. There are many things we can do to assist our dogs. As discussed in Chapter 8, crates are sometimes nonnegotiable, specifically for the dog's safety. For Oaklee, we didn't have a choice. He was destroying furniture beyond repair and ripping off the wall molding to get out. We were extremely fearful that, if given the chance, he would try to eat through a door or window to get outside. So we had to crate him. Four crates later, we decided on an industrial crate he could not bite, and that did the trick.

When it is essential to their safety, the first thing we have to do is create a safe haven for them. A crucial step in alleviating this anxiety is providing a safe, comforting environment. The right crate is not just a place to confine your dog; it's their den, their castle, their sanctuary. Size matters. (Yes, men, you heard me!) Just kidding, but seriously, the crate should be cozy enough for them to feel secure but roomy enough for them to be able to stand, turn, and stretch. Place it in a quiet, relaxing location, shielded from the hustle and bustle of the household. Most dogs will freak out more if they can hear and see you but cannot physically get to you, thus reinforcing the separation anxiety. The goal is to create a positive association with this space, making it a place they look forward to—not one that they dread. Never use the crate as punishment! *Never.*

If a crate is a hard no for you for whatever reason, try to find a room your dog is comfortable in and won't destroy. Some dogs are not destructive when anxious. If this is your dog, congrats! You got terribly lucky and should appreciate that. Instead, maybe your dog just shuts down and doesn't eat. Maybe they shake, bark, drool, or cry. Whatever the symptoms, the first thing to do is find a room or area where they feel most comfortable. I usually suggest closing off other rooms of the house to make it a smaller area. Many dogs that are anxious about being left alone do worse with more space because it's just more responsibility, a bigger place to pace around in, or more room to have an accident in.

Next, use soundscapes and enrichment. The ambiance of the sanctuary plays a pivotal role. A sound machine can mask the jarring noises of the outside world, offering an auditory blanket of comfort. This one can be life-changing. Many people go for music or a TV playing in the background, but sound machines are the big guns. They block sound getting in but also sound getting out. Music and TV cannot do this. This is clutch for apartment living and especially helpful if you work from home! Not to mention, the soothing quality of the noises these machines supply can help dogs relax more quickly. We love ours!

Couple sound with high-value enrichment. As previously discussed in Chapter 5 about filling their cups, enrichment is a necessary resource that engages your dog's mind. These tools can turn the tide of anxiety. They're not mere distractions but bridges to a world where being alone doesn't mean being lonely. Many people say their dog will not eat anything when they are gone, and this is not surprising! As we've touched on, when dogs are in fight or flight, they are not likely to eat because they are too concerned with not dying. Food is no longer the highest resource. They're thinking, *If I am dead, I can't eat, so I should focus on staying alive.* But still offer this food! If you never offer it, they can never take it.

But we do need to focus on significantly reducing their stress prior to expecting any different behavior. Regardless of all our efforts, we sometimes need a helping hand in the form of medications. Unfortunately, this is a topic not every pet parent wants to hear, but it is a must-have conversation prior to separation training.

Medications are not about sedation but about providing relief from the overwhelming fight-or-flight response that our dogs cannot fix on their own and have zero control over. They allow your dog to access a calmer state of mind, where the seeds of new, positive associations with being alone can be sown. If your dog is injuring themselves, is destructive, or is in a panic in the crate—screaming, crying, barking on a beat, and drooling—no matter what interventions you create to get them to realize they are okay, it will be for nothing.

Earlier in the book, we discussed how you would feel during a panic attack if someone told you, "Calm down. Everything is fine." You would get more panicky and frustrated, maybe even angry, because they just didn't understand. If this describes your dog, they most likely need medical intervention. And let me make this perfectly clear: it is okay if they do! It is *not* the end of the world, and the meds will *not* be forever!

This sort of anxiety is extremely common but usually undiagnosed, so many dogs go through life suffering. There is one thing to be cautious about: if your dog needs meds but doesn't get them, the anxiety can get much worse—especially if you are still leaving them and trying to work through the systematic desensitization without giving them the mental relief they need. This is dangerous.

Some of you may be highly against medication. I get it! Prior to Oaklee, I didn't believe in medication either. After destroying and eating his way out of four crates due to extreme abandonment and separation anxiety, the last straw was when he put that hole in the metal door, got his head stuck, and almost died. It was an extremely terrifying wake-up call for me. Someone explained to me that Oaklee had a chemical imbalance and that in this extreme time of stress, he would go into fight or flight so severely that his body was no longer experiencing pain. His reality was altered. He thought he was in more danger in the crate than out of it. So, almost killing himself trying to get out was his best solution.

None of my regular methods were creating any positive change for Oaklee. I had to put my own ego and personal beliefs aside and realize that the only way I could help him was to get him the medication he needed. By making this choice, I had to put my own thoughts about medication aside and decide to love Oaklee *more*. If that time came for you, could you do the same?

It is important to note that not all antianxiety medications are created equally. And not all are safe to use in behavioral training. I warn you about this because, in my professional experience, behavior medication is, unfortunately, not something every general veterinarian is well versed in. Working closely with a veterinarian who only suggests fear-free training and deals with behavior often or a veterinary behaviorist who specializes in this to find the right medication is a step toward giving your dog the peace they deserve. When navigating behavioral meds for our dogs, it's essential to approach this topic with an open mind and a clear understanding of the options available, including their potential benefits and considerations.

Fluoxetine (Prozac) is usually my go-to suggestion for severe separation anxiety cases. It emerges as a beacon of hope for many dogs grappling with anxiety (and aggression). As a selective serotonin reuptake inhibitor (SSRI), fluoxetine works by increasing serotonin levels in the brain, which can help stabilize mood and reduce anxiety. This medication is particularly beneficial for dogs that experience relentless anxiety symptoms, offering them a chance to experience calmness and openness to learning new, positive associations with being alone. The key to success with fluoxetine lies in its ability to help dogs step back from the edge of panic, allowing behavioral training to be more effective. Unfortunately, this life-changing and life-saving medication takes about three to four weeks to kick in fully. So, in the meantime, if leaving the house is absolutely necessary but you are afraid for your dog's safety, you might need an as-needed medication (one that does not need to be used daily or at the same time each day).

Clomipramine (Clomicalm), a tricyclic antidepressant, offers another avenue for treating dogs with separation anxiety, obsessive-compulsive disorder, and aggression. By affecting neurotransmitter levels in the brain, clomipramine aids in alleviating the distress that leads to these behaviors. Its role in behavioral modification is to create a foundation upon which dogs can build new, healthier habits and reactions. For dogs trapped in a cycle of obsessive behaviors or relentless anxiety, clomipramine can be the key that unlocks the door to a more peaceful existence. Similarly, this medication takes three to four weeks to see positive changes.

Gabapentin (Neurontin), while primarily known as an anticonvulsant medication, has found a place in treating anxiety and aggression in dogs. Its effectiveness in reducing pain also extends to a calming effect on the nervous system, making it a valuable tool for dogs with anxiety that manifests physically. Gabapentin can be particularly useful in creating a serene state of mind for dogs, enabling them to better cope with stressors that previously triggered their anxiety or aggression. This one is an as-needed medication. It can be useful for dogs that have a milder case of separation anxiety, but it cannot help fix chemical imbalances or anxiety disorders for good. It relieves anxiety only for the amount of time it is in the body, which is usually six to eight hours.

It's crucial to navigate the use of these medications with caution and awareness. Trazodone (Molipaxin), for instance, underscores the need to carefully consider a medication's effects. This one is often suggested, but can be unnecessary and dangerous. While trazodone has sedative properties that can be beneficial in certain contexts, it is not recommended for dogs that are prone to biting. Its ability to lower bite inhibition poses a significant concern, as it can inadvertently increase the likelihood of biting incidents. This highlights the importance of choosing the right medication based on a thorough understanding of each dog's specific needs and behaviors.

In the realm of addressing canine anxiety, particularly those cases that might not warrant prescription medication but still significantly impact the quality of life for our pups, high-quality CBD emerges as a promising ally. Cannabidiol, or CBD, derived from hemp plants, has gained attention for its potential to soothe and calm without the psychoactive effects associated with THC. For dogs experiencing milder forms of anxiety—be it due to social situations, noise sensitivity, or general nervousness—CBD can offer a gentle nudge toward relaxation. The magic of CBD lies in its interaction with the endocannabinoid system, a complex network within the body that plays a key role in maintaining balance across various biological processes, including mood regulation. By supplementing this system, high-quality CBD can help ease the underlying tension without the need for stronger pharmaceuticals. It's akin to providing a comforting hand to hold during moments of distress, offering a sense of calm and security that allows dogs to navigate their anxiety with more ease.

However, like all things consumable, it's crucial to approach CBD with discernment, prioritizing products specifically designed for pets and ensuring they are of the highest quality and free from contaminants that could harm your dog. The concentration of CBD, the presence of third-party lab testing, and clear dosage guidelines are essential factors to consider, ensuring you're providing your dog with a safe and effective supplement. Currently, as I am writing this, true CBD cannot legally be purchased at big-box stores. Of course, that may change so always do your research! Any hemp products you find at your local pet store are not what we are looking for. Doing your research and finding the best-quality product is imperative. I offer our favorite suggestion on our website to ensure people get the good stuff and aren't bamboozled by the many crappy companies out there.

While CBD is not a cure-all, its potential benefits for dogs with less severe anxiety make it a valuable tool in the comprehensive approach to canine wellness. By offering a natural means to enhance relaxation and ease stress, high-quality CBD can be a part of empowering our dogs to lead happier, more peaceful lives.

Let's talk about Oaklee's medication journey for reference so you can get an idea of what this can look like. But remember, Oaklee was a severe case! He was prescribed fluoxetine because of the intensity of his anxiety and the markers we saw that suggested he had an abusive history that resulted in horrible abandonment triggers. Because the fluoxetine would take four weeks to kick in and we did not want to risk him injuring himself, we added trazadone to the mix. This is *only* because Oaklee has zero drive for aggression. He is a happy dummy through and through. He would rather run for the hills than injure anyone, no matter how horrible they were to him.

Honestly, it is so sad, but this is the only reason we allowed trazodone. And even then, I was hesitant. I don't like sedatives, but we quickly realized how high of a tolerance Oaklee had to this medication. He was on the highest dose for his weight and still looked like he was ready to party. It was astonishing! I couldn't believe it. So we had to add gabapentin too. Thankfully, we needed it for about only two weeks. Then the fluoxetine was ready to go, and it was all he needed. We didn't have to use more as-needed meds other than a few doses of CBD on days when he was particularly amped up.

What a relief! He was *finally* able to be home for thirty minutes without intense panic and stress. As the days went on, we were able to add ten minutes at a time to his exposure therapy. Over time, we got to six to eight hours without stress or injury to himself or the crate! We eventually got to the point where he no longer needed the crate and could be left in our bedroom for up to eight hours with no issues or destruction! I say again, what a relief!

We got to this point by working with the fabulous Dr. Samantha Mammen, and I couldn't have been more grateful for her. I still am, to this day, since she's helped our family with every hiccup, every question, every sickness, every loss, and every celebration. She's the friend and veterinarian who talked me through learning about behavior meds, what they do, and how they can help, thus making me a better behavioral trainer for my clients and rescue dogs trying to get adopted. She helped me educate myself on proper, safe, and updated studies, which led me to become IAABC certified as a behavioral consultant. I am forever grateful to have her in our lives as a colleague, but mostly as an amazing friend and companion!

Without this pivotal moment with Oaklee and without Dr. Mammen there to assist us and educate us through this hopeless time, I honestly don't know where we'd be. I know for a fact that the universe works the way it should—most of the time, anyway. I know in my heart that even though Oaklee was otherwise *perfect*, any other family would have surrendered him back to the shelter immediately with how intense his separation anxiety and destruction were. He was meant to be ours, and he is the happiest little boy ever now, feeling so safe and content in our bedroom with his sisters.

I bring this up because sometimes you just need that one special person in your dog's life who is in the profession for the right reasons and is good at their job. That person *cares* about your dog's well-being, not just the money. The people we choose to take care of our family members can dictate how our future with them goes. This includes dog walkers, doggy day care, groomers, and, obviously, vets and trainers, etc. They need to love it. They need to care. They need to always make sure they are putting the dog's safety and mental health in front of egos and personal gain. We need to ensure that your dog receives the appropriate treatment tailored to their unique situation. Which means we all *need* to advocate for our dogs and do our research. Just like we should be doing for ourselves! We should always research diagnoses and cures that are promised along with it and get a second opinion if it doesn't feel right or add up.

If you're starting with a general vet before upgrading to something more serious, like a vet behaviorist, seek a vet with a strong background in behavioral issues, and don't hesitate to ask for recommendations or referrals within your community. I find it great to ask in your town's Facebook group for personal recommendations and referrals before even calling a doctor's office.

To finish up our medication discussion, remember that incorporating medication into your dog's treatment plan isn't a sign of defeat. It's a step toward empowerment. It shouldn't be the last resort if all else fails. It should be used first and foremost if your dog likely is struggling with trauma or a chemical imbalance. Or both. It's about providing your dog the support they need to overcome their anxiety and enabling them to live a happier, more peaceful life. As we explore these options, remember that the goal is not to change who our dogs are but to help them become the best version of themselves, free from the shadows of anxiety. This is our end goal, and it is possible.

Again, if Oaklee can do it, I swear, any dog can!

So, what is the game plan moving forward once we get all our ducks in a row? systematic desensitization! systematic desensitization is about gentle, gradual introductions to being alone, turning a source of panic into one of peace. It's a slow dance, a balancing act if you will, starting with just moments apart, then short durations behind a closed door, and gradually increasing. It's crucial to never rush this process, to monitor their comfort, and to celebrate the small victories. Each step should be associated with positive experiences, reinforcing the idea that solitude can be safe, relaxing, and even rewarding.

Clients ask me constantly about using a camera to keep an eye on their anxious dogs and if this is okay. I always say yes, but on one condition: do not use the camera to check in on your dog when you cannot go to them. What good is it to look in on your dog shaking and freaking out when you know well and good that you can't leave work? All it does is stress you out and make you panic as well. The camera should be used to help us work on the issue, not be a catalyst for continued stress. Cameras can be super useful. They just need to be used properly and appropriately. Setting one up to see how our dogs are improving over time and when exactly they start to stress through the process so we can make tweaks and time our arrival properly is important.

Here are two examples of how to start systematic desensitization for a dog that *will* eat enrichment when left alone but, the second it is finished, slips into anxious territory, pacing, barking, drooling, shaking, destroying, etc.

Set up the crate or the room appropriately for them with whatever they need to be comfy, then drown out the chaos. Give them their enrichment, either locked in the crate or on a bed or couch. Then walk away. After that, you can choose between two options:

- If you have a camera on your dog, stay gone and watch the screen until the enrichment looks like it is coming to an end. Come in before any stress indicators appear. Let your dog out, and praise them like crazy with tons of treats!
- Stay out for fifteen seconds, then come back, quietly drop a few treats into the crate, and walk away again. Stay away for thirty seconds, then come back and drop treats. Leave again for forty-five seconds, come back, and drop treats. Then sixty seconds. A minute and a half. Two minutes. So on and so forth so that you are slowly increasing the time you are gone.

With the first method, adding extra enrichment to the crate once the first enrichment toy looks like it's coming to an end and then walking out again can extend the amount of time your dog spends in the crate without added anxiety. With the second method, you can do the same thing, but eventually stay away for longer and longer times.

What if your dog *will not* eat the enrichment?

Offer the enrichment anyway, then walk to the door and back several times, dropping treats every time you return. Randomly do something unrelated in the vicinity. Come back and start walking away, treating again but with more time in between. Walk out of the room for a few seconds, then come back, repeating and increasing the time in between ever so slightly. This whole exercise shouldn't last more than five minutes if your dog is stressed and unable to eat the treats. If your dog will eat the treats, you can do this for a bit longer—ten to fifteen minutes.

Your dog may do best if you put them in with enrichment and simply walk out without returning for a few minutes. You can start with one to five minutes, depending on their stress level, and come back and let them out. In twenty minutes, you can attempt again and add a minute or two to the duration. Keep in mind that anxiety can differ from day to day. If you have a good day and then the next is crap, try not to get discouraged or frustrated. Some days, a dog just wakes up more anxious! Just like people, it is unavoidable sometimes. Just keep rolling with it and stay positive. With consistency comes progress, and progress is never linear.

Realistically, there are many variations and ways to do this. You just need to figure out what kind of balance is good for your pup. Take your time, and do not ignore added stress, expecting them to be desensitized over time. They won't just get over it one day or get used to it because the situation hasn't changed. They need all their needs met, antianxiety relief, and proper systematic desensitization for their specific anxiety in order to make new associations with being left alone. Combining these strategies creates a comprehensive approach to managing separation anxiety. It's about understanding, being empathetic, providing a safe physical space, and offering a mental space where calm can flourish. When needed, medication is a bridge to better days, not a solution. And through systematic desensitization, we teach resilience and build up their ability to cope in our absence for longer and longer periods.

As we embark on this journey with our anxious companions, remember that progress is measured in steps, not leaps. Patience, consistency, and love are your greatest allies. Separation anxiety is not overcome in a day, but with time and dedication, your dog can learn to find peace in solitude, knowing that though you may leave, you will always return.

And please remember, I know how hard this can be and how difficult it is to not want to throw in the towel. Just be kind to yourself, give yourself grace, but always keep in mind what you would want someone to do if it was you with the anxiety. Would you want someone to give up on you when you needed them the most? Most of us just want to find a loved one who finally says, "Oh yeah, you are worth all the bad times. I'm not leaving." Set yourself up for success and persevere. You got this!

Social Anxiety

Welcome to a subchapter that delves deep into the world of social butterflies with clipped wings—dogs that navigate the tumultuous waters of social anxiety.

Just as humans can feel overwhelmed in crowded places or anxious in social settings, our pups can experience similar feelings of unease, fear, threat, and stress when faced with other dogs, people, or unfamiliar environments. It's a journey fraught with challenges, but together, we can guide them toward becoming more confident and comfortable social beings. Our role? To be their gentle guide into the social whirl at a pace that respects their comfort and boundaries.

Social anxiety in dogs can manifest in various ways, from the dog that hides behind their parent's legs at the park to the one that growls or snaps when a friendly hand reaches out to pet them.

Understanding the root of this anxiety is key. Was your dog not socialized properly as a puppy? Have they had negative experiences with other dogs or people in the past? Did they come to you terrified? Are they a rescue, and you have no idea what they have gone through?

Identifying the cause is the first step in addressing and overcoming their fears, but it can also enlighten and empower you as the parent.

One of the main things I am compelled to make clear when I talk to new clients about this type of behavior is how normal and common it is. This, by no means, means that a dog can't live a beautiful social life eventually, and it definitely doesn't mean a dog is broken. If your dog can warm up to you and trust you, they can do it with others. But they are experiencing fear-based social anxiety. Fear-based reactivity is different from saying, "My dog is aggressive."

The first step in recovery is creating a safe space for socialization. Just as with separation anxiety, the foundation of helping a dog with social anxiety is creating a safe and controlled environment where they can learn, grow, and feel safe without force.

This doesn't mean throwing your dog into the deep end with a sink-or-swim approach at a crowded dog park. (In fact, no dog park, ever! They are so dangerous.) With the sink-or-swim approach, the damage will just continuously be reinforced. Instead, it's about gradual exposure to social situations in a way that feels safe and manageable for them. This is to ensure they come out of every single situation moving forward, thinking, *Oh, that wasn't that bad!* It is important to manipulate the situation to work in your favor. The duration of time and how intense the distraction or trigger is should be something you can control.

Choosing the right people and animals (guests) for the job is tough, but it can be done! Not all dogs or people will be the right fit for your anxious dog, and it is our job to identify who will help and who will hurt. Look for calm, friendly, but indifferent dogs that are known to be good with others, ones that can coexist and not pay your dog too much mind. Similarly, introduce your dog to people who understand dog body language and will give your dog the space they need to warm up in their own time.

When you play your cards right, these positive interactions can slowly build your dog's confidence around others.

What you *don't* want are people who say they are dog lovers and that all dogs love them. *Red flag*! You want people who you know are dog *savvy*, can follow directions, and want to help with no ego involved. These are non-pushy people who have great social awareness, aren't loud, and don't talk with their hands. If the person looks like someone who will reach over a dog's head to pet them or put their face in a dog's face, swipe left!

This is, yet again, something that should be done with the help of a professional behavioral trainer. Just like with Oaklee's journey through separation anxiety, enlisting the help of a professional can be invaluable. A skilled dog trainer or behaviorist who specializes in fear-free or positive reinforcement training methods can work wonders. They can provide you with tailored strategies and support, ensuring your approach is both effective and compassionate. You may be missing key triggers or something that's so simple to tweak that it will improve the situation with less fear and reactivity right from the first second. Or maybe the guest needs to do something different and unorthodox, and it is something you would never think of because you are too far in it and emotionally involved.

This is why doctors aren't allowed to treat their own family members! We don't think clearly or logically when it is our own. Myself included! Anytime something goes on with our dogs, I have to talk it out and back it up with John, my mom, or Dr. Mammen to make sure I am not letting my emotions cloud my judgment or make me miss something important.

Of course, medication needs to be brought up multiple times, as all anxiety can be due to a chemical imbalance, and we cannot expect a dog to improve or give us the desired emotions and behavior if their brain is literally fighting them. Though this topic makes some uncomfortable, it's crucial to understand that, for some dogs, medication can provide the necessary support to overcome their social anxiety. However, it's important to remember that medication should always be considered alongside behavioral modifications and not as the sole solution.

I have to urge some parents to do zero socialization and stressful situations until the medication is on board because pushing the socialization too soon can be extremely damaging. Their dog cannot physically and emotionally handle these interactions.

Medications like fluoxetine and clomipramine, which we discussed in the context of separation anxiety, can also be beneficial for dogs dealing with social anxiety. They can help reduce the overall anxiety level, making social interactions less daunting.

Gabapentin and a high-quality CBD, which are known for their calming effect, can be particularly helpful for one-off stressful events, like a guest coming over for a short visit, a visit to the vet, or a grooming session, which we will discuss more a little later in this chapter.

Again, trazodone should never be given in social situations if a dog is extremely fear based and feels they are trapped or threatened. Remember, this is a sedative and can make them more agitated and vulnerable, causing them to act in a way they might not if they were not on the medication. I call trazodone the "beer muscle drug." If you are at a bar and someone picks a fight with you, you are way more likely to engage in that fight if you're drinking beer than you would if you were sober.

Why?

You are impaired, and your inhibitions are altered, making you feel vulnerable and confident all at the same time. Horrible combo for dogs and people!

We can see the light at the end of the tunnel when we manipulate the power of positive associations with a gentle approach! Creating positive associations with social situations is key. Start small, with short, positive encounters. Treats and praise can go a long way in helping your dog associate other dogs and people with good things.

The exercises I usually suggest are similar to the ones described in Chapter 11. But they are usually done inside, so they are tweaked slightly and are usually cut off quicker because the distance is much shorter. This means the dog may see the trigger as more dangerous and threatening because they are in their home, the trigger is closer, and we are usually sitting and stationary inside.

Remember, it's about baby steps—celebrating the small victories as you gradually increase their exposure to social situations. This could look like a friend stopping over for a quick five to ten minutes for a cup of coffee and your dog has only a mild reaction! Small wins are still wins! Slow and steady is a saying for a reason!

systematic desensitization for social anxiety involves carefully controlled introductions to other dogs and people. This might not be everyone's cup of tea because having a friend over for five minutes and then kicking them out feels rude. But you have to keep in mind that your emotions don't matter. Besides, if your friend offered to help and you explained the situation, rules, and expectations properly, they would not be shocked at being booted after a short period of time. They wouldn't have agreed if your dog wasn't in their best interest. Don't be hesitant to let good friends and family aid you in this process. The pace should always be dictated by your dog's comfort level. Never rush or force interactions. If you are worried about offending your helping hand, either they're not the right hand or you need to work some more things out emotionally with yourself first.

Addressing social anxiety in dogs is not a quick fix; it's a journey that requires patience, understanding, and a lot of love. Every dog is an individual with their own fears and challenges. But with the right approach, your dog can learn to navigate social situations with confidence and calm. Remember, the goal is not to transform your dog into the life of the party but to help them feel safe and secure in the company of others. Do not put expectations on them that they might never meet. If you do so, you might stunt their progress with frustration and hopelessness. Many times, they are making positive changes, but you are so blinded by your own disappointment that you don't see it all paying off.

As we embark on this path together, remember that progress with anxiety of any kind is measured in steps, not leaps. With patience, consistency, and the right support, your dog can overcome their social anxiety, opening the door to a world filled with friendship and joy. Just as Oaklee found his way through the storm of separation anxiety, your dog, too, can find their place in the social world, one paw at a time.

Noise Anxiety and Sensitivity

Ah, the symphony of life—thunderstorms, fireworks, construction sites, kids screaming and crying, and even the humble ding of a household appliance. To us, these sounds might be background noise or minor annoyances, but for dogs with noise anxiety or sensitivity, they can be downright terrifying and constant.

This subchapter dives into the whirlwind world of noise anxiety, offering insights and strategies to help your dog find peace amidst the chaos.

Noise anxiety in dogs isn't just about being a little scared of loud noises; it's a full-blown, paw-trembling fear that can lead to destructive behavior, dangerous escape attempts, or even self-harm. From the booming wrath of a summer thunderstorm to the festive explosions of New Year's fireworks, these auditory experiences can turn your dog's world upside down. But fear not, for understanding and preparation are the keys to tranquility.

As always, first and foremost, recognizing the signs is crucial so you can start to be as proactive as possible. The usual signs of noise anxiety are panting, drooling, pacing, hiding, or even attempting to burrow into furniture and closets. These are not acts of disobedience but cries for help from a pet struggling to cope with their fear.

Remember when we discussed you having a panic attack? No one can simply save you from it just by telling you everything is fine. This type of anxiety is similar to separation anxiety because it leaves parents feeling helpless while the dog's brain is panicking in a manic way.

There are no cues or training exercises you can do consistently every day to cure this because this anxiety is usually sparked by variables outside your control. You never know when a thunderstorm may roll in, when someone may set fireworks off at eleven p.m. on a random-ass Tuesday, or the next-door neighbors may put an addition on their house. We cannot account for all of these things, but we can try!

Much like dealing with separation anxiety, the first step in managing noise anxiety is to create a safe space—a cozy, sound-dampened sanctuary where your dog can retreat when the world outside gets too loud. This could be a quiet room in the house, away from windows and external walls. It could be the bathroom or your closet. Furnish it with their favorite bed, toys, and perhaps a piece of clothing that smells like you for added comfort. This does not work for every dog because some cannot stop pacing, but it can't hurt to try! Wherever this safe haven is, it should feel super safe and be accessible to your pup at all times.

To minimize the intrusion of external noises, consider soundproofing the room with heavy curtains, acoustic panels, or even just blankets over the windows during high-noise events. A white noise machine is the best option. But a soft music playlist can also work wonders in masking the jarring sounds of thunder, fireworks, or construction, providing a soothing auditory buffer for your dog. I prefer the sound machine because the ambient noise drowns out all noise coming in, which is way better than music or TV. If you choose music, classical is said to be the most calming to dogs!

If you want something you can do to be a little more proactive and feel like you are making a difference, think about desensitization and counterconditioning.

Desensitization involves gradually exposing your dog to the sounds that frighten them, but at a much lower volume, and slowly increasing it over time as they become more comfortable. We have done this with the majority of our dogs since day one, solely because before we had kids and started listening to the sound machines through their baby monitors, John and I slept with thunderstorm sounds playing on our Echo. Because our playlist was relaxing and intended for sleep, it was absolutely perfect for desensitizing all our dogs at an early age. This set them up for success. By the time they heard a real thunderstorm, they were pretty unfazed because they'd heard similar noises every night before and during sleep.

This is just one way to desensitize. If you don't like sleeping with anything on at night, you can play these sounds on a low volume for your dog once or twice a day, maybe when you are crate training them or they are peacefully taking a nap on the couch during the day.

The proactiveness doesn't have to stop here! Counterconditioning pairs the scary sound with something positive, like treats or playtime, to change the negative association to a positive one. So, put the thunderstorm sounds on again while giving your dog treats and praise every so often. Or let them have frozen enrichment the whole time the thunder is playing. Not only will they get desensitized to the noise and be unfazed, but they will start to subconsciously associate the thunder with positive, fun things. So when real thunder hits, they may just stay asleep or look around for some fun enrichment to keep them busy!

Together, these techniques can be powerful tools in reducing noise anxiety. However, like all the other techniques we've covered, they require patience and consistency. Obviously, we used thunder just as an example here, but these techniques can work for many different types of noises—fireworks, vacuums, and household appliances your dog is sensitive to—and get them used to the cries of a newborn baby before the baby comes home from the hospital.

Timing is everything when it comes to some of these sounds and situations, but that doesn't mean it is always possible for us pet parents to anticipate or time properly.

For dogs sensitive to thunder and fireworks, trying to stay ahead of the game and knowing when these things will happen is the best way to help. Unfortunately, we can't always do this because the weather is unpredictable and sneaky. Similarly, humans who set off fireworks outside the normal fireworks holidays are also unpredictable and sneaky. Oh, and inconsiderate. Your plan for fireworks and thunder should be safe haven, patience, and interventions.

Interventions help because, yet again, behavioral modifications and practices cannot always penetrate a mind in full-on panic. High-quality CBD or prescribed medications can provide additional support that helps your dog start to make lasting changes with decreased anxiety. As discussed in previous parts of this chapter, these options can help reduce overall anxiety levels, making it easier for your dog to cope with noise and start to recover emotionally.

For this specifically, Sileo is a great option to discuss with your vet. It is an oromucosal gel formulation of dexmedetomidine hydrochloride indicated for the treatment of canine noise aversion. In short, you can squeeze this gel into your dog's inner jowl area to seriously reduce stress and anxiety in a matter of minutes. It is pretty incredible, especially when a dog is inconsolable or unrecognizable during these troubled times. Only drawback is, this is not something to be used daily if your dog is agitated by normal daily sounds.

Now, other types of noises or noise-sensitive situations can be a little more tricky. Planning walks during quieter times of the day or choosing routes that avoid known construction areas can be helpful. I had a client who would walk their dog only at nine p.m. because most everyone was inside, construction noises rarely ever happened, and the delivery trucks were rarer. This is always a great start, but our goal should always be to get over the hump and gradually move toward times with more normal noises.

Also, so many parents are walking their dogs so much longer than the dogs can emotionally handle. We have this idea that to be good parents, we have to walk our dogs three times a day. COVID and being home consistently with our dogs didn't help much with this because it was the only real socialization some of us humans got. And since the stimuli were so low, the dogs didn't seem to mind back then. But now there is way more chaos out on the streets, and stacking can happen easily. This is something all pet parents should avoid.

Stacking is when a dog experiences a stressful encounter and essentially travels up the ladder of reactivity or stress. The more situations they encounter without time to emotionally recover in between, the worse and worse the reactivity or stress will get.

Picture a tower of blocks built by a toddler. The more blocks stacked on, the more fragile the whole structure becomes. For example, your dog may hear three different loud noises in the distance and start to panic. Each time, their stress meter goes up a little more. The fourth time, they just hear a neighbor close their garage door in the distance, which is not as loud as the previous three loud noises. But the dog tries to take off for home, and you are confused and frustrated because the garage door on its own wasn't that big of a deal. But because your dog was stacked emotionally, they did not have the bandwidth to handle it.

This happens a lot with reactivity on leash, as well. The longer they walk, the more fearful and reactive they become, making them less and less tolerant.

This is similar to kids! We see kids on vacations or in restaurants having a full-on tantrum, and we say to ourselves, "What's wrong with that kid?"

Well, truth be told, we don't know. But if I can make a guess? That kid is not in their normal home or bedroom, so they are out of their element and probably exhausted. Some parents of young kids are overzealous with vacations and always schedule a busy itinerary.

I'm some parents. I'm talking about myself.

Maybe that kid didn't get to nap like they normally do. This is a recipe for disaster. Then, as parents, we are frustrated and mad even though *we created this outcome*. If we can't avoid the busy schedule, we at least need to not get frustrated and add to the chaos. Because that kid's chaos and flip-out make all the sense in the world. Stressed, overstimulated, overtired, overwhelmed kids tend to melt down, and so do dogs. But as parents, we don't get to get upset about the messes we are responsible for with the tiny humans and the adorable dogs that can't speak up and say, "I'd like to go home now!"

My main advice: stop walking for so long.

Start with five to ten minutes, and as your dog's issues improve, you can try to extend for longer. But truthfully, if you do not identify this, your dog may start to negatively associate walks and not even want to get leashed up or leave the house anymore due to this fearful stacking. This is not only extremely isolating, it's also dangerous. What if there is an emergency and you need to get them in the car immediately, but they won't get the leash on or leave the front door?

You do not need to walk your dog every day to be a good dog parent. I'm gonna say it again. *You do not need to walk your dog every day to be a good dog parent*! In fact, you don't need to walk them at all. But you should keep up on the things that will help you avoid delay in an emergency situation, like periodically leashing up and walking out front or in the backyard for a few minutes and then back in the house. Or leashing up, getting in the car, having a few treats, and then immediately going back in the house. These little activities help in stressful, time-constrained situations when we need our dogs to go with the flow. We've got to set them up for success to do so!

When discussing unavoidable, everyday noises in the home, like fire alarms, appliance dings, doorbells, etc., preparing your dog ahead of time with treats and distractions can help mitigate their anxiety. I'm currently working with a dog that was terrified of the noises the dryer makes when it's finished. His parents had just moved to a new place with a new dryer, and he panicked the first time he heard it. He never got used to it. Mom and

Dad were managing the issue by doing the wash only when he was out of the house or asleep in their bedroom with the door closed. We wanted to push past this, so I had them start small! (This method is great for vacuums and hair dryers as well!)

They did have to get him on an SSRI medication first because his anxiety was through the roof. Also, he was afraid of many other noises and situations. But once the meds kicked in, we got started.

First, we used frozen bone enrichment to help him relax in these situations. He would be in their room with a bone with the door open and hear the noise in the distance. Mom and Dad would be near him, going about their business but nonchalantly keeping an eye on him to make sure he was recovering when he heard the noise. If he heard the noise and paused his licking, they would praise him and throw treats while continuing to fold laundry or do similar chores. This let him know that the dinging signified great things but that Mom and Dad were not going over the top and coddling, which would agree that the noise was scary.

Once his anxiety decreased in this situation, we moved him a bit closer to the noise. This was decreasing the distance and increasing the stimulus because the noise sounded closer, which meant it was louder and more prominent to the dog. Every time Mom and Dad moved a bit closer, they did the same thing until he was ready for the next step. After only a month of doing this exercise a few times per week, they can now run the laundry whenever they feel like it, and he is either unfazed or just puts more distance between himself and the noise, which is amazing progress!

We can work our asses off as parents, and our dogs can make great progress. But sometimes, despite our best efforts, an unexpected noise event can send our dogs into a panic. Having an emergency plan in place—whether it's a ready-to-go safe space, a calming supplement or medication on hand, or a quick distraction technique—can make all the difference in these moments. Always keep in mind that life is a gamble, we can't account for every variable, and setbacks are inevitable, at least at one time or another. Expect it so you aren't disappointed. And when it doesn't happen, you'll be elated!

Last, never underestimate the power of a support system. Connecting with fellow pet parents, trainers, and veterinarians who understand noise anxiety can provide additional resources, tips, and moral support. When we are able to discuss our struggles in a judgment-free environment, we can vent and ask questions about progress without feeling like we are the only one in the world feeling or dealing with the same thing. Why suffer in silence? There are plenty of parents who have been where you are and are now on the other side, eager to help you achieve the same thing!

In conclusion, managing noise anxiety and sensitivity in dogs is about preparation, patience, and understanding. By recognizing the signs, creating a safe environment, employing soundproofing and desensitization techniques, and knowing when to seek additional help, you can help your dog navigate their fears so they come out on the other side braver and more tolerant.

Remember, the goal isn't to eliminate their anxiety but to equip them with the tools and support they need to face the noisy world with confidence and the ability to recover. Together, you and your dog can find harmony in the chaos, one soothing sound at a time.

Travel Anxiety

For the wanderlust-stricken among us, the thought of a road trip with our dog conjures images of joyous exploration. Yet for our canine companions with travel anxiety, the journey is anything but joyous. They are not picturing rainbows and sunsets, that is for sure! Travel anxiety in dogs is a road less desired yet frequently encountered by pet parents. It intertwines with the fabric of other anxieties we've explored—separation, social, noise—but it takes its own unique form in the context of car rides, public transport, or any form of travel that takes a dog out of their comfort zone. This subchapter is a concise guide that draws from our discussions on other anxieties and steers you and your pup toward smoother travels.

Travel anxiety can stem from a variety of sources: unfamiliar motion, motion sickness, the sound of the engine, confinement in a moving vehicle, not being able to get to you while you drive, or negative associations with car rides (like going to the vet, being surrendered to a shelter, or being dumped on the side of the road). For some dogs, the mere sight of their harness and keys together can trigger anxiety as they anticipate the stress and anxiety that often comes with it.

As with other forms of anxiety, the principles of a safe space, behavioral modification, and, when necessary, medication hold true. The goal is to transform travel from a source of stress into an opportunity for calm, fun, positive experiences.

When anxiety impedes progress, consulting with a veterinarian about the use of medication or CBD, as touched upon above, can provide the necessary calm to facilitate behavioral training. It's not about sedation but rather reducing the anxiety to a level where learning and adaptation can occur. For this topic, I am not just talking about antianxiety supplements. If your dog is experiencing motion sickness, they need something to help them. Imagine feeling super sick every time you get into the car. I can relate so hard to this, as I have motion sickness from a car accident I was in. And if anyone is driving other than me, it is god awful. When I fly on planes, I have to take a high dose of Dramamine to get through it, and I still don't feel 100 percent. Even though I do not have a fear of flying, I don't fly often for this reason. I hate how I feel. It will take me half a day to feel like myself again.

A dog experiencing the same thing will absolutely associate that horrible feeling with the car if they feel sick every single time. So, you need to make sure they aren't experiencing actual nausea during this time. And if they are, you need to get the necessary medication from the vet. Not all nausea ends in vomiting. Sometimes it's just drool or wobbliness. Keep a lookout for these symptoms, and try to reduce food before a car ride.

In addition to making them mentally and medically comfortable, you can also start by making the vehicle a welcoming place. Introduce your dog to the car in a stationary state, allowing them to explore and find comfort with treats and praise. Similar to the other techniques, keep it short and sweet, like two to three minutes tops, with just treats, praise, and exploring.

Once they aren't showing any real aversion to the car being stationary, you can sit in the driveway with the car on and just continue with the praise and treats without movement.

When they don't seem to mind that, you can go for a slow ride around the block and come right back. This drive should not exceed two minutes, especially if your dog is showing stress.

Gradually progress to short, pleasant drives to nearby fun destinations. I'm talking McDonald's for a vanilla cone or Wendy's for a vanilla frosty! Drive-through, super fun, yummy, and fast! And then head right home. This builds a positive association, dismantling the fear brick by brick.

What if you can't get your dog physically in the car?

You are not alone. So many clients come here to my farm, and the struggle is real. I have to help them get the dog back in, but the situation can be remedied with a positive, excited attitude that does not waver or get frustrated easily; high-value treats; and less pressure. Yes, less pressure!

Many times, we corner our dogs to get them to jump in the car. They dislike this! They will push back every time. Instead, sprinkle high-value treats in the car, where they can get them before jumping in or up. Then put a bunch farther in, where they can see but can't reach till they get up there. Keep replacing a few treats that are easily attainable. This motivates them to want more.

Using a long line can be helpful too. Especially if the door to your back seat doesn't open far and it is close quarters. Now, if your dog puts their paws up and comes back down, still praise and get excited with more treats! That is a breakthrough! They are getting more comfortable.

If they are still struggling, you can try to have a second person go to the other side of the car and open the other door. This person can reach through and try to lure the dog with treats inside. Once they do jump up, give tons of praise and treats, then let them jump back down. Let them practice going up and down! For some dogs, it's a confidence about jumping up, especially as they get older.

Funny and pathetic story time! Oaklee is a therapy dog, and for about two years before having kids, I would take him to a school once a month to do the Read to Dog Program. He had two other dog friends there, both female. He loved them, and we called them his girlfriends. Well, when we were leaving one day, Oaklee was feeling pretty good about himself as he said goodbye to his ladies. We went to get into my Ford F-150 pickup, which is a jump for him. He wasn't fully paying attention because he was so jazzed about his friends. So he missed the jump, smacked his cute, little face on the floor of the truck, and fumbled up into the cab. Thankfully, the only thing that got hurt was his ego! The poor boy had a hard time jumping up for a few months because he remembered tripping, and it was tough on his confidence. It was so sad, but we worked through it with a lot of patience and encouragement. Now he is as good as new! But just that one simple time made him self-conscious about doing something he'd successfully done thousands of times.

Behavioral modification techniques like desensitization and counterconditioning play a crucial role. Gradual exposure to the elements of travel, combined with positive reinforcements, can change your dog's emotional response to traveling. Just like with noise anxiety, playing familiar, soothing sounds can create a calm environment within the vehicle. And we want to play our cards right and keep all the interactions super short in the beginning, then work our way up to normal times in the car.

Why do I emphasize travel training? Beyond the joy of adventure, it's about necessity. In emergencies, the ability to safely and quickly transport your dog is paramount. Whether you're evacuating during a dangerous situation or rushing to the vet, the last thing you need is a panicked pet who won't get in the car. Training for travel is as much about safety as it is about well-being. So, get creative with your techniques!

The strategies we've outlined—creating a positive travel environment, employing behavioral modification, considering medication, and recognizing the critical nature of this training—offer a path forward. Like any journey, it begins with a single step. For our dogs, that step is toward a vehicle, not with trepidation but with trust, guided by our understanding and patience. Together, we can shift the world from a place to fear to one to explore, one calm ride at a time.

Veterinary and Grooming Anxiety

Ah, the dreaded vet and groomer visits. Necessary for our dogs' health and well-being, yet sometimes feared like that damn monster under the bed. Our challenge is to make these outings less about the destination and more about the journey—filled with, you guessed it, treats, praise, compassion, and understanding.

Vet and grooming visits are essential aspects of a dog's life. However, these experiences can be incredibly stressful for some pets, leading to what's known as vet or grooming anxiety. This type of anxiety stems from fear of the unknown, previous negative experiences, or the discomfort of being handled by strangers.

Recognizing the signs of anxiety in your dog during vet or grooming visits is crucial. These can include excessive panting, drooling, shaking, hiding, stiffness, shutting down, or even aggressive behavior. It's important to understand that this anxiety is a natural response to what the dog perceives as a threatening situation.

Dogs secrete stress hormones, and the vet's office is one of the places where this happens the most, for obvious reasons. Your dog steps into the lobby, smells the intense cortisol, and immediately thinks, *Get me out of here. Something is wrong!* This is a normal survival skill. We just need to be a little more understanding of that immediate reaction because we don't know what they are experiencing emotionally. They are acting appropriately to what their body is telling them to do to survive.

Thankfully, there are many ways to reduce vet and grooming anxiety, but we need to tread lightly. Pre-visit preparation, which is gradually getting your dog accustomed to being handled, can be helpful. Regularly touch their paws, ears, and tails so they become used to the sensations they might experience during a vet exam or grooming session.

But I do not suggest doing this like many of the other dog trainers out there suggest. What do I mean by this? By just touching and asserting ourselves without taking note of how the dog feels about it or making the situation a positive experience, we can do a lot of harm—very similar to sticking our hands in a dog's food and getting a food guarder as a result. I say this because I know this from personal experience.

Poor Pudgalina. She is our first baby, and we adopted her as I was getting my first certification. She was essentially, for lack of a better word, our guinea pig. We used the old method of touching her paws, ears, tail, butt area, etc. In the beginning, it was fine. But as she got older, she began to have an aversion to all things handling and grooming. She is a long-haired Chihuahua mix, so she needs to be shaved just on her body and her feet. She's good about most of it, but that's because I worked for a groomer for over a year. She received baths, trims, and full haircuts regularly. And she started disliking it as she hit her eighth-month mark. The feet are the worst, such as cutting nails and her grinchy toes, which consist of the long hair that grows out from her paw pads. She *hated* these two things.

That is when it dawned on me: you can't *just* desensitize. You have to do counterconditioning simultaneously and create some structure. And this can differ for each dog. Pudge hates her feet and her butt being slightly touched. She's tiny, so I get it! Some dogs are weird about being touched around the head, held, or restrained. These are all things you can practice prior to going to the vet so your dog not only has been desensitized but has good associations with it.

Use treats and affection to create positive associations with the vet or groomer. You should never enter the vet's office without your treat pouch on! Consider taking your dog to the vet or grooming location for social visits that don't involve exams or grooming to build positive experiences. I have a client who has a small Chiweenie. He's a little guy—eight pounds, if that—and prior to us working together, he was basically terrified of life. One of the main things we needed to accomplish was muzzle training and creating an improved relationship with vet visits. He would get so worked up that even the vet was nervous he was going to have a heart attack or seizure from the stress. Mom worked from home and had a light schedule, so she was able to take him in the car two to three times a week to the vet's office. She's so dedicated to him that it makes me want to cry.

At first, we started with just driving there, sitting in the parking lot, giving lots of treats and praise (and maybe some ice cream), and heading home. The next step was sitting in the parking lot for a few, getting out, walking in the grass for a few minutes, getting back in the car, and heading home. About a month in, she'd go into the lobby, circle around, get some treats from the receptionists and techs working up front, go back outside, and head home!

Each time, Mom spent a little more time without any negative outcome. He got to the point of enjoying these little struts into the lobby and getting treats like it was Halloween. He wasn't shaking or hesitant anymore. It was a miracle. Not really—it was proper training—but it was pretty fucking awesome!

She then started to have him walk around with his muzzle on to help him associate the muzzle with fun. This worked for him! Then we got to the point where Dr. Mammen would allow him into a room, and nothing bad would happen—just treats and praise. They just kept working to a good place. So much so that he was able to go into a room, get a quick shot with minimal restraint, and recover quickly.

Mom was so proud of him, but I was proud of her. She put so much time and energy into his health. Yes, his anxiety, but truly, his health. Before this, he needed to get sedated every time he needed to be looked at, and it wasn't healthy for him to go through that every few months. But she got him to such a good place. Yes, it took time, but it was so worth it!

Now, everything I just discussed will *not* work unless you master this next one: choosing the right professional! You should *never* settle when it comes to a vet or groomer. Search for professionals who are experienced in handling anxious dogs. Some are specially trained to work with fearful pets and can make a significant difference in your dog's comfort level. These professionals are certified in fear-free training!

On the other hand, *run* from vets and groomers if you see these red flags:

- They want to immediately muzzle without giving you time to desensitize your dog first.
- They want your dog on trazodone before they see them again simply because your dog growled at them.
- They want to restrain your dog by holding them down on the floor no matter what your dog's response is.
- They want to take your dog in the back for a nail trim.

There are so many better ways to handle all of these things. Which vet do you think I described first?

Dr. Mammen!

I send the majority of my local clients to Dr. Mammen specifically because she takes her time and is not fearful or intimidated by fearful, reactive dogs. She *wants* to help them overcome this and get better at going to the vet. This is why she became a vet! So she and her staff put the work in, grab peanut butter and treats, get on the floor, and do whatever else is necessary to keep the dog happy and stress-free. They even do something called the dog lift, which is a little trapeze situation where they hoist the dog up in the air, safely using the doorframe. The vet tech is feeding the dog peanut butter and treats while the doctor is behind, quickly clipping all twenty nails. No restraint, limited stress, and no risk of injury to anyone. The whole ordeal takes maybe two minutes. The dog lift contraption is genius, in my opinion. This is a great way to improve nail trims.

But what if this isn't available to you? There are many ways other than taking your dog into the back and doing God knows what!

There are the nail file boards, which I find pretty inventive. This is basically a big nail file on a board that you can train your dog to scratch, thus allowing them to file down their own nails at their own pace. The only drawback is that it can take a long time if you are starting with really long nails. Plus, you need to remember to do it often if your dog's nails grow fast. This tool is better for maintenance and needs to be done consistently! Your dog also needs to be willing to do the scratching. Not all dogs love this or are food motivated enough to do it consistently, so make sure your dog has the right personality for this type of training.

We have worked through it with Pudge using patience and systematic desensitization. We will make sure she is feeling safe and loved, and then we will clip only one nail at a time. Then we leave it alone. This way, she isn't stressed and freaking out as we try to get all twenty at one time. We get one nail, praise and treat her like the queen she is, and let her go back about her business. This works for her and a lot of other clients, as well. We have also figured out that she does so much better when John holds her and I am the clipper. She feels safe with John, so we roll with it!

Now, I have some clients who push it and will go for more than one or two nails at a time, even though that isn't the protocol. Then they tell me that the next nail trim after was a disaster. The dog won't come out of the crate and won't go back on the couch where they attempted to cut the nails.

Well, yeah! No shit. I create a protocol for a reason. I am trying to show your dog that:

- It doesn't hurt.
- It will be quick.
- They can trust you to stop before they get too stressed. If you ruin that for your dog, I can't force them to believe it.

I have this one dad client who means well, but he is just so rough around the edges with expectations. He's a first-time dog dad, and I think he was raised in a matter-of-fact way. He'll say, "I should be able to do _______!"

In reality, no. You shouldn't be able to do anything just because you are a human and your dog is a dog. Your dog doesn't like nail trims! If your doctor wants to give you four vaccines, it is your right to say, "No, I am fearful of shots. I can only handle one or two right now." What if they said you needed to have the four because they are the doctor and you are the patient?

Anyone who says, "I should be able to do it all at once," is putting their own convenience over their dog's fears and discomfort.

Think better, be better, do better. You wouldn't want the same thing done to you if the roles were reversed.

This technique goes for all grooming—ear cleaning, teeth brushing, wrinkle cleaning, nose moisturizing, butt cleaning, paw wiping, removing a tick, etc. Some dogs do not like these things and may even land a bite over it. Getting your dog more comfortable with these necessary services may take some time, but we can get there. Try having them sit in the same spot, giving a cue like, "*Paw*," then giving treats and praise without doing anything to the paw except holding it. Ears, same thing. Have them sit and wait while you touch the ear, praise, and treat! Then you gradually get to the point of doing what you need to do. You just need to be patient and take your time so they can get more comfortable. Adding a cue can help them know what to expect as well!

Anxiety aids may be needed here. If this is the only anxiety your dog experiences, I suggest a high-quality CBD that you can use just in time for systematic desensitization sessions! Products like calming collars, anxiety vests, or natural supplements can help soothe your dog's anxiety as well, but I am not overwhelmed by their success. Still, they can't hurt! Consult with your vet about these options and whether medication might be appropriate for severe cases.

Ultimately, we have to stay calm and positive. Dogs can pick up on our emotions, so maintaining a calm and positive demeanor during visits can help ease their anxiety. If you are nervous and scared, your dog will be too. If you don't feel comfortable doing basic husbandry techniques that are necessary for your dog's health, reach out to the consultant to get you kick-started in the right direction.

As pet parents, our goal is to ensure our pup family members live happy, healthy lives. Addressing the various forms of anxiety they may face, including vet and grooming anxiety, is a testament to the depth of our love and commitment to their well-being. It requires (*a lot*) of patience, understanding, and sometimes a bit of creativity. But the rewards—a happy, confident dog—are immeasurable.

Remember, managing anxiety is not only about the immediate comfort of our dogs but also about building their overall confidence and trust. Each small step we take to help them overcome their fears strengthens the bond we share. It helps us lay the foundation for a resilient, trusting relationship with those who have the ability to put their health first. Like our vets, dog trainers, dog walkers, and groomers. Which is so unbelievably important!

In closing up all this anxiety talk, let's remind ourselves that dealing with dog anxiety, much like any aspect of pet parenting, is a journey. It's filled with ups and downs, successes and setbacks. We have to accept this part! But with each challenge we overcome together, we forge a deeper connection with our beloved dogs. So let's continue to approach our dogs' anxieties with empathy, patience, and unwavering support, knowing that our efforts are building a safer, happier world for them. Your dedication to understanding and alleviating your dog's anxieties not only improves their quality of life but also serves as a powerful reminder of the incredible bond between dogs and their humans. Real talk—we have the ability to make their lives *better*. What a gift!

Ignore any family member or friend who is giving their uneducated two cents, and advocate for your dog. Show your kids, grandkids, nieces, and nephews how to properly take care of, respect, and unconditionally love a dog, no matter what—just like you would do for them!

Chapter 14:
How Dogs Socialize

Ah, now we get to the meat and potatoes that every dog parent should be wondering about at one time or another: the art of dog-on-dog socialization! This is a delicate dance, but most parents treat it like the Macarena.

Am I dating myself? I swear I am not that old. If you are too young to know what the Macarena dance is, grow up and educate yourself! No one needs that kind of negativity!

Socialization is not just a part of dog training; it's a cornerstone of raising a well-adjusted, confident, and happy dog. It's about more than just playing or interacting with other dogs; it's about teaching your dog the nuanced language of canine communication, understanding boundaries, and fostering positive interactions. This chapter delves into the dos and don'ts of dog socialization, drawing from years of experience and the horrible social media content we see on the daily.

Socialization is a complex, essential process in dog development, encompassing much more than mere exposure to other dogs and people. It's about understanding and facilitating your dog's ability to communicate, interpret, and engage with their world respectfully and confidently. This chapter integrates crucial aspects of dog communication, play, greeting etiquette, and signs of trouble, providing a comprehensive guide to nurturing a well-adjusted canine. Unless you want to have to reread about reactivity in Chapter 11 months from now and kick your own ass for not doing this the right way, please pay attention!

How can we expect our dogs to understand dog communication if we don't? Dog communication is multifaceted, involving a combination of visual signals, vocalizations, and body language. Recognizing and interpreting these cues is fundamental to successful socialization. For our dogs' sake, we have to help them through the trials and tribulations.

Visual communication: Dogs convey feelings and intentions through body posture, tail and ear positioning, eye gaze, facial expressions, and more. A play bow, for instance, signals a friendly invitation to engage, while a stiff body and a side-eye may indicate discomfort or be a precursor for a correction.

Auditory communication: Vocal cues, like barks, growls, whines, and sighs, provide additional context to a dog's emotional state. Understanding the nuances of these sounds can help you better interpret your dog's needs and warnings.

The importance of proper play is huge! Regular interaction with other dogs is vital for maintaining social skills, especially for smarty-pants dogs! Happy dummies can kind of pick up where they left off with socialization if they had a good upbringing. Play allows dogs to practice communication, learn to control the intensity of their bites and bodies, understand the concept of taking turns, and figure out when to stop play appropriately and without force. It's essential for parents to ensure their dogs are paired with appropriate playmates and to supervise these interactions closely to prevent play from escalating into aggression. This is something our society tends to not do. We don't know what to look for and what to avoid. We also tend to easily get distracted and complacent.

Do you know how to look at another dog and spot characteristics that do not jibe with your dog? You need to know all these so you do not put your dog in a tight spot and so your dog doesn't accidentally piss off another dog.

When I am looking for appropriate play, there are a few markers that I know are solid. The best one is the double play bow! I mean, it even sounds adorable. Play bowing is when a dog lets the front half of their body hit the ground while they keep their butt up in the air. Their face will be low and in the middle of their front paws while they look up at the dog they are trying to engage with. I say this marker means they are gravy. In other words, there's no conflict here. But the other dog needs to reciprocate. Not every dog gives up the fun play bow that easily. Some dogs may be more reserved, aren't big players, or don't like to coexist with others.

Other physical signs to look for are loose, relaxed bodies and loose tail wags. You don't want to see stiff bodies and tense tail wags. Playful tail wags are wobbly and wacky—they have no rhyme or reason to them. A floppy tail is what you want!

Another is inhibited biting, which is play biting that does not produce pain on the receiver. You can spot this by seeing the bite happen without a physical or emotional response from the other dog. For instance, if one of your dogs bites your other dog in the neck and the bitten dog just keeps walking or ignoring their attacker, you can bet there is no pain involved. The dog that's biting isn't using any pressure. This is an amazing skill to have.

The last thing to look for is reciprocal actions. If your dog is making attempts and is all over another dog, and the other dog is playing back, it's gravy. If the other dog is stiff and giving the cold shoulder, it is a no-go, at least for now. I always tell my clients that if both dogs are actively playing, switching between dominant and submissive stances (one on top and one pinned on the bottom, then switching without issues), running away, coming back, giving each other the breaks they need, and no one is bleeding or crying, you are usually in the clear! All these signs indicate that all dogs are enjoying the interaction and learning valuable social skills.

Greeting other dogs properly is usually where the downfall starts. As discussed in Chapter 11, proper introductions are critical in preventing conflicts and fostering positive relationships between dogs.

Start in a neutral territory, and always avoid face-to-face greetings on leash, which can lead to heightened emotions and misunderstandings.

So, if we can't let our dogs meet face-to-face, what do we do?

Pair walking!

Walking dogs together but at a distance allows them to get accustomed to each other's presence gradually. Use treats and praise to reinforce the presence of the other dog. Give them a few minutes to self-regulate. If they're excited or nervous, give them a beat. As you walk and get closer, the dogs can sniff the ground, go to the bathroom, and focus on something other than each other, which helps them make better decisions when meeting.

When they meet face-to-face instead, it is all about the dog in front of them, and they have nothing to help them split their brain. They can make bad or impulsive choices, make the other dog feel overwhelmed, or feel overwhelmed themselves because they are too fixated. Any of these can lead to a disaster. Dogs should always feel like they can retreat when socializing, especially on leash.

Try to picture yourself walking. Having someone on your right while you face forward feels a lot better than someone staring you down and making you feel stuck because you can only move forward. All my awkward, introverted, "I don't know what to do with my hands while I talk" readers know exactly what I am talking about! It's awkward! It's way better to have an activity to do while getting to know someone new.

Moms and Dads, you gotta read the body language! Observe the dogs' approaches. Polite dogs usually sniff each other in a curved path rather than straight on and directly. Oaklee will legit stand sideways and just gently tilt his head a little to get a sniff. It is the most innocent thing I have ever seen. He especially does this when he knows the other dog is nervous. He doesn't want to undo the trust he's gained by going in aggressively for a butt sniff. Oaklee is truly a socialization wizard! I'm impressed by him daily.

Watch for signs of discomfort or aggression, then intervene if necessary. If your dog abrasively approaches another dog for a sniff, this is not your dog being friendly. This is your dog being *rude*, and you are allowing it. Stop it. You are making other dogs feel uncomfortable and putting the other dog and your dog in jeopardy of having an issue. Again, do not just pass this off as friendliness. It's just abrasive and obnoxious!

Just remember, all behavior is communication. So, if your dog or the other dog reacted randomly, do not reprimand. Fight the urge! Something spooked them, and that's allowed and valid. Maybe they didn't like how the situation felt. Or perhaps their stress hit its limit, and they needed to get it out. You don't get to tell them no about that.

For example, Oaklee was helping two Frenchie brothers socialize in a session at the farm one day. It was going well, and everyone was chill. They all went to smell something in a similar spot, and Oaklee made the mistake of flapping his ears. I think a bug flew by. Luigi, one of the brothers, growled and lunged at him. He didn't make contact, and it was just a warning. Oaklee gave a little growl back, and they both did a stress shake, which is excellent and necessary regulation. Nothing needed correcting. Luigi just got scared! Oaklee is *huge* compared to him, and he got nervous. He let Oaklee know, then they both shook their stress off to start over and recover, and they went back to hanging out. All good!

So many parents get nervous about this and want to make sure it never happens. But that's just not real life. If we want to have dogs and socialize, then we need to put our own limitations aside or not put our dogs in situations that we emotionally can't handle. Socialization between dogs is natural, normal, and necessary! The necessity is to make sure that the punishment fits the crime! If Luigi had bit Oaklee multiple times for shaking his head a few feet away, it would have been a different conversation. But he did everything right.

If you are choosing to be a dog parent who socializes your dog with a lot of dogs, recognizing signs of trouble is imperative. Understanding when an interaction is going south is crucial for preventing conflicts and ensuring the safety of all dogs involved. We don't want any scuffles or PTSD moments for your dog!

Signs of trouble include avoidance, prolonged standing over and staring, excessive yelping, mounting, stiffness, hard staring, escalating growls, and warning barks. The second you start to notice any of these behaviors from your dog or another, intervene excitedly to distract abruptly. Or distract calmly if you feel you don't want to spook the other dog.

This kind of social interaction for humans is tough too. Like ridiculously fucking tough because humans are struggling severely with communicating right now as a society, let alone monitoring another species. Another parent might not be paying attention at all and just be on their phone the whole time. Or they might say, "Oh no, my dog is super friendly. That's just how they play." Or maybe they say, "They're dogs. They'll work it out!"

Red flags. Red flags. Red flags. This is not the time for you to be people-pleasing, nonconfrontational, or passive. Get your fucking dog out of there ASAP! You don't owe these random people anything. You do owe your dog a second perspective and safety. When something doesn't feel right, it's because it's not. Trust your gut and go home! In no way does whatever they *think* about you and your dog have anything to do with you or actually matter, so put that shit aside and get out of there.

That leads us to the key considerations for socializing your dog.

Is the dog park really necessary? Is it worth it?

I avoid dog parks altogether and at all costs. The unpredictable nature of dog parks can make them hot spots for negative encounters. I'd rather opt for controlled environments where interactions can be closely monitored.

Day care is a great alternative. I know that not everyone wants to spend the money on that. Or maybe you want to physically be there with your dog and make it a fun experience for both of you. I get it. There are alternatives. If the dog park is a must or if it's the only place where your dog gets real exercise, try to avoid the park at the height of the insanity. Exchange numbers with a few other parents you like and whose dogs your dog likes, then plan to meet up at the same time each week when no one else is usually at the park. Manipulate your situation to work for you!

Another alternative is renting a Sniffspot. This is basically Airbnb for dogs, so you rent the whole park to yourself! We have one on our farm, and we love it. It's a whole acre where dog parents can come with their pups and just let them run. A lot of these dogs live in apartments and do not have backyards, so they don't have a place to roam and get the exercise they need. Some of them are extremely reactive and can't be around other animals, so this is a sanctuary for them. If you still want your dog to play, have those other dog parents you met and like split the small cost of renting one with you just for your pups, then have an uninterrupted blast! We've had family reunions and doggy birthday parties here as well! Our Sniffspot has running water, picnic tables, an umbrella, a 120-foot line, toys, a poop station, and a baby pool! My next goals are some lights and a firepit for some extended summer fun out there!

If you choose to go the day care route, ensure that it's reputable and practices positive reinforcement and proper socialization techniques. Just like any other profession, not all doggy day cares are created equal. You want a place that's clean, has cameras, and maintains a proper dogs-to-attendant ratio. The first place I worked at when I was starting in this field had four separate "parks"—two small-dog sections, one for medium-sized dogs, and one for big dogs. There were anywhere from five to fifteen dogs in each park.

Guess how many attendants there were per park.

One half.

Yep, that's correct. Only two attendants were watching all four of the parks. So, if you were in with the medium-sized dogs and a fight broke out in the big-dog section, you had to open the gate without any of the medium dogs getting into the big-dog section and get to the fight within seconds.

Do you know how difficult that is?

It was ridiculous but also dangerous. This was obviously so the owner could save on paying employees. Horrible, in my opinion. So, always ask a lot of questions. Don't just assume that all companies do things the correct way or follow the laws.

You also want to make sure that the attendants are nice to the dogs. I worked with one girl who kicked the dogs. I was mortified. One, I can't even fathom kicking a dog. But two, why do you work at a doggy day care if you are going to kick a dog for it jumping on you? You are in the wrong profession. Please go home.

So yes, cameras are a must. You also want a place that communicates properly about how your dog is doing and makes sure its employees are gentle and sweet with your dog, even when you are not there.

Regardless of what, where, or who you turn to for socialization, advocating for your dog in all capacities is most important: You know your dog best. Trust your instincts, and remove your dog from any situation that feels off or unsafe. This is the best frickin' thing you can do for them. Second-guessing any situation for even a second more could turn a small issue into a full-on traumatic experience for everyone involved.

So many clients come to be with dog reactivity or aggression, and it always starts with, "This one time at the dog park . . ." That's honestly all I need to hear to know what we are dealing with. It is just so unbelievably avoidable! No more dog parks or unsafe socialization on the side of the road with strangers! Just say NO!

Communication and boundaries are good! Say it with me! *Communication and boundaries are good.* This goes for humans too. Speak up! If you feel uncomfortable telling someone to stop doing something to you, it's most likely because, somewhere along the line as a kid or young adult, you were told not to stand up for yourself, whether directly or inadvertently.

Parents sometimes quiet their kids so they're not embarrassed by "inappropriate behavior" or to avoid inconveniencing other people. For example, if you didn't want a shot when you were taken to the doctor, your parent might have made you just get over it or told the doctor to do it anyway without helping you through it mentally or emotionally. In little situations like this, kids learn that their emotions aren't safe or wanted. They learn to clam up and just let people around them do whatever to appease them. They think that's how they achieve love and affection.

This is garbage and also extremely dangerous! Do we want our kids to do what some adult tells them to do just because the adult is older? Do we want our kids' safety features to be turned off so they blindly follow anyone?

Our dogs can start to show the same people-pleasing tendencies that we were unfortunate enough to accrue. We pass our shit down to our kids and our dogs, and it is time to stop now.

Never reprimand your dog for communicating discomfort or setting boundaries. Instead, understand what they're trying to convey and respond appropriately. If a dog is playing in a way your dog does not like or is getting in your dog's face when your dog is done playing, your dog *needs* to be able to say, "Please stop." But a dog's only way to do this is usually by growling, barking, or showing teeth, which provokes us humans to immediately say, "Hey! *No*, don't do that. Play nice."

Well, the nicest thing your dog can do is give a clear warning. Would you rather them sit there and take it until they finally lose their shit and bite the other dog? Or, if you have a dog that would never take it to that level, would you rather they just be emotionally suppressed into a depression and learn to hate socializing? You pick, because when we reprimand our dogs for using proper communication, those are pretty much the only two options you are left with.

Now, does the punishment fit the crime? This is a big question. I briefly had a client who had a dog-aggressive dog. This dog got out of the house multiple times and went after other dogs. The parents did aversive training with her using a prong and shock collar. It did not improve her behavior. It only increased her anxiety and aggression. Shocker. They moved multiple times in two years, and the dog was ridiculously stressed. Then they decided to get a puppy.

Oh yes, a puppy. The stupidity still knocks me off my seat every time I think of this case study. Our life is in shambles, and our current dog is one reaction away from a nervous breakdown. So *let's get a puppy*! It was just so irresponsible for so many reasons, but I will stop myself and save you from another angry rant.

Anyway, the older dog obviously did not like the puppy and hated the whole situation. The parents were reluctant to start her on meds even though her chemical imbalance was clear as day. I gave them a set protocol: until we get the older dog under control, by no means should the puppy and the older dog be near each other unattended.

Within two weeks, the older dog was on the couch one day when the puppy walked into the area for a drink of water. She was on her way out and passing the couch when the older dog attacked her. The dog gave no warning because these communication techniques had been trained out of her. Multiple bites and a trip to the ER—simply for walking by the couch.

They are lucky the puppy didn't die.

Then the parents were talking about euthanizing the older dog after they had literally put this dog through hell and set her up to fail by unnecessarily bringing a puppy into the house and not following my protocol! They didn't *need* a new puppy. And now, because the older dog did exactly what we knew she was going to do, she has to die?

So many things are wrong with this situation, including the unnecessary pain and fear the puppy went through. Now we have another dog that will most likely hate other dogs because of this incident, which was avoidable.

Sorry, back on topic. I knew that bringing up this story was going to make me rage! Simply speaking, the punishment did not fit the crime. The puppy was just walking by the couch, and the older dog attacked. Yes, the older dog absolutely needed medication for her chemical imbalance and was untreated, so it's not her fault. But I use this as an example to show what this looks like.

If a dog is extremely stressed, anxious, and fearful, their reactions might not fit the situation. People can get like this too! We can blow up in a situation because stress and anxiety have been building all day. The majority of us are never taught to offload our emotions appropriately, safely, or in a healthy, healing way. So we just hold it in our chest until someone says something so small, and we inappropriately release all that tension on that person who was undeserving.

Our dogs do the same thing! That old dog lost it, and that puppy was the unfortunate target of years of aversive training and stress simply because she walked by the couch. Both of these dogs deserved so much better.

We need to make sure we allow our dogs to express their needs, wants, likes, and dislikes from the beginning. When they can do this, they can communicate clearly and efficiently. If not, it gets messy. Their emotions get pent up, and they usually do not accept rejection well either, which is *huge*.

Here's a question for you straight females reading. Have you ever had a guy hit on you, and you were scared to turn them down because you were getting weird vibes? Like you knew the rejection was going to make this kid lose his shit?

Yeah, terrifying. It can be similar in dogs. (And men, I'm sorry. I'm sure men have felt scared to turn down a woman as well, but I'm a lady, so I'm rolling with this example.) But in this human scenario, the girl tries too hard to be polite and nice so she doesn't destroy the dude, but he doesn't take the hint. He starts making her uncomfortable even though she repeatedly says, "No, thank you." So she needs to get more abrupt with him. Then what happens? He gets pissed and insulted and calls her a "bitch who isn't that hot anyway."

I know my ladies are nodding. We've all been through it. Many individuals never learn how to handle rejection. Our dogs can fail to learn this as well—especially if they are the abrasive, never-give-up type and have socialized only with passive or playful dogs.

Like I said earlier, Oaklee is the socialization wizard. We had an excitable husky mix come to the farm for an in-person session. She was young, only about seven months old. She also had a sister at home who was petrified of her because she was too much. Granted, the sister was much smaller and didn't get much socialization, so it all made sense. Huskies have a tendency to be extra!

Well, she came here and immediately jumped on Oaklee's head and was all over him. He was not about that life, so he stood still in the beginning and didn't engage much to show he wasn't feeling it. She continued, so he gave a little growl, and she immediately was submissive. I think it was the first time anyone had ever growled at her in her life. He noticed how sad the rejection made her, so he gave her a kiss on the nose. He did this to communicate that they were still okay but that he didn't like what she was doing. He helped her recover and deal with that rejection. He then play bowed to her, and she reengaged nicely and appropriately this time. They played calmly for a few minutes, and her dad was floored.

When we teach our puppies how to socialize, it is important to find a good teacher. Sometimes, littermate siblings aren't the best teachers. They may need an older, regulated, tolerant dog to help out. Now, I realize that getting access to an Oaklee isn't the easiest thing in the world, but if you do have it at your disposal, use it!

Puppies should learn from an early age how to:

- Engage in a nonabrasive way
- Understand play cues
- Understand when to stop play and listen to minor corrections appropriately
- Personally give corrections appropriately
- Access rejection
- Recover from rejection

When a dog is good at all of these, I say they can "play to style," which is rare outside big cities that have dogs together twenty-four/seven, like New York City.

In conclusion, this is a lifelong journey for most pups! Socialization is an ongoing process that plays a crucial role in your dog's ability to navigate the world confidently and peacefully. By understanding and respecting the nuances of dog communication, facilitating appropriate play and greetings, and recognizing signs of distress, you can support your dog in developing and maintaining the skills necessary for positive social interactions. Remember, you are your dog's advocate and protector, ensuring their social experiences are safe, positive, and enriching.

As parents, we are the decision-makers. Our dogs can't raise their hands and ask to leave. So pay attention. Listen to your dog and your gut. Don't fuck it up!

Part Three:
From Start to Finish

Chapter 15: *How to Pick the Right Dog for Your Family*

Let's dive right into the shitshow of choosing the perfect canine companion for your family, shall we? Because, let's be honest—picking a dog is more complex than choosing what to binge-watch on Netflix next, and you can't just switch it off if you don't like it.

First off, picking a dog is a big fucking deal. It's like choosing a new family member, but one that poops in your yard and might chew your favorite sneakers. You want a fluffy buddy that jives with your lifestyle, or else you're signing up for a world of frustration, chewed-up couches, and maybe a bitten mailman or two.

You have a real gift here! With babies, you get what you get most of the time and don't get to choose anything about them. With dogs, you get to take your time and look at personalities and what you want your life to look like!

At the beginning of the book, I spoke about why I wanted to pursue this career. One of the main driving forces was *Pit Bulls and Parolees*! With every single adoption, they asked the adopter what their life was like and if there was anything in their life the new dog would *have* to be okay with. They would then test out the dogs to see which was the best fit. For example, one guy was heavily into motorcycles, and the dog would be around them often. So they tested the dogs out around a motorcycle to see which dog reacted the least. Another episode was about a family with kids, so they tested the dogs with strollers and kids to see which one did the best!

You have the opportunity to do similar things to find a dog that would *love* to be a part of your life and lifestyle. Why give up this beautiful gift?

Breeds, breeds, breeds—there are so many, each with its quirks. It's like a dating app but for pets. Understanding different breeds is important, but what is most important is understanding that just because something is written about the breed does not mean it is set in stone. When you read up on a breed, these characteristics and personality traits are stereotypes. They are not law! Some dogs are laid-back, like the dog version of a couch potato who loves Netflix marathons more than you do, while their sibling may have enough energy to power a small city and could make you question your life choices. *It is a gamble.*

Here's the scoop: do your homework on the breed you are interested in, but take everything with a grain of salt and do not have set expectations, ever!

If you're a marathon runner, a border collie might be your spirit animal, but there is a slim chance they will give you the middle finger when you try to get them off the couch. Are you more of a "let's chill and watch the world go by" person? A bulldog might be your speed. Or they may bark at you to get up and play with them.

Researching breeds, temperaments, and personalities is always helpful, but I always want new parents to remember that a dog might not be exactly what they read about. For example, doodles are all over the place. Every breeder and their mother are taking poodles and breeding them with other breeds—goldendoodles, sheepadoodles, Bernedoodles, etc. Buyers are thinking they are going to get the most happy-go-lucky son of a bitch this side of the Mississippi, and what they really get is *straight-up poodle madness.*

Nothing against poodles. It's not *their* fault at all, but they are not typically happy-go-lucky or go-with-the-flow dogs. I have never met one that was, unfortunately. It's a result of bad breeding. But we are mixing them with these big ol' happy-dummy breeds like Labs and goldens, and we expect those personalities to shine through over the anxiety poodles are prone to.

Genetics are a gamble! You could get the most neurotic goldendoodle on the planet and not be prepared. Again, this dog still deserves love, but I want parents to understand all the risks of focusing just on breed characteristics.

Now, if you have kids or plan to have kids, you should take into consideration many aspects before picking the right dog. Kids and dogs can be the best of buddies or a recipe for chaos. If you are going for a purebred, look for breeds known for being patient and not too fussed about loud noises, overstimulating atmospheres, or a toddler who thinks they're a living, breathing, slightly drooly horse. Typically, but *not always*, golden retrievers and Labradors often ace this test. But they are more excitable and energetic, so keep that in mind. Meanwhile, more sensitive or nippy breeds, like poodles and Dalmatians, might not be thrilled with your mini-me's shenanigans.

Again, these are stereotypes! I am not saying that I haven't met a Dalmatian that was good with kids, and I absolutely know a few disgruntled goldens that do not love kids. Salt everywhere. Take it!

There are no guarantees, but you should do your research and make the best choice for your family and the future you envision. I will discuss dogs, babies, and kids more in Chapter 17!

What about rescue dogs vs. breeder dogs? Yes, the age-old debate: adopt a wise, possibly house-trained older dog, or get a puppy with a bladder the size of a peanut and the chewing instincts of a beaver. Get a breeder puppy and have them mostly from the beginning, or adopt a dog that may have emotional or physical trauma from a questionable past.

Rescues can be amazing companions and are often grateful for a second chance. Puppies? Adorable, but they're basically four-legged babies that need a ton of work. Choose wisely, or you'll be up to your elbows in . . . well, you know.

If you haven't noticed, I am pro-adopting for multiple reasons, but the reason most pertinent to this topic is that you're able to pick the right dog for you. When you rescue, you can foster to adopt and take your time finding the right fit. That's true with puppies as well! If you want a puppy, you can still do that by rescuing. Not all rescues offer foster-to-adopt options, but many do! By adopting, you just have a lot more versatility in picking the right dog. Breeder puppies usually require a deposit months in advance, and you don't get to meet them or pick the one you gravitate toward. It's more of a "you get what you get" situation.

Now, let's discuss allergies and health concerns. Allergies—the buzzkill word of pet ownership. Some breeds are more hypoallergenic than others, but remember, there's no such thing as an allergy-free dog. If your kid sneezes at the mere mention of fur, you can look into hypo breeds. But again, this is not a guarantee. You could think you are getting the most pristine bloodline goldendoodle while, in reality, you purchased from a puppy mill, and the dogs are not as they claim. This happens all the time! Once you purchase the dog, the dog is yours! Regardless, you should invest in stock for tissues and antihistamines, just in case.

Also, it is extremely important to note that you can find hypo breeds in the rescue system as well! It is a little more time-consuming to find one that fits your lifestyle, but they are there. Purebred dogs are rehomed all the time. You just need to know how to find them. Petfinder.com is a great resource! It can search thousands of rescues and preferences all at one time, including size, breed, temperament, age, and more! It's a pretty impressive site.

Like I said, rescuing takes a bit more time, but you have a gift, and this decision should never be rushed. You want a chemical bond with this pup! Why not take your time and find the absolute most perfect fit for your family and lifestyle? I always say that the perfect dog comes along at the perfect time. But if we don't give the universe time to give us what we need, we might make bad choices and be led to things that aren't meant for us.

Rescuing can take longer because rescues are way pickier about adopters than breeders are. Breeders don't give a fuck who they give their puppies to as long as they got the cash! Is that who you want to get your dog from? Or do you want to work with someone who is going to make sure that dog is the *right* fit for you and you are the *right* fit for them? This is for the long haul. We should take our time.

Next, we'll discuss the financial and time commitments that come along with getting a dog. These two things are terribly overlooked, and, to be frank, I am fucking over it.

Here comes the real talk: dogs cost money. Like, sometimes, a lot of fucking money. Sometimes "Why did I think this was a good idea?" amounts of money. From normal checkups and vaccine vet visits to those surprise "I ate something I shouldn't have" surgeries, make sure your wallet is ready for the adventure—especially with puppies or hyperactive dogs.

How about training? Do you know that good, proper training costs a decent amount of money? I mean, if you play your cards right from the beginning, the amount shouldn't be too bad. But if you make the mistake many others do and go with aversive or board-and-train programs first, you may be already $4,000 in the hole—and it was all bullshit, and you are worse off than you started.

And time? Puppies are time vampires. Cute but utterly exhausting. Do new parents with a newborn baby expect to keep their normal sleep schedule? If they do, they're insane. There is a reason maternity and paternity leave is a thing! If you are getting a dog that is a year old or younger, make sure you've got the bandwidth to deal with midnight potty breaks and a creature with the energy of a caffeinated squirrel.

I literally loathe hearing how exhausted puppy parents are and how they didn't think it would be like this. What did they think it was going to be like? I want to know. Maybe a family member or a friend got a unicorn dog, and their expectations are from a pool of one dog, but they are setting everyone up to fail. Young dogs are *work*!

My parents' pittie puppy, Sage Marie, is about a year and a half now. She is still work. Thank God she is good in so many categories, but they still need to keep an eye on her outside, watch her crazy zoomie behavior, make sure she doesn't accidentally hurt Gatsby when she gets worked up, and keep her from digging ginormous holes in the yard. There is no guarantee the puppy stuff will end after the eighth-month mark, so you must be prepared for this and be *okay with it.* It is okay to vent, but don't you dare give up because your puppy is being a puppy!

Now, space is the final frontier. Or at least it should be when considering a dog. Apartment dwellers, fear not—size isn't always the deal-breaker, but energy level definitely is. I am going to say this once: *stop getting Aussie shepherds*! A Great Dane would be a better fit for an apartment than an Aussie, but it's still a questionable choice due to size. A Great Dane might be a gentle giant that's perfectly content and lazy in a one-bedroom flat, while an Aussie Shepherd turns your living room into a NASCAR track and barks at every noise they hear the neighbors make. If you're living in an apartment that's so cozy you have to step outside to change your mind, then maybe reconsider that Saint Bernard. Yes, they're sweet, but unless you're planning on saddling them up for a ride to the fridge, you might want to think smaller. Know your space's limits and choose a breed that fits—both physically and energetically. Again, by not taking this into account, you could set both you and your dog up for total failure.

For the high-rise dwellers, you can still have a dog, but let's be strategic. Breeds and mixes that are quieter (because your neighbors will thank you), more laid-back, and lower on the energy scale are your best bets. Think more along the lines of a chill bulldog that looks at your elevator like it's his personal chariot rather than a hyperactive husky or Lab mix that's ready to sled race up the stairwell.

John and I live on a nine-acre farm, but I am more of an inside person. We run two businesses that have many different moving parts, and there are about eleven frying pans that are going all at once. We have two toddler boys under four and are expecting another in a few months. We have a crazy, time-consuming lifestyle. This is exactly why we chose the *laziest* dogs on the planet! Tishi is thirteen years old and can hardly go up and down the stairs. She is the ultimate couch hippo. Oaklee is probably around eight years old and has an enlarged heart. If he has a spurt of energy for a toy that's been thrown, he coughs and gets out of breath. He is also a couch hippo. Pudge is going to be eight years old. Even though she looks like a puppy when she engages in play, she is around twelve pounds. So, when she gets the zoomies, all she needs is the square footage of our king-size bed to get that energy out in a matter of two minutes. We picked dogs that fit our lifestyle, and it works in their favor as well!

At the end of the day, choosing the right dog for your space isn't about just making sure they physically fit in your living room without you having to move to the second couch (which you don't have). It's about ensuring their happiness and energy levels match your living situation. Because nothing says, "I might have miscalculated," like a border collie trying to herd your Roomba in a one-bedroom apartment.

So, when considering space, think less about whether they can fit and more about whether they can thrive. Remember, a happy dog makes for a happy home, even if that home is less sprawling estate and more intimate living situation. Choose wisely, and may your floors be free of unexpected indoor zoomies. Unless you're into that sort of thing, in which case, zoom on, my friends, zoom on!

Another *real talk* moment: Before you commit, do a gut check. Are you ready for the early mornings, the training challenges, and the commitment to another life for the next decade or more? Are you ready to treat this dog like your natural-born child? Dogs are not accessories or phases. They're living, breathing beings with needs and emotions. Be honest with yourself about the commitment you're ready to make.

I never get more upset than when I am working with a client who had no right to get a dog. Whether someone works full-time without a second to breathe or is retired and expects the dog to stay on the couch and be perfect from day one, they need to have proper expectations. But mostly, it's vital to realize that these unrealistic expectations and decisions made on a whim affect another life! You need to understand and grasp the gravity of that. I believe that if humans took this into account, there would be no rehoming or surrendering. The shelters would be much less crowded!

If I haven't said it enough (one more time can't hurt), choosing the right dog for your family is a big deal. It's like adding a new, slightly hairier member to your clan. It requires thought, research, and an honest assessment of your current lifestyle and future plans. Whether it's a sprightly puppy or a wise senior dog, a purebred or a mix with mysterious origins, the right dog is out there, waiting to fill your life with joy, laughter, and a bit of controlled chaos.

Go forth, choose wisely, and embrace the incredible journey of dog parenthood. And remember, when in doubt, choose love—it's the one decision you'll never regret.

Chapter 16:
Senior Dogs and When to Let Go

Ah yes, senior dogs—the grandmasters of napping, the seasoned sniffers of smells, and the wise, old souls that seem to look at us with decades of doggy wisdom.

As our beloved pups enter their golden years, we embark on a bittersweet journey. It's filled with tender moments, a few more gray hairs (for both of us), and the inevitable reality of saying goodbye. Buckle up, buttercup—it's going to be an emotional ride. But I promise to sprinkle in enough silly to keep us from flooding the room with tears. I know this is going to be a tough chapter for some, or maybe all of you, but I believe it is necessary to discuss, rather than avoid, this topic.

First off, aging in dogs is like aging in humans who are hitting retirement: every day is a weekend, and naps are nonnegotiable. But it's not all leisurely strolls and dreamy snoozes. Senior dogs start showing their age through slower movements, a general decrease in energy, and a bit more grumpiness. I mean, who wouldn't be grumpy with arthritis? You might notice them taking the stairs more cautiously or hesitating before jumping off the couch or bed. And just like your Uncle Bob, who can predict rain with his knees, your dog's discomfort might become more apparent with bad weather.

I feel that pain is the thing we most need to keep an eye out for. Recognizing pain and discomfort can be harder than it looks. Dogs are stoic creatures, often hiding their pain like a poker player with a winning hand. Some of the pain tolerances I've seen in dogs are the exact opposite of the man flu. (Sorry, men. You can't deny that the majority of you act as if you are dying when you have a simple head cold. But I digress.) Like I said, our dogs are usually the exact opposite, never letting on that anything at all is wrong.

Signs of discomfort in your aging pup can include limping, difficulty standing up after lying down, loss of appetite, or a sudden dislike of being touched in areas they once enjoyed, like hips and the neck area. If your previously cheerful dog now seems as grouchy as a cat forced to wear a sweater, it might be pain speaking. Take note of their appetite and water intake to see if they are also struggling in other areas.

Many female dogs suffer from chronic UTIs as they get older. This usually goes undiagnosed until we pick up on a huge change in behavior. Keep an eye out for the telltale signs: straining to pee, making more pit stops than usual, or leaving behind urine that smells like it could knock out a skunk. The smell of UTI pee typically smells like ammonia and may have a reddish tint to it. Blood in the urine is as big a red flag as finding your dog googling "bladder discomfort." So, give a look every so often if you tend to not follow them outside or watch them pee.

Don't play the guessing game. If you notice these signs or your dog seems off their game—like licking their bits more than usual or showing signs of discomfort—it's vet o'clock. UTIs can range from "I'm a bit uncomfortable" to "Holy hell, this is the worst," so getting a professional diagnosis is key. Remember, catching a UTI early can save your dog a heap of discomfort and you a mountain of stress (and cleaning supplies). So, keep a watchful eye and stay on top of those bathroom behaviors. Your dog's urinary tract will thank you, and so will your carpet.

Now, as dogs age, some may lose their sight or hearing or even develop cognitive dysfunction (doggy dementia), leading to confusion or anxiety. It's heartbreaking to watch, but there are ways to adapt. Create a safe, comfortable environment for them, keep routines consistent, and have patience thicker than the last slice of Thanksgiving turkey! Let's dive in a little deeper into each so you know what they look like.

Arthritis: The creaky bone tango. The bane of canine existence. It's like your dog has aged into a grumpy old man overnight, complete with the "get off my lawn" vibes. Stairs become their Everest, and getting up looks like a slow-motion replay. Regular vet checkups, pain management, physical therapy, and perhaps even doggy yoga (yes, it's a thing) can help manage those aching joints.

Dental disease: This is more than just doggy breath. Dental disease can turn kisses from a sweet gesture to a stinky assault. But it's not about just bad breath; dental issues can lead to serious health problems. Imagine your dog's mouth as like that one neglected room in everyone's house, but instead of clutter, there's plaque and tartar. Keeping those chompers clean is crucial, so regular dental checkups are a must.

Our family *loves* putting a water additive in our dogs' water bowl, and it has been a game changer. All three of them and the cat have decently nice breath regardless of their ages.

The biggest misconception about doggy teeth brushing? That we need to *brush* the tartar off. Wrong! The goal is to get that enzymatic toothpaste on the tartar so it can break down over time. You can't brush away tartar with a toothbrush, so the water additive and frequent brushing are the best ways to avoid spending an arm and a leg on dental work. If your dog needs dental care and it is ignored, they can get an infection, and that can be deadly. So, do not ignore the roadkill breath.

Historically, purebred dogs, especially little dogs, have notoriously bad teeth genetics. Thankfully, our little Pudge has had only one dental issue so far, and that was due to a cracked canine tooth, where the root was exposed and painful. Cracked teeth are something to keep an eye on in general, but even more so when dogs get older. Pudge's personality changed drastically when this happened. She wasn't eating well, was rigid and stiff all the time, was quick to get upset, and didn't want affection from us. We knew something was up! John picked up on it and checked her mouth. Dr. Mammen fixed her up, and she was right as rain again in a few days!

Vision and hearing loss: As dogs age, their eyesight and hearing might start to fade. One day, they're catching frisbees like a pro, and the next, they're bumping into furniture and looking confused when you call their name. Patience, adjustments in how you communicate, and a safe, obstacle-free living space can make their life easier. I had a blind dog, so I can say it's not as bad as it looks and sounds. Although our Opal was born blind, so she didn't know any better. When older dogs go blind, the main thing is to make sure you help them navigate the house safely. Also, do what you can to anticipate and be proactive about their inevitable anxiety. They will, of course, be confused as to why they cannot hear or see (or both) and will feel scared and vulnerable.

Obesity: The chunky monkey syndrome sneaks up like a thief in the night—if the thief was made of treats and reduced exercise. It's all fun and games until your dog resembles a furry beach ball and has a hard time getting up on their own. Keeping an eye on their diet and ensuring they get enough exercise (within their limits) can help keep the pounds off. Also, watch food intake. Many dogs slow down as they get older, thus burning fewer calories. If you are noticing this, it might be time to cut back on their amount of daily food! Being heavy in old age can increase pain and arthritis, so your dog should stay at a healthy weight.

Kidney and liver diseases: These are the ninjas of the dog medical world—silent but deadly. Symptoms can be subtle at first, like increased thirst or changes in bathroom habits, but these conditions can seriously impact your dog's health. Regular blood work can be a game changer in catching these issues early.

Cognitive dysfunction, better known as doggy dementia: This condition makes seniors forget why they walked into a room (we can all relate, right?).

They might seem disoriented, bark at the wall for no reason, have sleep disturbances, or even forget their potty training. While there's no cure, medication and environmental enrichment can improve their quality of life.

Navigating a senior dog's health challenges is like being their personal health detective, minus the cool hat, magnifying glass, and paycheck. Making regular vet visits, keeping an eye out for signs of these common issues, and providing a whole lot of love and patience can make their senior years more comfortable. And remember, every gray muzzle and slow step is a badge of honor. So, celebrate the journey you've shared and the love that only grows stronger with time!

Now for the not-fun discussion: the end-of-life cues.

Knowing when it's time is easier said than done, and we always think we'll be able to think more clearly than we do when we're in this scenario. Let's be real. With my age group (the millennials) choosing more and more that they do not want human children, their dogs are what we call "dual-income dogs." Meaning they are the sole beneficiaries of two active, loving parents, as well as their time, love, and money. No kids to cut the resources!

I bring this up because there is a running joke that the women of my generation will have a full-on meltdown, crying and sobbing about their dog passing away when they are only two years old, healthy as an ox, and sitting right in front of them, confused as to why their mom is being so dramatic. I believe the younger generations do a better job of treating their dogs like family and are better overall at making sure they live a healthy, full life. Because of this, the end will be massively hard for these types of parents. I've been one of these parents. It is life altering.

Here comes the tough part—recognizing when your dog's quality of life has diminished to the point where letting them go is the kindest option. It's a decision no pet parent wants to make, but it's an act of love—the final vow to protect them from suffering.

End-of-life cues can include consistent pain that medication doesn't alleviate, severe mobility issues, incontinence, loss of appetite, and a noticeable disinterest in life's joys, like that tail-wagging enthusiasm for their favorite squeaky toy. Or, in Oaklee's case, I would instantly know something was really wrong if he wasn't hungry for a meal.

Deciding to let your dog cross the Rainbow Bridge is a personal, heart-wrenching choice that only you, in consultation with your vet, can make. It's about them, not us. Yes, it's going to hurt like hell. Yes, you'll question if it's the right time, if you are doing the right thing, and if there is anything else you can do to help them live longer. But remember, it's the final act of love and courage you can show your loyal companion. Don't chicken out.

I swear I am not trying to be insensitive, but there is nothing that upsets me more than a dog parent not being able to handle physically being there for their dog during this last milestone. Be there for them, hold them close, and offer comfort and love as they take their final breaths. It's the least we can do after years and years of giving us unconditional love and kissing away our tears. Please don't drop your dog off and make the vet tech's eyes be the last ones your dog sees before they cross over. Those last moments should be calm and filled with you telling them, "I will miss you so much, but it's okay. You can go now. I will be okay, I promise."

I am crying right now as I am writing this. I didn't think I would since I am not currently in a situation of letting anyone go right at this moment. But I have been there. Many times, in fact. It is something you never get over. The shitty reality of grieving is that losing a dog is losing a family member, and don't let anyone tell you differently. Grieving is a messy, nonlinear process filled with "I'm okay" moments followed by ugly crying into a tub of ice cream because you heard a noise that sounded like them or found an old tumbleweed of fur under the couch. And that's perfectly okay. Everyone grieves differently. Allow yourself to feel all the feels, reminisce about the good times, laugh at the silly moments, and cry over the loss.

A few months after losing our beloved Opal Marie, I walked into our bedroom, and, before I clicked on the light, my eyes played tricks on me. I thought I saw her napping on her bed. When I clicked on the light, she obviously wasn't there. It was like I had lost her all over again in that moment. I was inconsolable, even though I'd been happily having a normal conversation with John in the kitchen just moments before. Grieving can hit you anywhere and anytime. No one is safe unless you are a sociopathic monster, in which case, I feel bad for you because you will never know the beautiful pain that comes with loving someone so deeply.

Losing Opal was one of the hardest things we'd ever had to go through. She was only a little over a year old, so she was a baby. She wasn't old. We weren't able to say, "She lived a full life," to make ourselves feel better about the choice. She was born blind, and when she was around seven months old, she started having seizures. She did well on meds for a few months, but they quickly stopped working, and she would seize in these horrible clusters. She'd have one every few hours for one to two days, and there was nothing we could do to stop them. Once the cluster subsided, she would be a shell of the dog she'd been. She'd forget the map of the house in her brain, need to be re-potty trained, and be disoriented and confused. It was devastating each time to watch her start from scratch and not know why. My poor girl worked so hard each time to get back to normalcy, but we could see how tired she was getting. Watching her suffer like that for days was more than we could handle. After talking with her neurologist and Dr. Mammen about any possible remaining options (there were none), we had to make the choice.

We told ourselves we didn't want to do it while she was in the throes of a cluster, when she was not herself, and when we could not give her the proper love and send-off she deserved. So we had a goodbye party for her. All her friends and family came to give her lovin', kisses, and treats one last time. It was beautiful to see how many people's lives she had touched and how happy she was to be with them all.

The next day, Dr. Mammen and Danielle (our favorite vet tech) came to let her cross the Rainbow Bridge in our home. This way, Opal could stay comfortable and be with her big brother as she crossed over. They lay on the floor together, we said our tear-drenched goodbyes, and, within moments, our baby girl would never feel pain again. It was a pain like I never thought I'd feel but also a strange relief that I was able to end her suffering for her. It was the last great act I could perform for her. As awful as it felt, it was part of my job, and I had to follow through, for her.

Now, another thing we don't learn in school but should—navigating through grief. You don't learn about it until you are in it, and even then, some don't learn how to navigate it. Some people like to avoid or push their feelings down so they don't feel them. This is dangerous. When we numb sadness, we also numb everything else, including joy. Many people don't do well with the normal suggestions, like seek support from friends, family, or pet-loss support groups. This can be because they don't enjoy or aren't good at talking about their feelings. That's okay too. Watching YouTube and reading articles can also be a huge help if you tend to not like to open up to others. Remember, it's okay to talk about your dog, celebrate their life, and keep their memory alive.

I am a decently spiritual person and believe in spirits. We have an amazing medium named Nicole Glosser. She's the real deal—so easy to talk to and ridiculously good at what she does. The first time we had an appointment with her, John and I hardly spoke, and she told us things she could have never found out by reading our social media or looking us up. She immediately connected with Opal's spirit, which obviously had me bawling. But what happened next had me on my knees. She said Opal wanted to thank us for the legacy we created for her and that her short time on Earth should be used to help others survive what she went through. Nicole then asked if we had started a foundation for her.

John and I both had our jaws on the floor. The night before we had our reading with Nicole, John had started working on the Opal Foundation, which is now a 501(c)(3) foundation that raises money for dogs like Opal that need MRIs. MRIs are extremely expensive, usually $4,000 to $6,000. And after all that money, it is not a cure. It only helps the doctor diagnose the dog's condition. Nicole could never have guessed what we'd done the night before. No one else knew. It wasn't even finished yet. It was incredible.

I am not telling you that you need to book a medium reading and connect with your dead dog, but it absolutely helped me feel better and know she was out of pain but still with us always.

I brought up this story partly because I believe our dogs are with us all the time. I know that anytime I think about or talk about Opal, she is right there, wagging her tail because she's so happy that I am thinking of her. It may hurt to think of them. It can even feel like there is an ache so deep that you will never be whole again. That ache can feel like a dagger in the heart. But they love to know we are thinking of them and keeping their memory alive.

We had to let Opal go two weeks before I had my first son, JJ. I was devastated he would never know her. But that was just never the case. JJ is four now, and when he goes to bed and is having a hard time sleeping, he asks Opal Marie to help him fall asleep and keep the bad thoughts away so he can rest. He knows her, watches videos of her, and talks to her photos on the family room walls. He knows her and will always know how loved she was despite the disability that almost had her unnecessarily killed at three weeks old. He will always know her because I make sure he has that choice.

It is so hard, but the pain gets easier to handle. Creating a memorial or a photo album might seem like too much if you don't want to be reminded of the loss. I get it, but by shutting out the bad, you silence the good too. All the good times deserve to be remembered. And when you're ready, don't be afraid to open your heart to another deserving pup. It's not about replacing your beloved pet; it's about offering love to another in need, yourself included. Putting off loving again does not change the life you had with your old dog. It won't bring them back. Your old dog would have wanted you to be happy because dogs love unconditionally. They'd never want us to hurt or grieve for them for too long before having something else to help us along.

Since I was young, my family has always believed in the two-dog-household rule. Which means we always have at least two dogs at one time. We have been lucky enough to have this work well. I didn't know if we were ever going to round that corner with Gatsby (who loved being an only dog), but he pulled through and let Sage Marie into his heart. (Yeah, we like Marie as a middle name!) When I was little, we had Chips, our chocolate Lab. When he was around eight years old—overweight, lazy, and slowing down—my parents got me Dottie for my sixteenth birthday. A beautiful white pittie mix. (Yes, we also love our genetically challenged white dogs too! Unfortunately, it is a blessing and a curse that I will get to in just a moment.) Dottie is the unicorn puppy I spoke about way earlier in the book. She needed five seconds of training and was a perfect angel. She got Chips off the couch and kept him active, and he lived to be fourteen! Sadly, a year after his passing, Dottie was diagnosed with bone cancer in her cheekbone at age seven. I was devasted. Chips was my dad's dog. Dottie was mine. I would have taken her to college with me if they would have let me!

Right before Dottie's diagnosis, my boss had a baby and didn't want her two-year-old American black Lab anymore. Here's where Gatsby Boy enters the chat. He loved Dottie. She tolerated him, with love. She was always super nice to him, but he was more than twice her size and abrasive with his love for her. She passed five months after we adopted him. He was heartbroken and didn't want any other dogs around him after that, becoming extremely reactive. Poor boy.

Losing Dottie was my first real heartbreak from losing a dog. I was twenty-three years old, and it was like losing a child. I cared for her day and night. I cleaned the blood from her face and mouth as the cancer got bigger and bigger. I was the one who had to make the call, not my parents. She looked at me one night, and I just knew she was telling me it was time.

Funnily enough, I had just met John the previous month, and though we were not together yet as a couple, something told me she was ready to let go because she knew I would be okay with him. Dogs are so much smarter and more spiritually aware than we give them any credit for. We celebrated her eighth birthday, she had her Frosty Paws ice cream, and we let her go the next day. I thought I'd never recover, but it just made me want to help dogs more, specifically pit bulls.

Weirdly, Opal Marie was plopped into my arms on February 22, 2019, during a rescue transport that John and I volunteered for in South Carolina to save twenty-two dogs from euthanasia. It was three years to the day after we'd let Dottie cross the Rainbow Bridge. I knew my Dottie Girl had sent me Opal.

And when did Opal pass?

On February 22, 2020. The same day, only one year later. You can't tell me all of that is just coincidence, and if you choose to do so, I will choose to keep believing in spirits and the universe having a hand in these beautiful things. Let the universe guide you. Let it bring the right dogs to you. It might make the grieving part even harder, but how lucky are you to have something so special that it is devastating to say goodbye? It is a blessing and an honor.

In closing, navigating the senior years or the last few months with your sick dog is a journey of love, adaptation, confusion, helplessness, gratitude, and, ultimately, heartache. But it's also filled with moments of pure joy and the kind of deep, unconditional love that only our dogs can provide.

When the time comes to say goodbye, do it with the same, if not more, love, empathy, and devotion they've shown you their entire lives. And as you grieve, remember that the pain eventually eases, leaving you with cherished memories of a well-loved dog that left paw prints on your heart.

To my crossed-over pups: thank you for the love, the lessons, and the laughter. I wouldn't have missed it for the world, and I'd do it all over again.

My sweet girls,

'Til we meet again. <3

Chapter 17:

Dogs and Kids

Welcome to the grand finale of our dog-centric odyssey, where the tender worlds of Frito-scented puppy paws and small, sticky jam hands collide. This isn't merely about preventing your living room from turning into a scene reminiscent of a toddler-piloted, dog-chasing drone gone wrong. No, it's about fostering a bond so profound between your dog and your children that it rivals the most epic tales of friendship known to humanity (or caninity, for that matter).

I'm talking *My Dog Skip*-type shit. You know, the beautiful book about a beloved dog that helps his boy navigate his entire childhood? Every parent should want their kid to have that type of unbreakable bond with a pet. As cats tend to not reciprocate our obsession, dogs are the obvious choice here!

As we draw the curtain on this long, informational journey, let's delve into the art of blending the chaotic beauty of dogs and kids into a masterpiece of mutual respect, understanding, and, inevitably, a bit of mess—but the good kind.

Dogs, babies, and kids are kind of my specialty. I was featured and interviewed on the *Pregnancy Podcast* three times. This podcast is the *bomb*! It's super helpful for all those first-time moms who are so confused and have no idea what is about to happen. Vanessa Merten is knowledgeable, but she doesn't just feed you what she would do. She gives you all the sides of the story so you can make your educated decision, which is what I love most about her and her work!

Additionally, I created the Dogs & Babies: A Complete Online Course For New & Expecting Parents. It's like I literally wrote the book on how to handle dogs and kids successfully! It's my most loved passion because I absolutely love babies and kids but also treat my dogs like my babies. So I have perfected how to help expecting parents navigate this Narnia of the unknown. Because you don't understand parenting until you are a parent!

It is also extremely important to note that even if *you* do not want or have kids, someone close to you may. For instance, my sister is simply cool Aunt Nikki, and she fucking rocks that title. She loves the shit out of my kids but also absolutely loves to hand them back over to me when she's done and can go home! Which is fine too! But her dog, Jackson, struggled with JJ's toddler stage, and rightfully so, because he had never been around a toddler. He would look at my sister like, *Okay, what the fuck is that, Mom?* My sister had a hard time dealing with his reactivity at first because she had no idea what to do, and I think she was embarrassed he was acting that way.

It's been almost three years since the first time Jackson walked down Toddler Nation Lane and struggled. I can happily say that as I am writing this last chapter, Jackson is happily spending a month at my house while my sister traipses around New Zealand like the kid-less bitch she is! (Just kidding. I love the shit out of my sister, and I am happy to care for Jackson while she has that amazing experience.) But in short, Jackson overcame his toddler reactivity regardless of not living with kids himself. So, even if you do not want kids, this chapter can still be necessary for you to pay attention to so you can help your dog prepare for what your life may have lurking for you!

Pre-baby prep, we call this the groundwork. Before the stork parks its metaphorical self on your doorstep, there's a critical preparatory phase that often gets overshadowed by nursery paint colors, stroller reviews, and perfectly picked-out registries. Your dog, the first baby, deserves a briefing. You should never skip this step, but many do because it just isn't on their radar.

Start by slowly introducing your dog to new smells, sounds, changes in routine, and baby paraphernalia. It's like easing them into the idea that their monopoly on your affection is about to be shared. But hey, they're gaining a lifelong friend, so the trade-off can be beneficial if you don't let your kid turn into a little monster. (Just kidding. Kind of.)

Use recordings of baby noises to desensitize them to the upcoming cacophony of joyous baby sounds. It is important to use newborn baby sounds, not just regular baby sounds. Newborn cries are *very* different from bigger-baby cries. Gradually adjusting your pup to these changes can transform potential jealousy into curiosity and protectiveness.

Don't ban them from visiting the nursery or investigating new baby gear. We want them to love this frickin' kid, right? Do not fear everything that comes along with it! Let your dog get comfortable with all things baby and become desensitized to all this new stuff so that once the baby comes, it's no big deal that this stuff has been in your house for weeks. This one is a bigger deal than it sounds.

Why?

Because a lot of baby and mama gear is terrifying.

Story time! One of the first expecting couples I ever worked with ran into this little snafu. Thankfully, no one was hurt, and I get to use it in my training to help other expecting couples not make the same mistake. This poor couple came home to their two dogs with their new baby boy. Things weren't going poorly, but Mom had a tough delivery, was in a lot of pain, and was emotional and stressed. To top it all off, she was struggling with breastfeeding. God, it's so tough sometimes as a brand-new mom. On day two, they decided to bring out the breast pump for the first time. This was something they hadn't desensitized their dogs to because they hadn't thought anything of it. Well, baby was sleeping in the bassinet in Mom and Dad's bedroom, but Mom and Dad were in the nursery with the breast pump. Now, most of the breast pumps that insurance covers sound like you are landing a fucking plane. You can hardly hear anything when you are using them.

So, what happened?

Their sweet female dog associated Mom's distress with the new baby, and the loud-as-hell breast pump was the last straw. She went into their bedroom, got up on the bed, looked into the bassinet, and started growling at the baby.

Again, no one was hurt. Dad had noticed her leave the room abruptly and followed her, catching her only after a few seconds. He was able to keep his cool for the most part and call her to him sweetly, but they realized quickly that they had to get back to basics. They realized that their dog had figured all of this upset was the baby's fault. As far as the dog was concerned, he was the only thing that had changed, so he must be the culprit!

That's why this part of the groundwork is huge.

All the changes that come with a baby need to happen *long before* the baby shows up so there is no correlation. That includes all the baby gear—stroller, bassinet, breast pump, baby swing, etc.—as well as changes in routine during the day and at night. If you aren't going to be walking your dog three miles a day after baby shows up, change that routine before baby shows up. If you don't want your dog sleeping in bed anymore because it makes you nervous, change up the sleeping arrangement way before delivery day. We have to be proactive way before the baby makes an appearance.

Pregnancy, the joys! So many changes. And not just little ones. There are also drastic, life-altering changes! As your family anticipates its new arrival, your dog will undoubtedly sense the shifting tides. They're tuned into the changes in your body, smells, and routine, so maintaining a semblance of normalcy for them is crucial. Keep up with their mental exercise, cuddles, and simple training. This means trying to come up with a way to ensure these things don't falter when you come home with the new bundle. In some cases, it is absolutely inevitable that you will miss a beat. You are human.

Well, not really. You are a new mom, and that means you are basically a zombie—a milk-producing, sleep-deprived, surviving-only-on-oxytocin hot mess. I know, I make it sound so good, right? I swear it's amazing, but some parts kinda suck. I just like to be honest and realistic about it, especially with my clients, so they know what to expect.

I worked with one mom whose dog pretty much hated everyone other than her and only tolerated his dad. Mom dealt with the dog and was fine with that. She didn't mind that he hated people. She didn't like people too much either, so fixing that reactivity wasn't a bucket-list item for her. She just wanted to make sure they had no problems with the baby and that her dog still felt like number one. Part of their routine was walking for multiple hours every single day. She thought she would immediately be up and about the day after she came home from the hospital.

Unfortunately, I had to shatter her dream. Not because I wanted to be one of those "just wait till" moms. I hate that. I had to tell her the facts because her dream had also been my dream prior to JJ's arrival, and it got ripped out from under me. I did not have proper expectations about possibilities, and I couldn't believe it happened to me.

I had wanted an all-natural birth—no meds, no epidural, no stirrups. I was gonna labor like a beautiful goddess and have no pain.

Ha! Bullshit. That was the opposite of my real story. I am not telling you this to scare you or discourage you from having babies. Have all the babies! Babies are the best. But I tell you this story because it can happen, and everyone should be prepared.

I was five days over my due date and fucking ready for JJ to not be inside me anymore. Like really fucking ready! I finally went into labor, and my water partially broke. I got to a delivery room, and boom, my water broke all over the floor like in the movies. And then, back contractions! Like, really? It was horrible. I wouldn't wish it on my own worst enemy.

Anyway, long story short without going into the whole thing, I became preeclamptic and came down with a fever and an infection. I labored for twenty hours and pushed for four hours, only to have the discs in my neck bulge, basically temporarily paralyzing the top half of my body and leaving me unable to push. Yeah. So, emergency C-section it was. I had no choice. It was the last thing I wanted, but there I was. Thankfully, I was fine once they got JJ out. He was fine too but needed NICU for five days for no reason other than what happened to me. They needed to make sure he wasn't sick.

I tell this story because I told myself there was *no way in hell* I was having a C-section. So there I was, at home with my stomach split open, unable to get up from the rocking chair by myself, and unable to lift anything heavy or drive for six whole fucking weeks! Not what I was expecting, that's for sure.

So, back to the client mom. I had to tell her. I had to let her know that sometimes, the unexpected happens, and you can't bank on anything. So we had to come up with a game plan in case she couldn't walk her dog the next day. I told her I thought it was wise to have Dad get more involved in the dog's routine moving forward. It was the only way to ensure that her dog didn't feel neglected or stressed once the baby came around. He would already be used to these changes.

Always talk to other moms to get a proper perspective. Not your dramatic, woe-is-me moms, but your realistic, this-is-hard-but-I-love-it moms. Those are the ones to ask!

This is also an opportune time to reinforce basic commands and some decent manners—essentials that ensure your dog remains confident and clear-headed amidst the forthcoming whirlwind of change. My favorite cues for all dogs to know are *sit*, of course. *Look*, which means, "Look at me real quick." *Wait*, which means, "Hold on a second. I will release you. You just need to have patience." *Touch*, which is my version of "C*ome here*," but works so much better. *Leave it*, which means, "That's dangerous, don't touch it ever." And the classic, *drop it.*

I teach these mostly so our dogs know what the hell we are asking from them on a day-to-day basis while we humans are talking a mile a minute. Cues are not the end all be all, and they are not mandatory for having an awesome dog. But if your dog has high energy, low impulse control, or any amount of energy and spatial awareness, cues can be ridiculously helpful. Otherwise, you just have a dog that gets words yelled at it that they never learned, and they get more and more desensitized to those words by the second. Cues can be extremely beneficial for all dogs, but especially for one with a baby on the way. It allows everyone to communicate more clearly and kindly.

When you teach these cues, keep it fun. If you get firm and frustrated while training, I'd turn my nose up at you and ignore you too! Do you notice that I called it a cue and not a command?

Why?

Because it should be an ask, not a demand. You'll quickly learn that toddlers and dogs will oblige much quicker when you use a sweet tone and not a nasty one. Pick which type of parent you wanna be!

Now for the meet-cute! Have you seen the movie *The Holiday*? Amazing movie. Watch it! They have an adorable scene where an old director explains what a meet-cute is. In a film or TV show, it's an amusing or charming first encounter between two characters that leads to a romantic relationship.

Imagine the scene: you're back from the hospital, baby in arms, and your dog's tail is wagging with uncertain anticipation. This moment deserves the finesse of a seasoned director! But sometimes, it's not as picturesque as it sounds. Let's go over the ways this scene *should* be conducted.

First, we have some logistics to figure out! Figure out who is taking care of your dog while you are at the hospital, in the birth center, or laboring from home. Whether it's your parents, a sibling, a friend, a dog walker, etc., have them be there when you get home. If your dog will be at a boarding facility, make sure someone can bring them home *before* you get home. Provide a step-by-step process that your helping hand can follow before you get home so your pup is ready to go. This will include appropriate exercise, relaxation, serotonin- and dopamine-boosting enrichment, sweet, loving affection, and high-value treats and extra enrichment that's ready to go in the freezer or cabinet!

Remember, there is no rush. This situation should be calm and peaceful. There should be no pressure to hurry it along. If you think your helping-hand person is going to rush or tends to be flakey, this is not the right person. Find someone else or try to handle it without the extra hands. Rushing this situation can be detrimental to everyone involved but mostly your dog and baby. We want to set your dog up for success!

Make sure all adults involved are ready beforehand and feel confident! Talk it all through with each other. There should be no tension between partners or adults involved. For instance, if someone is feeling anxious, have a plan B and figure out how to defuse the situation. You are not getting frustrated with one another.

Okay, it's *go* time!

Step #1: Once your helping hand has taken care of your dog's needs, you will arrive home and pull up in front of your house. The partner who did not have the baby will go inside, greet your dog, say hello, and do whatever they like to do together when they have missed each other. For example, a little bit of calm play or lovin's on the couch. This can take ten to fifteen minutes. Mom will be in the car with baby. If you need to feed or change baby, this is a good time for that. The goal is for baby to stay asleep during the entire introduction inside, if possible. But don't panic if they don't!

Step #2: Once your pup has settled a bit with the first parent, it is time to switch, and Mom should go in. Baby stays in the car with their other parent. Mom repeats Step #1—greeting the dog, loving on them, and helping them self-regulate and calm down naturally. This can take ten to fifteen minutes! If your dog is acting a bit weird, they may know something is up or realize you have recently been through something stressful—especially if you had a tough delivery or C-section. Don't be concerned by this! Dogs are intuitive. If they are extra hyped because of this, maybe spend a little more time with them before the next step.

Step #3: Bring that baby in! Once your pup has calmed down and received ample attention from Mom, it is time for the partner to bring in the car seat with the baby in it. The car seat is essential for baby's safety in the beginning! Some dogs have very low impulse control and do not realize their size. Come in calmly. Let your dog sniff the bottom of the car seat briefly while you give tons of praise and treats! Place the car seat on the kitchen counter or table. It needs to be a place where your dog cannot jump up easily or stick their head inside.

Step #4: Take your motherfucking time. I mean it!

Step #5: Safely get baby out of the car seat and hold them against your body. Be sure to tuck baby's limbs into your body and against you. The goal is to protect baby at all costs with your arms and hands. They should look like a little turkey ready to bake on Thanksgiving Day! Again, it is usually best if the baby is asleep for this, just so the crying doesn't spook your dog. Walk around with the baby, allowing your dog to follow and be interested. Have your helping-hand person treat your dog while everyone in the room is praising them. Have the extra person make sure the dog doesn't jump too much. During this time, Mom should be resting and not moving too much! I know that might be frustrating. I get it! But you just brought a baby into this world, and you need to physically rest. It's great practice for allowing people to help you moving forward. You're welcome!

The partner holding the baby can choose whether to do this on the couch, do it at the kitchen table, or remain standing and just crouch down, but now you're going to move to your pup and let them get a sniff of your newborn's butt or back area.

Step #6: Let your pup sniff, max three to five seconds. Everyone will say, "*Yes*! Good boy! Great job!" the entire time they are sniffing or are close to baby! This is important! Once the three to five seconds are up, detach the baby from your pup's nose by moving baby over to the other side of you, standing up, or having another human call them in a positive way to receive pets, love, and a reward. Short and sweet! Don't let them stay too long in the beginning. They are *super* new at this, and we don't want to overwhelm them.

If your dog is a little more fixated than you'd like—meaning they are unable to break focus and are staring, yawning, and licking their lips—this is a good time for someone to take them for a little walk or let them sniff in the backyard. Maybe give them some time away in a crate or bedroom. (Always with high-value enrichment so they don't think they're in trouble). Another option is some exciting mental enrichment given near all you humans.

Do not force the situation by making your dog interact with baby if they are scared, avoiding, or fearful. This can look like backing away, running away, barking and retreating, turning their face and eyes away when you bring baby over for a smell, yawning and pacing, or being unable to settle. If you are using the methods in our Dogs & Babies online course, you will see all the ways to improve this. If you force it, they will believe your baby just brings fear, anxiety, and discomfort. Have someone give them a break using the same techniques described above!

What about kissing? Your dog kissing your baby is safe, I promise! Again, short and sweet. When dogs kiss consistently for too long, it can be related to OCD or stress, or they can work themselves up and feel pressure and start to feel fearful, as if they can't retreat. Help them through this by monitoring and talking positively the whole time. If their body posture changes and the kissing speeds up, detach positively with a look cue or praise. We have to help them realize on their own when it's the right time to stop!

If your dog is overexcited, this is not a time to use a forced place, stay, or go-to-your-bed behavior. Take them out of the situation so they can come down and self-regulate with the tips above. All new behaviors, emotions, or rules will be associated with the baby. *Everything* needs to be positive! Forced stay cues can produce a lot of stress and anxiety and should not be used around baby.

For example, I had a client's dog that was obsessed with the new baby. But every time someone stood up with baby in their arms, she would go to nip. Naturally, the parents were terrified and called me. We figured out that she was being overly motherly and basically telling the guest to sit the hell down with that baby so he wouldn't get hurt! They kept putting her in a forced *stay* and *down* on her bed, which only made her *more* protective when she was out of that state. Once we got her on antianxiety meds and helped her be a part of baby's life safely, she was like a built-in babysitter!

If your dog acts negatively, combat everything your body is telling you to do. Do not reprimand or yell! If you yell at your pup for having negative feelings, you will only make those bad feelings about baby more solid. That's because the only thing that has changed is you bringing a baby home, and now your dog is being yelled at. They will associate your abrupt change in behavior with the baby, and this is the number-one thing we want to avoid. Give them the space to have their feelings, and feel confident that there is much time to improve their feelings about baby.

Step #7: Try, as much as possible, to give your dog as much attention as you normally did prior to having a baby. This is not the easiest thing in the world after having a baby because this is so new for all of you, but if you are set up for success and ready prior to coming home from the hospital, all you need to do is execute! This includes meal prepping. Everyone always stocks the freezer with easy meals to heat up prior to baby coming home, but we have to do the same with enrichment. This way, in those first couple of weeks, you can head to the freezer or cabinet without a thought and just hand something off to your dog multiple times a day!

Step #8: Relax and enjoy! After you get the first interaction out of the way, try to relax as a family. The goal is to get your dog to settle and coexist. Go about how you would have relaxed as a family prior to baby, like having a relaxing night on the couch or cuddling in your bedroom, etc. It's time to enjoy the new siblings! It may not be perfect all the time, but you can always get a handle on it and fix it. You are blessed. Congrats, parents!

Now, let's dive into navigating baby's milestones. Or better yet, let's dive into your dog navigating your baby's milestones!

As your infant morphs into a mobile, curious explorer, the dynamic with your dog will face new tests. Teaching your child how to have gentle interactions with the dog from the get-go is paramount. It's about instilling a deep-seated respect for the dog's space, emphasizing that, despite their fur coat, they're not another plush toy. Establishing and enforcing boundaries is nonnegotiable; it's what keeps harmony in the household and ensures everyone's well-being.

When I am dealing with a baby from three to nine months old, I am helping them through this process. I leave nothing to chance! They are still trying to learn how to use all their dexterities properly. So whenever a baby is interested in petting a dog that likes being petted by kids, I have the baby on my lap and hold their wrists so I can control the movements. But I also put my thumb in the palm of their hand. By doing this, I am making sure I can push against the baby's finger if they unexpectedly decide to grab anything they shouldn't, like fur, skin, ears, or tails.

Little mishaps like this can scar a dog for a long time and lead them to not trust all little ones or tolerate or trust petting from them. So it's a big undertaking, and we should always make sure we are protecting our pups with these kinds of interactions. They should not be taken lightly. All parents, grandparents, family members, and friends should be briefed about this if they are going to spend time with both dog and child without you present.

It is baby steps to boundaries pretty much immediately. Or at least it should be. From the wonky first crawl to the assertive strides of a toddler, each phase of your child's development is an opportunity to teach and reinforce the sanctity of boundaries with your dog.

It starts with simple directives like "Gentle touch" and evolves into more complex lessons of empathy and respect for another being's comfort and signals. In the middle, we set boundaries for babies who don't yet understand our words but will start to understand the routine, as in things we do and things we definitely don't do. Your baby should eventually realize, *Oh, I never crawl toward Bailey*, or *Mom never lets me play with Bailey's food. It must not be a toy*, or *Bailey's toys are Bailey's, and I should never take them out of her mouth!* These lessons are invaluable, shaping not only your child's relationship with the dog but their approach to all living creatures. Kids learn by words and phrases way later on, but they see how you treat your pets *immediately*! If you never allow your kids to crawl all over your dog, they eventually stop trying. If you never let them take enrichment or toys from your dog, they'll stop trying. If you never let them make your dog uncomfortable by approaching them quickly and abrasively, they stop doing it.

I know this firsthand from our Chihuahua, Pudgalina. JJ thought she was so funny, like a stuffed animal. I let him know early on that we did not touch Pudge unless she wanted to be petted. As he got older and more adventurous as a toddler, he thought it was funny to run toward her on the couch and hit his body into it because this made her growl and run away. I explained over and over again that my job was to keep her and him safe at all times and that if he continued to scare her, she was going to eventually give him a boo-boo. I explained that he was scaring her and that we did not do this to our pets. He got slightly better around age three, but he would still provoke her a little. Anytime he would do that, I would calmly remove him from the situation and put him in his high chair. I would again explain that I had to keep them both safe and that if he continued, she would bite him, and I wouldn't be upset with her. We were getting close to the fuck-around-and-find-out stage of their relationship, but I didn't want to get her to that point. It wouldn't be fair to her.

When JJ was around three and a half years old, things changed. Pudge became his favorite, and instead of trying to get her to growl, he decided to be sweet and respectful to her. It took her a while to trust him again, but he stuck with his consistency. I told him he had scared her in the past, so he needed to make up for it and prove he was trustworthy.

Now, when he climbs into bed to wake us up, he gently comes in to make sure he doesn't scare or hurt her and says good morning to her. He asks her if he can have kisses, and she will either not move, which is a no, or she'll flutter her ears and move her head toward him, which is a hell yes!

Now that he is four, he finally understands her and respects her boundaries and vocalizations.

So, in short, it does not happen overnight. I had to explain things over and over again in different ways and with different phrases that he could understand. I calmly held boundaries to keep them both safe and stuck to my guns about his behavior toward dogs in a matter-of-fact way instead of yelling. I needed him to understand that if he couldn't respect her space and calm himself around her, I would need to remove *him*, not *her*!

Why would I make her leave the room he's in if she's peacefully minding her business? She lives here too. If he wants to play freely and have physical freedom, he has to respect everyone else who lives here. I am proud of him, and I think she is too!

Empathy is probably the most underrated personality trait. It is the keystone of coexistence for all living creatures, but I feel it is one of the biggest things humans are struggling with right now. We are demanding that everyone have empathy for us without reciprocation. Teaching your children to have empathy for the family dog transcends basic pet care. It's about nurturing an understanding that animals have emotions, needs, and boundaries just like humans do. If those needs are not met and emotions and boundaries are not respected, there can be consequences. Kids need to know what their accountability looks like. I believe that building this skill starts super young and needs to be taught. Some people come out naturally empathetic, which is great. But some kids need some extra help.

It's teaching them to notice when the dog is happy, anxious, or in need of space and respond with kindness and respect. This empathy, cultivated early, enriches not just their interactions with animals but their interpersonal relationships throughout life. I was able to teach JJ to have more empathy for Pudge and to not upset her or scare her. Now that JJ is a big brother, he's had to relearn all over again with his little brother. When we successfully teach kids how to have empathy for animals, they can be better human beings to each other and have an easier time with that. Practicing patience, love, and empathy for animals will help our kids struggle less around each other, but it must start extremely early.

Now, let's talk more about how we are handling our dogs during these situations. Raise your hand if you thought I corrected Pudge for growling or snapping at JJ when he was acting like a fool.

If you raised your hand, put this book down and get a refund. You have learned nothing!

I praised the *shit* out of that little dog. Wanna know why?

Because she did nothing wrong.

She verbally communicated: check!

She air snapped when she could have made contact, and she's fast as fuck: check!

She ran to me because she knew I would protect her, and she trusts me to respect her space: check!

If she *had* bitten him, I still wouldn't have corrected her. He would have deserved it after the millionth time she'd nicely corrected him.

Again, kids tend to put themselves into fuck-around-and-find-out situations. Did I *want* him to get bit? Of course not! Did I *want* her to have to bite him to demand some damn empathy and respect? Absolutely not. She shouldn't ever be put in a position like that. If it *did* happen, though, I'd never blame her for defending herself against a thirty-pound toddler who just wouldn't leave her alone.

Now, let's switch it up! Maybe your dog is just anxious, jumpy, and reactive around the clock. Maybe they didn't like your kid to begin with. Or maybe you are in a situation like my sister was in with Jackson, where he had never dealt with a toddler until the thing was right in front of him. The premise in all of these situations is mostly that your dog is simply untrusting, and the toddler had no involvement in that lack of trust.

So, what do you do?

Well, reread Chapter 11 on reactivity! What do we do when our dogs are scared, fearful, and reactive? We praise, we treat, we get excited! Turn that damn child into a resource giver, not a resource taker! Help that kid do everything in their power to not freak out that dog or spook them. Let your dog eat the food that drops from the high chair as the kid throws it all over the floor! Let your kid throw that dog a shit ton of treats! Let your dog know that they are super safe and everyone loves them when that kid is around!

Dogs and kids are a delicate dance and should be taken extremely seriously. I mean, if your kids get bit, I am not blaming the dog. I am going to blame you. Is that something you are prepared for?

For those thirsty for more nuanced guidance on melding the worlds of dogs and babies into a harmonious life symphony, my comprehensive online Dogs & Babies: A Complete Online Course For New & Expecting Parents awaits. It is the blueprint for a peaceful home. Well, as peaceful as it can get with toddlers running around. Half the time, it feels, sounds, and looks more like the Cirque du Soleil, and I am not sure who the ringleader is. But regardless, this course was written by a veteran—someone who has helped hundreds of families keep their dogs in their homes once they have a baby! It's your deep dive into every conceivable aspect of this transition, ensuring you're equipped to foster a relationship between your dog and your child that's both safe and enriching. If you are expecting, want kids, or might be around other people's kids more often, this course covers everything from start to finish, soup to nuts. It even covers how to deal with guests when your dog is reactive or overexcited and how to deal with your dog becoming overly protective of that kid. It goes over every single kind of dog personality and behavior and all the ways you can make sure that the bond between dog and child is deep and true!

Now, for the full circle of dog training and beyond! As we reflect on the journey we've embarked upon together through this book, it becomes evident that training our dogs is as much about educating ourselves and our offspring. It's a generational commitment to breaking cycles of outdated, punitive training methods and embracing approaches that are grounded in understanding, patience, and love. I am urging you to start passing the torch of compassion to your children, your family members, your friends, and random people on the street, right now! Scream it from the rooftops! The legacy we leave for our children in how they interact with and treat dogs is monumental.

It's about choosing to be the pivotal change in a lineage of dog parents. This responsibility, though heavy, paves the way for a future where the bond between dogs and humans is rooted in *mutual* respect that is free of force.

How cool would it be if you were the person in your family to say, "Enough is enough. We are not doing this anymore!"? Sounds pretty fucking empowering to me! Just think. If you change and show your kids how to induce positive change in others as well, dogs fifty years from now will be living the life. They'll be so calm, just going with the flow, trusting, and being happy-go-lucky. Ugh, the thought of that makes me tear up!

We've been saying for years that our children are the future, and there is no denying that. Teach them to be nice individuals who care about others and don't ever put their ego before someone else's boundaries and needs. Also, do that for yourself as well. We can say it. We can try to teach it. But until our children *see* us do it ourselves, they don't believe a wink of it.

As we close this book, remember that the change starts with us. The lessons we teach, the examples we set, and the love we share with our dogs will echo through generations.

The age-old saying goes, "Treat others how you would want to be treated." This should count for our furriest family members too.

Here's to the future—a future where dogs and kids not only coexist but thrive together, bound by an unbreakable bond of mutual respect, understanding, and a boatload of unconditional love. Let's raise the bar, set the stage, and create a legacy of compassionate dog lovers. Because, in the end, it's not just about training dogs. It's about shaping hearts and minds.

It has been a true honor educating you. Thank you for the opportunity to change your life and your dog's life. Now, go forth and be the change. Be a kickass parent! Your dog, your kids, and the world will thank you.

Here's What to Do Next

I have more to give. Whenever you're ready, here are four ways I can help you live a better life with your dog:

1. Access All Your Free Bonuses

By choosing this book, you've taken a significant step toward deepening your connection with your dog and understanding their behavior. Along with the insights within these pages, you've also gained access to every bonus and resource included to help you and your dog live your best life ever.

Visit: **pawsomeuniversity.com/bonus**

2. Use your FREE Behavior Evaluation

If you're still facing challenges with your dog's behavior, I'd love to offer you a **free behavior evaluation**. Visit me at **pawsomeuniversity.com/book** to set up your call.

3. Tune into My Podcasts

The Podcast for Dog People: hosted by me and my husband, John, where we dive deep into the world of dogs and their people. Explore expert tips, inspiring stories, and practical advice to enhance your life with your beloved canine companion.

Paws & Pacifiers: hosted by me, this podcast is a must for expecting families who are dog parents, offering guidance on preparing your pet for the arrival of your baby and ensuring a harmonious home for all.

4. *boop* The journey doesn't have to end here. I'd love to connect with you.

You can find me on social at @JaimeTheDogTrainer and @PawsomeUniversity

See you on the inside.

Make a Lasting Impact in Real Time

Dear Reader,

Thank you for joining me on this journey through the pages of this book. It was a blast spilling my head and heart to you. I hope it has enriched your understanding and enhanced your relationship with your best friend.

If this book has made a difference in your life, or in the life of your dog, please consider leaving a review. Each review helps more dog parents discover these methods, potentially transforming the dog training industry and improving the lives of dogs and their families. Your feedback not only supports my work but also contributes to a broader change, advocating for positive and informed dog training practices.

Let's help others learn the joy and effectiveness of these approaches. Your review could be the beacon that guides another dog parent out of frustration and rehoming into fulfillment and forever.

Thank you for your support and for being a part of this important movement. Together, we can make a lasting impact.

Warm regards,

Jaime Caponetta

About the Author

Jaime Caponetta is an author, IAABC Certified Canine Behavior Consultant, ABCDT Dog Trainer, and the proud owner of Pawsome University, an online and in-person canine education company she founded with her husband, John. Her most important title, however, is Mom. She has two small boys with another on the way, and three amazing rescue dogs and one cat, who she also considers to be her children.

In addition to operating her nine-acre farm and rehab facility where they rehabilitate rescue dogs for adoption, Jaime provides behavior and operations solutions to shelters and rescues around the country. She also provides humane education both in person, through online courses, and via her two podcasts, the *Pawsome University Podcast* and *Paws & Pacifiers Podcast*.

Her journey to a career as a dog trainer began at the age of sixteen when her family rescued a Pitbull who became the light of Jaime's life. That dog introduced Jaime to the need for competent and compassionate pet professionals. She knew one day she would become a dog trainer and help more abused animals find their forever homes. After college, she harnessed that dream and went all in.

She cut her teeth at a doggy daycare and soon started working as an animal care technician at the Monmouth County SPCA. This quickly became her favorite job of all time, a true trial by fire. While at the SPCA, she simultaneously worked on getting her ABCDT Dog Training certification through Animal Behavior College. She also met her future husband.

Soon after, she started her first company, Pawsome Walks, offering dog walking and petsitting services. Her focus was on pet care with the highest standard of care. She continued to gain experience and knowledge, eventually earning the certification of Canine Behavior Consultant from the IAABC. She and her husband founded Pawsome University in 2017 and soon became a prominent name in positive reinforcement behavior modification.

Jaime thinks of herself as a therapist/detective hybrid for dogs. She looks at the whole picture—not just what's happening through the eyes of their human companions. Where other trainers practice abusive behavior suppression or management techniques, she works with dog parents to identify the root of the problem and change the behavior properly, leaving you with an emotionally regulated, behaviorally sound, ridiculously happy dog. She knows how to crack the code and figure out what is preventing your pup and you from bridging the gap in your relationship, fixing the problem for good.

Made in the USA
Las Vegas, NV
18 July 2024

92564112R00194